I WANT YOU TO KNOW

A Posthumous Story Told By A Nineteen-Year-Old

Sandy Speers Markwart

Legacy Book Press LLC

Camanche, Iowa

For Michaela—
Who always acknowledged my grief
Never attempting to pry it from me
The light on my path

TABLE OF CONTENTS

AUTHOR'S NOTE

My brother Jarett will tell you the tale that I have longed to tell. Jarret is dead. I have spent many years off and on writing and rewriting the words on these pages. When I found the fictional voice of my brother, the words came to me with such ease — the tragic spilling forth in poetic prose — the people and the place in descriptive narration. The voice I struggled with over the years was my own and now it is clear to me why. This was never my story to tell.

Jarett died suddenly September 17th, 1998, in a car accident on a country dirt road. He was on his way to meet our sister Tricia at the university they both attended. This is Jarett's story, and I hope that I have depicted him in a manner that he would agree with. Others may tell this story differently, but their words are not the ones I hear in my head.

I know that at some point — fleeting or long standing — Jarett suffered horribly, knowing what his absence would do to us. This narrative is about that horror.

Based on a true story

THAT DAY

I see my sister — the youngest — the one who waits for me.

I see her discontentment rising and the inkling of fear that blossoms within.

I see her drive aggressively, leaving the place where I am not, but should be.

She takes the road that is not a road,
the dirt path lined with sunflowers that smile and wave at me.
Their tall stalks stand sturdy in the wind.
They, like me, will soon lie twisted in the sun.

I didn't see it coming.
I didn't understand the magnitude of its force.
Please forgive me.

We live on the Saskatchewan prairies surrounded by undulating waves of wheat in the summer and the same waves of snow in the winter. The beauty of this flat land is something that I love and will long for.

My family farm sits amid a tall stand of trees four miles northeast of here. The road home looks like this: Head straight east until you hit the grid that travels north and south between Richardson and Kronau. Take a left and enter the "S" curve where the gravel twists away from you in both directions. When the path straightens out, take your first right. This is our private access, half a mile long, and when the lane curves to the left, the house and the yard will present themselves to you. There is a dip in the lane at the point where the barbed wire fence reaches out to touch the ditch on the right side. If it has rained recently, this low-lying part of the road will be consumed by a large puddle and there will be deep, rutted tire tracks veering to the right and the left. You will see the pine posts from this vantage point as they follow the banks of the creek bed on both sides in an orderly manner — they confine the space where our horses roam. My sister Sandy, the one who wanted to be a cowgirl, strung most of that wire and hammered the u-shaped fencing nails with the determination of a hired hand.

A quarter mile from the grid, the rows of caraganas begin. These bushy, fast growing trees are the choice for many farmers who attempt to divert the wind and the snow. At the approach road that enters the wheat fields to your left and your right, you will see the woodpile. Beyond the orderliness of the stacked and aligned wood lies the horse graveyard. *The worms crawl in and the worms crawl out*. There are sinkholes where their bodies rest, as the earth has succumbed to their decay. *Buried six feet deep*. I say their names: *Pal, Chief, Raider, Summer…*

Where will my parents place me to rest? Will the weight of the burden I have placed on them ever allow them to forgive me?

Follow the fence line, and you will see all the farming equipment spaced evenly and parked just so. I know each of the implements, the tractors, the swather, the combine. I know the sound of the tractor starting up on a crisp fall morning, my breath visible before me. I breathe it in deeply. Surrounding me is the beauty and the peacefulness of a life in the country. It fills me up inside, for I am a farm boy at heart.

The world has been muted.
I have left my anatomy and departed with my soul.
I hear things, but for now I am unable to process them.
My brain sits battered and bleeding in the fractured skull below me.
My mind is not my own.
But, my spirit, my inner being, my life force is.

My life flashes before me on a mini screen inside my mind — the reel winding tighter and tighter.

The frames keep flashing glimpses of a nineteen-year-old blond haired boy with dimples.

Me.

Interspersed with episodic glances of a crumpled car and a corpse.

Splicing the reel to the unreal.

The farm is my Heaven. It represents a simplicity that can only be expressed in sensory responses to the uncomplicated. I feel immense joy at the sound of a tractor chugging away on a hot summer day, straining against the pull of the shovels digging deep in the ground. The simple pleasure I feel when I see my mom carrying a thermos and cooler, walking out toward me in the field with a sandwich, some pickles, an iced tea, and homemade cookies (has to be homemade with my mom). I am thick with dirt and hot and sweaty, but the taste of that simple offering is as pure a pleasure as I can conjure up in my mind. The pride I feel when I see my dad take on the work of ten men and never complain. The gratitude I have for my three sisters — Bonny, Sandy, and Tricia — who allowed me to be the favorite without complaint. The affinity I feel for animals that wag their tails and lick your face every single time they see you. My friend Chris, who has known me since kindergarten and will extend his friendship to include my parents and sisters when I am gone.

My dad is a wheat farmer who works harder than most and expects the same from his offspring. He is a man of few words. He would tell you that there is no such word as "can't" and that hard work can produce anything you want. He would also tell you that having children is the most important thing that you will do in your life. He loves the country, the fresh air, the open spaces, and the hard work that it demands. He approaches any task with the determination and the work ethic of a Clydesdale. He stands tall in judgement and short in praise. He is the man who complains about the barn cats being under foot, but when you encounter him in the quonset alone, the cats are on the workbench, tails curled tightly about "henning" bodies, noses in the task at hand and my dad's calloused hands lightly touching arching backs. My dad will never fully recover from what I did today.

I was only three years old when my dad tore down the old barn and built the quonset in its place, a massive building to house farm machinery. There is a picture of me sitting on one of the tires of the old Minnie tractor. My face is filthy, like I had been eating dirt, and there in the background are the rafters being raised. The term barn raising is when a community comes together to build a farmer's barn, in this case it was a quonset, but the concept is still the same. My mom baked a huge pot of chili, there was garlic toast and coleslaw and pickles and beer. One at a time, the rafters were elevated against a clear blue sky, arches that formed the sides and the roof.

The quonset is a huge building and when I think of it, I think of my dad. As long as I can remember, he rose in the dark, a habit I thought he would never be able to break. I always imagined that even well into his retirement he would still be getting up before daybreak. When I was older, I often accompanied him, walking briskly across the expansive yard, the splendor of a sunrise ahead of us in the east. He always wore a pair of oversized coveralls and his hands with hardened skin were dug deeply into his pockets. His steps were quick and he always seemed to be in a hurry.

He will leave the farm like me one day and never come back. Neither one of us would have ever expected that.

My mom is a farm girl through and through, happiest with her hands in the dirt, the dogs resting in the shade of the trees around her. She is at her best when she is doing something for someone else; she oozes selflessness. Each morning the horses whinny to her, calling for carrots and bran mash, which she obediently delivers. She is the only one who doesn't ride, but the horses respect her just the same. To watch this petite woman amongst the slayers of the quarter mile is heartwarming. They paw at the earth, they root at her pockets; the biggest, the palomino, places his head on her shoulder — such tenderness, such admiration.

My mom is small in stature, but a strong and capable woman on the inside. She has been referred to as a "tough old farm girl" by my seven-year-old nephew and quite honestly, the portrait fits. She has not worked outside of the home for thirty years, but she can whip up a puppy Halloween costume right now if you change your mind about trick or treating; she can drive a three-ton truck like a champ; and she can infuse you, her child, with so much love that you feel buoyant. Her happiness depends on her children's. We are lifted and floating like balloons in the sky. She is our anchor. She walks beneath us, smiling, ready to catch us if we fall, holding tightly to the strings, releasing us a little when we are ready to venture farther.

And suddenly, SLICE.
The string is cut on one of the balloons.
It rises up and up.
She can't reach it, she can't help it, she can't live without it.
She lets go of the other three and clutches the limp string in her hand.

I have three sisters, all of whom are older than me. Two, Bonny and Sandy, have left the family farm to build their own lives, and the third, Tricia, is a university student like I was. I was on my way to meet her when it happened. Tricia and I shared the same parking pass and when we didn't travel to school together, we had a plan to meet in the parking lot for the parking pass trade-off.

I didn't ever use my seatbelt until I got to the highway.
These dirt paths that define the patchwork quilt of farmland that I lived on are the fastest route to the city, and I liked to drive fast.
I saw it at the last second.
The blur of green and brown, of headlights, the GMC logo, a silver grill.
I tried to brake.
Its size enormous,
its weight unstoppable.
It was transporting grain from a farm outside Balgonie.
Another teenager sat in the driver's seat.
I should have cranked the steering wheel away from it.
I would have rolled, but might have lived.

He was going too fast.
So was I.

My youngest sister Tricia and I are very close. Our bedrooms are directly across the hall from each other. She has grown up hearing me snore each night and I have grown up accustomed to her plugging my nose and mouth to make me stop. She is funny as hell and my dad is harder on her than he needs to be. Today she will lose so much of who she is. Goodbye carefree, goodbye hopeful, goodbye sister.

Tricia is still waiting for me.
She parks her car and runs inside to call home.
My dad answers.
"Is Jarett there, Dad?"
"No, but he didn't leave that long ago. Give him some more time."

This morning my mom and I spent the early hours crushing peppers for her to put in her homemade salsa. Picture me, six-foot-six, at the counter beside my five-foot-two mom — I smile at the thought. My mom single-handedly plants and maintains a garden that would fill a food pantry. She lovingly pickles and cans and preserves. This will be her last harvest. The jars in the root cellar will still sit on the shelves when my sisters sell the farm a few years from now.

I can hear my voice as I leave — *Bye mom* — And the sound of the door closing on my existence.

I left her with a smile and a wave and the heat of crushed peppers on my hands.

It is a magnificent fall day. A beauty. The path that brought me to where I am now is uneventful and as everyday as every day can be. Tricia left early this morning to get to her classes. I followed shortly after, but I will never become anything as a result of my education — a doctor, a lawyer, a farmer. I will, however, be the cause of my youngest sister's personal ruination.

My death will sever her heart and soul.
She will see the accident first.
She will come undone.

We met at the intersection.
I just a little before him.

I came from the east.
He came from the north.

My dad left the farm this morning after sharing a pot of coffee with my mom. He was off to Kronau, the small town where we get our mail, and then to the city to get the oil changed in his diesel truck. My parents drink 2.5 cups of coffee each and every morning together. This will be the last of their morning rituals that feels the calmness of a new day breaking. The parental bond they share will be severed today. A life they created together will rip them apart when it sits in an urn in their closet.

My dad is the proud father of only one son.

I will take that from him today.

My oldest sister, Bonny, busies herself with the mission of getting two elementary kids off to school. Lunch boxes, signed permission slips, and "Don't forget your sweaters!" She drinks tea because the caffeine in coffee is too damaging to her Zen-ness. She doesn't believe in vaccinations, or x-rays or medication.

She believes that what will be, will be.

She does not worry about things that haven't happened yet.

My middle sister, Sandy, lives far from us in Boston.
She rises early to get to the gym and then hustles off to work.
She will be the last to know.
The poison will seep quickly into the matter of her brain.
Paranoia and anxiety will reside there.
She will suffer my loss throughout all the days of her life.
In her mind, death begets death.

The next opportunity that my family will have to see me will be at the morgue. They will be advised not to identify me, as I will be too fucked up to look at. They will take the officer's advice, but grapple with the decision until they find themselves in the morgue. We snivel at the monotonous tasks that stupefy us day in and day out, again and again, but long for them in the face of tragedy. Oh how my family will yearn for the humdrum day.

Point of impact.

Red shards from my Taurus suspended against the blue of the sky.

Blood red.

A lifetime of blue.

Steel buckles, absorbing a life; plastic shatters, stealing hope; aluminum crumples and whines in pain; glass fractures, breaking a family in pieces.

On impact my head led the way through the windshield and my body followed.

I see my corpse lying on the hood of my car.

I see the glass and the blood and the broken bones.

The red liquid that circulates through my veins and arteries creates a kaleidoscope of color on the hot metal where my body stopped.

I see the distortion and elongation of bone and muscle.

I feel nothing.

I see the driver of the semi walk over to me.

He is a mess at seeing how fucked up I am.

I see him walk painfully toward the nearest house.

I know that house.

It sits beside the house of my best friend since kindergarten, Chris.

A nurse, well versed in applying pressure to stop the bleeding, mobilization, BP's, head trauma, setting broken bones, and saving lives, lives there.

She cannot help me.

I was dead before the other driver reached the house.

I am nineteen years old.

Primary impact — car meets semi.

Secondary impact — my organs collide with the front of my body.

Tertiary impact — my organs slam into the back of my body.

And back and forth my innards bounce.

I am alone.

I am surrounded by fields.

Sunflower, wheat, flax, and oats.

I am not aware of how much time has passed.
A first responder from the small town of Kronau arrives.
He is the father of a girl I am friends with.
An ambulance from the city arrives next.
They will make my death official.
They radio it in — *Code 5.*
It's that simple.
A life has ended.
No one who cares knows.

There is death all around me and I am acutely aware of its presence. There are grasshopper guts smattered against the GMC grill that drilled into me at about 110 km per hour. A collage of shapes: heads, wings, abdomens, and legs. Crunchy exoskeletons unable to protect them from the trauma they endured. Fifty feet from where I lay is a dead gopher — road kill — like me. A hawk sits on an abandoned building two hundred yards from here. I watch it take off from its perch, ascending rapidly, wings furiously flapping, then floating on feathers outstretched in the sky. It searches for movement, a sign of life. Again and again it descends aggressively. I am certain that each time it will slam into the earth, but it never does. It lands with such precision on its prey that I am bewitched to watch the ritual of death. Three times it soars from the fields, barely touching down, with a squirming ball of fur clutched in its prehistoric talons. I watch with uneasiness the tiny outstretched claws of two field mice and the thumping pink paw pads of a baby bunny grasping at the air as they rise and rise.

Tricia calls home again.
My mom answers.
"Jarett still isn't here, Mom."
"Well, he left an hour ago, about twenty minutes before your dad. I am sure he is on his way. Just wait a little longer."

Tricia and my parents think that my car has broken down and that I am stranded on the side of the road somewhere. I drive a piece of shit car, so that explanation is reasonable. I am also a pretty good mechanic, so I can fix most problems, at least temporarily.

The farm will mutate today into something ugly.

It will become the place that I am not.

I am the heartbeat of the land and I am too big a part of every particle of dirt that they walk on. They will see me everywhere.

They will see my lifeless body just up the road.

My dad will act as if he is cultivating me into the ground each time he enters the field to work the land. Each swath of the wheat will render him powerless to my absence.

Every furrow closer to the demise he secretly longs for.

The seeding in the spring will not bring promise and new growth, but rather drudgery and resentment. The fields will soon be filled with weeds. Fast growing, unwanted plants that will suck the life from the farm, as I have done to my family. The coroner has arrived and he orders a post-mortem examination. I died suddenly of unnatural causes and I am nineteen years old, so my body will undergo an investigation that requires gutting me like a pig at the slaughter. The pathologist will determine the cause of my death and whether or not I was drunk or high. I was neither.

They are taking my body away now.

I leave the site in an ambulance.

No sirens.

No urgency.

My car sits mangled at two intersecting dirt roads. The one I was travelling on will take you to Highway 33 and the other will take you to White City to the north and Chris' farm to the south. My red Taurus rests in stark contrast to the beast that killed me — a semi-tractor trailer filled with grain. It is fitting that I am the son of a wheat farmer and that the hardened kernels I have planted and harvested throughout my days rained down on me as I died.

Tricia couldn't wait any longer.

Her questions about where I am will be answered very soon.

My dad has left Kronau with the mail.

He takes route 33 straight into the city.

He passes Tricia headed in the other direction.

She waves, but he doesn't see her.

Goodbye father of four.
They are less than a mile from where I died.

My youngest sister turns east off the highway and I can see the wake of dust that billows behind her. The dry prairie dirt turned to powder from the lack of rain. She drives faster than she should, the dread coursing through her veins. She is vaguely aware of the coming change that will knock her on her ass and pin her down. It is unlike me to not arrive on time. She is angry at me because it is the only emotion she has right now, angry because she is scared, angry because she has a foreboding feeling. She knows the road I take to get to the city and she returns home that way, hoping to find me broken down on the side of the road with a flat tire. The closer she gets to the farm, the more panic stricken she becomes. She needs me to be. She waited as long as she could. The fear descending through her body, her thoughts unstable, hobbling her movements and her mind, the ground feeling unsafe, like loose wet sand giving way to the weight of her thoughts, yielding easily, sucking her in. All she could do was drive home and hope to find me en route. The path she takes will lead her to me.

Neither my mom nor my dad are currently overcome with the same worry that devours Tricia. Being completely unfamiliar with the parking at the university and having never participated in our foolproof system, their responses of, *Just look around, he is there somewhere,* don't help to calm Tricia's mind. I am glad that my parents' thoughts are so devoid of distress right now, because soon, those optimistic notions will be pried from their minds by ratchets and pulleys and chains.

Tricia crosses the railway tracks that run perpendicular to the highway.
She will be the first to see it.
She sees a fire truck, police cars, and numerous other vehicles.
Mostly she sees a mangled red car.
My car.
I see the red brake lights.
I see her heart slam into her chest.
It stops.

I see her running toward the chaos.

Four seconds of hope — *He is at the hospital.*

Police officers are pushing her backwards.

She is screaming.

"That's my brother's car. Where is my brother?"

One police officer kindly says, "I'm sorry."

Two police officers are physically restraining her.

"Is he okay?"

No answer.

"Take me to my brother."

She knows.

She flails and she fights them, lashing out and screaming because I didn't come to her.

I tried, but I didn't make it.

My mom is at home vacuuming.

She gave up her career for pablum and diapers, homemade costumes and curtains. The quintessential mom who suddenly doesn't like pie when there is only one piece left. A woman who takes pride in her home and washes her floors on her hands and knees.

She does not hear the banging on the door.

I don't want her to hear it.

But teenage death takes no prisoners. It will plough through that fucking door and effortlessly squeeze the breath from her lungs, immobilize her heart and mash her petite being onto the floor like a bug.

Don't open the door, Mom.

My dad demands respect above all things. He could never be accused of not practicing what he preaches. He completes no job "half-assed." His motto, if he had one, would be, "If you are going to do a job, do it right the first time, or don't do it at all." In the city that surrounds him, police officers search the local oil change shops for the man who drives the silver Silverado, license plate ANS 209. They start in the east because he entered the city on that side.

My dad sits at the Jiffy Lube where he waits for his oil change to be complete. He would normally do the task himself, but with all there is to do on the farm right now, he opts for the 20-minute service. You can hear the employees yelling short, informative phrases to each other as they empty the oil and then add the new. *All clear on two.* The chairs are utilitarian, with metal frames and orange vinyl seats, built for sturdiness and ease of care. *Draining four.* The air is heavy with grease and oil, which mixes with burnt coffee from the machine in the corner. *Filling two.* There is a basket under the table with obsolete toys for the kids and some outdated gossip magazines for the adults. *Starting engine three.*

I see the police officer approach the counter to inquire about the now sonless man. My dad thinks his name has been called because the oil change is complete.

"Are you Dennis Speers of Kronau?"

"Yes," replies the six-foot man who will soon seem small to all.

I see them go outside where the news of my accident will cripple the man I respect and emulate. I see my dad stumble and fall.

I look away.

I struggle with how this can all be playing out before me and I have no way of interjecting myself into the scene.

The shock shackles me.

Observing from above baffles me.

My heightened senses overwhelm me.

The black, bagged bodies don't enter the hospital through the emergency. There are obscure doors around the backside for cadavers like me. As we pass by, I longingly stare at an ambulance with red flashing lights. I let my physical body go on without me. I am drawn to the sounds and the colors and the promise, the siren dissecting me with its spinning reverberation, the swirling, the headiness, blood red blazes of light ripping into me, parsing life and death, alive and dead, here and gone. I want my body to go through those doors. I watch other people's families and I see the fear in their eyes, but I also see hope. Hope because they went through those doors. There is so much to offer inside — code blue, clear the airway, take him to the operating room, apply pressure, scalpel, suction — I want to have a chance too. I want to give my family more than a telephone call, a knock on the door, a policeman with the news of their worst nightmare. But life has slammed the book shut on my being and all of the characters in my story will soon lie flattened between the empty pages.

13

I return to see my body again.
Rigor mortis has started to creep in.
My joints and muscles are stiffening.
Rendering my escape impossible.

Three out of five family members now know that they will never see me again. My mom is at home with a female police officer — bewildered, mournful, shrunken. Tricia is being physically carried from the accident scene and my dad is being driven home from the city — a limp, lamenting man in the back of a police cruiser. All alone when they were told of my fate. They will collapse on top of each other just inside of the mahogany front door with the lion knocker and the brass plate that says D. E. SPEERS. The police officers will look away at the sight of so much pain.

What have I done?
How the fuck did this happen?

They call the eldest first, Bonny. She gathers her children, her wits, and enough clothing for at least a week. Her husband steadies and guides her. The anguish circles her, stalking her mental acuity. They drive the six hours in a blur, the children seated in the back with their educational toys to occupy them. Nothing plastic, nothing suggestive of perfect body types, and nothing gender specific. Bonny is an educator and she takes every opportunity to teach a lesson with numbers and letters and shapes. Always imparting wisdom, I have seen her make a lesson plan out of sledding down the creek banks in the winter. Crouching beside her children, she talks of friction and weight mass and gravity. She never uses baby talk, but rather, speaks to them as she would to an adult. She never adopted the cutesy names of bubbas or doo doos for all of the baby paraphernalia. There is no dumbing it down here. A baby bottle is a baby bottle, a blanket is a blanket, and a death is a death.

They will tell my sister Sandy in Boston last. They let the day squeeze the life from them while she lives on in blissful ignorance. They won't call her at work. They will wait until she is home and her husband is present. Many hours have passed. I died around 10 a.m. and it is now close to 4 p.m. How must that have felt for them, knowing that Sandy was smiling and laughing and still living life? My dad struggles to find the strength to tell the one who started worrying as a young child and has never stopped… He understands what this will do to her and how it will validate all that consumes her mind. Worry will cripple her now. It will take her hostage, it will fester, it will bloom. I watch as Tricia and my dad stand at the phone in the quonset and dial the number. My dad states to his youngest now, "We will need to be strong."

It's ringing.

My dad longs for the ringing to keep ringing.

Click.

Sandy's husband answers.

My dad asks to speak to my sister in the voice of a man who struggles to make the call — monotone, quaking words, stretching syllables to stall.

Her husband thinks nothing of it, even though my dad has never called their home.

He yells for his wife upstairs, not saying who is on the other end.

Sandy picks up.

She hears our dad's voice and knows something is wrong.

No prelude to what is coming.

No intro, no explanation, no laying it out gently.

"There has been an accident. Your brother is dead."

Sandy drops the phone and screams.

My dad and Tricia know that her heart beats to a new rhythm now.

They know what she wishes for.

Stop breathing and you will feel nothing.

The death of me — the young, the vibrant, the promising — rips into them again and again.

The pathologist cuts my clothing from my stiff remains. He starts with an external examination, noting unique identifiers. He will write in his report that I have a pencil lead mark under my left eye where Chris stabbed me when we were eight years old. When the gory shit begins — the cutting and the sawing — I leave. I return to find all of my organs in metal bowls. I watch as the medical examiner holds my heart in his hands and I weep as only the dead can weep — dry, paroxysmal whimpering that those blessed with life cannot hear or ever comprehend. I force my dead self to watch the process of examination that each of my inner body parts goes through. There is the making of a profound "SPEED KILLS" commercial in all that I see. I read the notes detailing which parts of me were damaged when my body crushed the steering wheel and the dashboard and when my head shattered the windshield. I wonder how all of the organs will fit back into my body. There is no attempt to return them to their rightful positions. Like meat at the deli, the pathologist piles them in haphazardly: a liver, two kidneys, intestines, a spleen, a bowel, a stomach, two lungs, and the heart that I loved with. They sew me shut and complete the paper work. I have been released for burial or cremation.

My mom calls one person — her only brother.
His exact words, "I don't know what I can do for you, Joan."
His words speak volumes for his future actions.

Next stop. Embalming.
The embalmer pulls me from a refrigerated drawer. I am covered with a sheet, which I am grateful for, as I keep returning to my body. I can't stop myself. I am in a state of shock. *Can that really be me on that table?* He cleans my body with a disinfectant spray and then makes an incision in my armpit to find an artery so he can inject the formaldehyde. As it courses through my body, I watch as the death grey color fades and my body plumps up. Very sci-fi. Finally, my blood will be suctioned from my body. There will be no attempts to create a life-like peaceful look on my battered face. My parents saw me for the last time this morning.

Sandy is pacing. I watch as she fidgets and twitches in agitation.
The shock is setting in.
She is alone, as her husband runs next door to the good doctor who he hopes will sedate her. *Numb the fucking mind and all will be well.*
Sandy will resent from the start that he tried to drug her.
She will resent that he tried to lessen her pain with narcotics.
She still has that prescription bottle.
None of the pills are missing.

She was brave that way.

My mom takes the pills 2,500 miles away.
She needs them to anesthetize the truth.
I am her only son.
I am her hope and her future and her strength.
She is a woman in her fifties who life has left alone on the farm.
The wandering husband, the two grown children with lives of their own to lead and two more at home making strides in the direction of the door.
She left her teaching career as an eager young parent and now she finds that everyone is leaving her.
I didn't mean to leave her like this.

Sandy sits alone on the floor of her closet in Boston.
Black garments burying her in her own grave.
Her husband sleeps soundly.

Tricia pulls all of her being into herself.
The transformation begins.
Twisting and turning, she flips inside out.
She emerges not as a butterfly, but as a vulture.
She has already begun to gnaw at herself in the name of guilt: *Why not me?*
She will devour all that she was before I left her.

Bonny is almost home.
My dad walks like a zombie through the yard.
He must keep moving or the stillness will swallow him whole.
The silence is deafening at night on the farm.
He listens for the sound of a car approaching beyond the trees.
The red Taurus with the muffler that needs replacing.
My body rests on a cold metal slab at the morgue.

SASKATCHEWAN

When I think about Saskatchewan, I think four-wheel drive pick up trucks, plaid shirts from Mark's Warehouse, steel toed work boots, and hard laboring people walking those work boots around. I think kind people. I speak mostly about the people who live where I do — rural life on the farms of Saskatchewan — people who choose to live where they can stretch their arms wide and never touch anyone else.

There is a shift in the people when you leave the urban city and enter the rural farmland. On any country road that you drive on, if you pass a person travelling in the opposite direction, whether you know them or not, they will raise their fingers from the steering wheel and give you a hello, while simultaneously nodding upwards or downwards with their head. Typically, it is the two-finger wave, with the pointer and index finger lifting straight up off the steering wheel, the ring finger and pinkie staying slightly bent. Sometimes the entire hand will depart from the steering wheel and this is usually someone whose land borders yours, so you owe them more of a wave. This is customary and everyone does it without even thinking about it, unless you are from the city, just out for a Sunday drive. You are part of a club out here with the animals and the crops filling the fields. You are different. My sister Sandy still does the wave after having left rural life and the farm many years ago. She does it without thinking. It is an homage to a way of life that one cannot forget.

Saskatchewan is referred to as the land of the living skies. It says so on every Saskatchewan license plate. It really does present the world to you as an open book — the spine resting flat and the edges of the pages stepping away from you — offering you more, inviting you to go farther. I often think of the childish pictures I drew of a flat ground and a rainbow reaching bottom left hand corner to bottom right hand corner; an accurate depiction of the flat land with a sky that touches it everywhere you look.

I have seen the sky here change in mere minutes. The blue reaching farther than you can see, suddenly becoming grey and ominous in the time it takes you to ride your bike from the house to the field across the creek. I have been caught many times in torrential downpours on the roads that border our land. Most often, I was returning from a quest to the quonset to get a specific wrench or screwdriver for my dad, the front wheel on my bike slowing in the mud, carving its own path, pushing through, the pedals sluggish to the resistance, my legs burning with each circular motion.

Storms arrive quickly on the prairies of Saskatchewan.
Great swirling masses of grey build and build.
Blotting out the blue.

The clouds move across the land in shapes of powerful animals stampeding to safety. I can tell of the storms I have witnessed from the safety of the porch at night. The stillness that hangs in the air as it approaches. The electricity so heavily charged you can actually see the zaps, the currents, the static. The sky on the prairies is capable of releasing great hailstorms and rainstorms in minutes. The thunder so booming that you feel it course through your feet and up through your hair. The lightning arrives in forks, in sheets, filling the sky. The northern lights streak the Heavens with color, painting the immense canvas with brushes of greens and blues and yellows. The sky on the prairies is alive with sounds and colors, movement and electricity.
Living beneath it is an honor.

The eldest, Bonny, is home.
The living skies fall around her.
She and her family arrive in a flurry, propelled by disbelief and shock.
My sister stands more or less upright and her husband is the prop that holds her steady.

He is her brace, her crutch, her cane.

Bonny is 5' 10" tall and carries herself like someone comfortable with her height. She has shoulder length light brown hair, never pulled back, and she wears current eyeglasses that give her an intellectual flair. She doesn't ever wear any make-up, so she has a natural look that suits her. When I see her now, I can recognize my mom in her strained face.

Bonny's kids, ages three and five, are wide-eyed and confused.

My sister has told them what has happened, but they do not understand the finality of what I have done.

They are too young.

Low lying clouds and violent gusts of wind press in on the land, and the people who live there.

THE NEW ME

I wonder if I can still call myself me?
Or does me only relate to the living?
I still feel like me, but in a transparent, see-through sort of way.
I move through and around things.
I am not tangible, but I am still me.
I can't touch my mom's shoulder to calm her.
She can't touch my hand to calm me.
But I am still me.

I feel, but very differently.
I feel through my memories, my life filling the horizon with me.
I feel through the anguish I witness.
The pain I have caused.
The mistakes I have made.
I feel through the love that pours out of my family, the love they have for me.
I am still me.

NIGHT

The first night.
Darkness falls around my family like a trap door, caging the rage within.
Like mice in the horse barn, they each scamper to their corners.
They lie in their tombs alone.

Sleep does not come to most.
I watch the body of my mom surge and plummet beneath the sheets.
She whimpers at times and bawls at others.
She can't stop the breath that she is trying to suppress.
Her eyes open to the darkness that surrounds her and now lives within.
She longs for an escape from the pain, and that will be forthcoming.
My dad tries to remain still, but is unable.
He moves with great limitation.
Slowed is the parent who will bury his only son.
He is unable to comfort my mom.
She offers him the same.
They are separate now.
My death will destroy them both.

My sister Sandy is out of her mind. She keeps calling home and telling them that they need to go to the morgue and that I am actually alive and that there has been some kind of mistake. She does not mean to torture my parents, but she is so far away, and she can't stop obsessing about the details and finding some error. She does not want to be alone with this information that she is unable to process. She can't be alone with the husband who sleeps so soundly.
Her obsessive behavior intensifies.

She is not a religious person, but she needs to be told that I am in Heaven and that I am "Okay."

She calls a childhood friend with whom she has recently reconnected. Someone very religious.

This conversation will cast Sandy's beliefs in stone.

She dials.

She tells the person her story and what she is seeking:

Some affirmation that her young, innocent brother is of course in Heaven, for he did no wrong, he respected his parents, he worked hard, he had goals, he was a good friend, and he was the pride and joy of our family.

The Believer: "Did your brother believe in God?"

The Non: "I don't know."

The Believer: "I can't tell you that he is in Heaven then, unless I know his beliefs."

The Non: "But, isn't Heaven open to innocent teenagers who have done no harm to others, aside from dying?"

The Believer: "Let's pray for you."

The Non: "But, I didn't call for me. I called for my brother. He's dead and I need to know that he is okay from someone who believes."

The Believer: "I can't tell you that."

Sandy will always regret having made that call.

Bonny, her husband, and kids have boisterously filled the void in my room. It is hectic and loud. They come often to the farm, but never do they sleep in the double long bed that is mine. Perhaps my parents like the thought of the space being occupied. Perhaps they imagine the footsteps they hear below in the kitchen to be mine. Bonny is rewarded with the distractions of motherhood that my other two sisters do not share. She left home at the age of nineteen when she tired of the rules laid out by my dad: *My house, my food, my rules.* He runs a tight ship and she became intolerant of the standards that would often say: *Not good enough Bonny.* We didn't see much of her after that. She lived in the city for a while, but then moved two and a half hours away for university. She became engrossed in her own life and loved being free from the judgment and the inquiry. Her studies would allow her to become a teacher and she would be unparalleled in patience, creating a love of learning and inspiring future generations.

She is the strongest of my three sisters.

Tricia receives a phone call from a very important friend from the past, Tyler Fawcett, who neither one of us have seen for over five years. The three of us were very close friends growing up. His concern for Tricia is genuine and he will travel to Saskatchewan from eastern Canada for my memorial. His desire to come and sit with Tricia in the front row means a great deal to us both.

In Boston, Sandy begins her long journey alone.
Her husband will book the flight and get her home tomorrow, but she will do the rest on her own.
She is still in the closet.
She can't seem to choose clothes to wear to her brother's funeral.
It is not the first time she has felt alone.
It will not be the last.

Sandy has always loved fashion. She went to school for pre-law, completed the four years and then went to design school. When Sandy was younger, she wore some clothes that people here in Saskatchewan didn't quite understand. She has toned things down over the years, but she still doesn't like to wear anything expected. Sandy's hair is always changing, a continual make-over adjusting to the times.

Tricia lies alone in her bed. She knows that I am not asleep in the bedroom adjacent to her and the thought unravels her methodically. My parents lie down the hall in their metaphorical coffins, side-by-side, unresponsive to the horror that chews greedily on their beings. The wind is whipping outside, as it tends to do on the prairies, but tonight it feels different. On this night the trees wail and whine and warp. They moan the same song as my sister. Our rooms are upstairs at the back of the house, and they are nestled into a ninety-degree belt of staggered evergreens, poplars, and dutch elm off the northeast corner. The thirty-foot wide belt of trees redirects the cold winds from the north. It is unable to redirect death.

Tricia loves make-up. She loves shopping for it and she loves wearing it. When she was in middle school, my dad wouldn't let her wear any, so she would put it on after we got on the bus in the morning. She has always been fairly adept at the art of adornment — no bright blue eyelids or anything too garish. Tricia has dyed her hair many colors over the years, and she always has the most current and funky haircuts. She is tall, like Bonny, and likes to experiment with her look: grunge, a little punk, maybe something retro.

My mom comes to Tricia in the dark of the night.
She pauses at my door.
She hates this end of the house now.
The two lie in the full bed together.
Entwined in a ritual of suffering.
The tempest outdoors calls my name.
J—A—R—E—T—T.
They are both aware that the farm is grieving me too.
It will begin to slip away from them today.
When the storm settles, it will have already begun its metamorphosis.

The sounds of the storm allow my dad to leave the house that constricts about him.
The wind beats him and each drop of rain impales itself upon him.
He walks, leaning into the gusts and the torrents, to the quonset.
I was raised in this building.
As a child, I watched my dad build, dismantle, reconfigure, reconstruct, and reinforce anything and everything with his skillful hands. He has large, strong hands. I have seen him change the spark plugs on Tricia's car in minus 30-degree weather without gloves. I have seen him pound fence posts with a sledge-hammer for hours. I have seen such productivity in his hands. Rugged, capable hands.
He closes the door behind him and his anger rises to meet the fury outside.
The crux of the farm for my dad is the quonset.
He hates it now, because all he sees is the little blond boy in overalls and the teenage boy with the capable hands like his.
He picks up a crowbar and hurls it into a stack of doors.
They fall flat like dominoes.
Silent.
Unmoving.

He clears his workbench in one fluid swipe with a two-by-four.

His cries reverberate through this expansive structure, through the trees, through me.

He picks up a hammer and pummels the old tire rim that we were reshaping.

He kicks at the blades of the upturned lawn mower until they lie deformed in the cavity of the John Deere attachment.

The sounds masked in the howls from the Heavens.

He rages against this assigned damnation.

I watch as his powerful hands destroy the things that we built together.

I watch as his hands grip the edge of the workbench and he slides to his knees, to the cold of the cement floor.

His hands come to cradle his contorted face.

The sobbing, with each breath, will chisel away at the man I know.

His tears, like acid, melt the strength within.

His hands define him.

He will completely lose the power of them one day soon, and I will be there to watch.

The horses in their stalls are unsettled and skittish. Sorrow storms the barn, moving through the hay in the loft, rousing the kittens. The dogs do not sleep in the doghouse my dad and I built. They lie on the front porch, as close to their people as possible, sensing that something is wrong, knowing that the movement and the moaning within the walls are not typical. The dogs stand guard. Shifting positions. Staying alert. Unable to fight the foe that moved in.

Before the sun rises, the three people that live on the farm — my mom, my dad and my youngest sister — have all merged together in the king size bed of my parents. One of them seeking safety in numbers, and two of them needing their new youngest within reach.

SANDY AND THE FARM

When Sandy moved from the farm, she hesitated. She wanted to go, but she wanted to stay. Tricia and I were very young, but I recall the crying and the phone calls and my parents encouraging her to stay in Boston. Whenever she lost her way in life, she would call and say, "I need to come home. I can always find myself on the farm."

The farm wields vast amounts of power over her now, pulling her back. But one day soon, she will feel very differently.

When Sandy was a young teenager, she decided that the quintessential farm most definitely needed a tire swing and she was intent upon adding one to ours. I remember the day that she hung the tire swing from that big ole tree. I followed her as she searched through the old tires and found the perfect one. She chose a rear wheel from a Harley Davidson motorcycle that I rode with my dad. I remember the wind in my hair and the bugs in my mouth as we raced out to the main grid and back. When Tricia and I were older, Sandy, Tricia, my dad, and I would have competitions and time each other to see who could return the fastest. I excelled at this. Sandy was too timid to push it, my dad the heaviest among us, and Tricia, my toughest competition, just couldn't take the turns like I could. My legs were so long that I could simply plant my foot and spin the bike effortlessly beneath me. With the tire chosen, Sandy searched for and found the thick rope with the braided strands, tinted green and long enough to reach the chosen branch. I followed her back to the tree, which was lacking in branches at the base of the trunk, so I watched as she used the rope to pull herself up from a lower limb. She was in the thick of the branches now. On and on she climbed.

From the eyes of a small boy looking up, she became smaller and smaller before me.

She surveyed the branches.

She surveyed some more.

She made her choice thoughtfully.

The handpicked limb needed to emerge from the others, in order to allow for an expansive swing. It needed to be high enough to provide proper momentum to the child who sought the feeling of flying. And it needed to be strong enough to support the weight of a teenager, as she was at the time. I watched as she shimmied out across the branch. Her legs and arms wrapped tight as can be. Sandy had thought to tie the rope around her waist as she climbed and now she would choose the spot where it would hang and swing the tire below. Carefully, she unfastened the rope and tied the double bowline knot as my dad had instructed her to do. Nimbly she descended on the rope. Next was the tire attachment. She would use the same knot, but needed to make certain that the height was just right. Too high and the legs of a child could not climb on themselves. Too low and the branch would give way, causing knees and toes to scrape.

It was done.

I got the first ride.

She pushed me higher and higher.

My slender body embraced by the tire that carried me across these plains.

My chin barely touching the top, where the knot of a sailor pulled tauter.

I leaned back, arms straight, as her hands left my shoulders.

Eyes to the sky and the clouds passing by.

I pulled in on the return, knees bent, feeling airborne.

My back to the wind and my eyes to the ground.

Higher Sandy.

Higher.

That tire swing will hang there for over thirty-five years.

The threads fraying and the treads on the tire wearing.

The branch drooping from the weight of devastation that the farm will feel over time.

CHIEF AND RAIDER

Tricia and I shared the hearts of many animals. Two horses named Chief and Raider came as a pair when they moved to the farm. One was a Palomino and one was a Bay. Chief had a blaze of white from his eyes to his muzzle and white socks to match. He was golden with a tail and mane of white. Raider had a stripe between his eyes and his coat was reddish brown. You could see yourself in the deep pools of their eyes. Both stood tall and thin — built for speed in their day — and both were as loyal and gentle as old sheep dogs. Raider was the elder horse, we were told nineteen, and Chief was twelve. Raider had a bad chronic cough. You could already see some bones protruding where muscles should have been. A horse gets a chronic cough from eating moldy hay. A friend had asked my mom if we would take the pair and let them roam in our lush, green pastures, in the hopes that Raider would rebound. Chief would accompany Raider, as the two had never been separated since Chief was born.

Tricia was ten and I was eight when they came to live in our pastures. The plan was for them to stay until Raider got well and then be returned to their original owners. They frolicked on the banks of the creek-bed with the other mares, the geldings, and the stallions. They waded deep into the muck with the cattails brushing their bellies underneath, pausing, moving back and forth, back and forth in an effort to quell an itch. My sister and I were determined to heal this horse with the smoker's cough, and the best patches of clover were beyond the confines of the pasture. We decided that Raider's gigantic lips should have access to the bountiful feast beyond the barbed wire. I remember the first time we took Raider through the gate in search of the low-lying plants with the white flowers. Chief was in a state of alarm. He raced back and forth, head high, tail arched, neighing high-pitched screams of protest. He needed to be with Raider. We offered the same exit to Chief and soon realized that we could let him out without being on a lead. He literally followed us like a little lost pup. Our initial intentions were never to buy the two, but rather to heal the ailing one. Time would change all of that. My sister and I wanted to bet on the old horse to win. We each offered to pay $350.00 of our own money to buy the pair who taught us about loyalty, love, and friendship. The original owner suggested, *Let's wait until the end of the summer and see how Raider is doing.* She didn't want to take children's money unless Raider could get better. Raider was skin and bones at the end of August and he would not make it through a harsh Saskatchewan winter.

The owner came while we were at school.

She came with the vet.

When the big yellow school bus rambled into the yard, we saw the unfamiliar red pickup parked left of the large pasture gate.

And there, beneath the blue tarp, were the feet of the beast we so loved.

My mom said that Raider went peacefully.

She said that the vet gave him a needle and that his long, knobby knees gently buckled beneath him and he fell softly to the ground.

She told my sister and me how Chief had run in circles, bucking and whinnying as the bucket on the tractor lifted his friend into the back of the truck. The same bucket that had already dug the grave where he would rest.

The fresh dirt piled high beyond the woodpile.

Raider was to Chief as I am to my family.

I remember that feeling of panic and shock knowing that Raider was beneath that tarp.

I remember the feeling of hopelessness and longing.

I think of Raider's death and I see my own.

Blue tarp in a pickup.

White sheet at the scene.

Both hiding the horror beneath.

The horror the eight-year-old boy and the ten-year-old girl imagined.

The horror the sisters and parents know to be true.

30

Tricia and I did buy Chief, and he roamed our pastures and our hearts for another eight years. He died alone on the sunny side of the creek bed, on the crest of the hill, with the tall grass about him, in the shade of the dogwood tree. Tricia found him on a crisp, fall day, just as she had found me.

DAY

Dawn breaks on the farm and the unblinking eyes still stare at the ceiling.

The start of the first day without me.

The sun in the east summons my parents for their morning coffee on the porch.

The dogs wait patiently beyond the gate.

They seem to know.

The cats stay away.

The land roils about them.

I am the farm and I toss them about wildly.

I am the wheat waving in the fields.

I am the weeds advancing posthaste.

Encroaching their livelihood.

Devouring their lives.

The farmer lives a simple life. He is an optimist at heart, a gambler of sorts, a fixer of belts and pulleys, cogs, and wheels. The elements of wind, cold, and sun are etched around his eyes and mouth. His work ethic has rendered his back unable to rest reclined after 5 a.m. The day starts as the opening front door creaks to tell us so. The farmer walks across the yard with purpose. Hands hidden in expansive pockets of tan coveralls. Dawn breaks through the trees on a fall morning veiled in frost. The quonset is his office. The walk across the farmyard his commute. The lab and the shepherd are his colleagues. There are wooden drawers at his workbench that hold every size of nut, bolt, screw, washer, and wing-nut. Above the workbench, hung on fabricated hooks, are the saws, the hammers, the screwdrivers, and the wrenches. The farmer is well versed in Phillips, the slotted, the hex, the Torx, and the tri-wing. He employs the 3/8 wrench, the crow bar, the soldering iron, the torch. Sandpaper will smooth it, a socket will tighten it, a chisel will reshape it. In the course of a day, the farmer will use a vice grip to compress, a welder to attach, a lever to lift. The farmer is master of them all. He moves benevolently across the land that yields to his way of life. The earth is the vocational device that allows him to live as he does.

I watch as Sandy boards the plane bound for tragedy.
She is unaware of anything around her,
led about like a calf to slaughter.
Sad doe eyes.
Head bent.
Noose tight about her neck.
On takeoff, the negative vertical acceleration pushes her back in her seat.
She stares forward.
Unblinking.
The climb is long.
She makes promises to me at 30,000 feet.
She will keep most of them.

Tricia succumbs to her sibling guilt.
She does not think she is worthy of being the one left behind.
Of my three sisters and me, she was the one that pushed back the most. I never crossed my dad or mom, but she has crossed them many times. Tricia's desires pulled her beyond the solitude of a life in the country. Her friends in the city — the ones who had never even cut a lawn — made her resent the chores she had.
She complained all the time.
She fought with my dad.
She defied my dad.
If my dad said, *Get up at five and plough the field across the creek,* I did it without question. She could only think of her friends in the city, sleeping in every day, going to concerts and having fun. In her mind, the perfect son died when the indignant daughter should have.

Tricia commuted with me into the city most days and now she can't make sense of why she wasn't with me yesterday. She thinks that she might have seen it coming or she might have encouraged me to drive slower, or she might have been late getting out to the car and then the semi tractor trailer would have already passed the crossroad where we met. She thinks that it is all her fault. She knows that if she had been with me, then my parents would be burying two children.

She welcomes that.

Not for them.

But for her.

My mom is drowning on dry land.

She is submersed in the vacuum my death has created.

Inhaling my nonexistence, she dies a slow death.

She tries with all of her might to be strong for my sisters.

But she can't breath.

Bonny is occupied with her demanding three-year-old daughter. The child only wants her and no one else will do. She basks in the glory of being needed, as the other mom in the house lies comatose. The parent, the grandparent, has become the child.

My dad is wearing a path in the lawn.

He walks as if confined, never passing beyond the trampled grass to his left or his right.

He stops at times and stands left of the lilacs.

The purple, flowering bushes that smell like my mom.

He waits again for the sound of a car.

The sound of another daughter coming home to her sonless parents.

At the curve in the lane by the weeping willows, Sandy sees him.

Head bowed and conquered.

Full submission to the dominance of teenage death.

He is distracted, and inanimate objects are calling to him.

He stands in a diorama of the farm that is unreal without me.

Throughout the yard the tools and machinery call to him.

The auger sits beside the rectangular grain bins that define the farmyard to the east.

During springtime planting I would pull the grain from the bin with the auger, its helical screw blade spiraling upward, dumping the wheat kernels into the bed of the three-ton truck. He imagines me there. He sees me prime the motor before pulling the recoil start that brings the auger to life. He sees me try two times, three times and he begins his approach, but I wave him off.

I got this, I yell.

On the fourth try, the motor roars to life.

The spiral blade coils itself around the shaft, as it digs out the memory and the marrow from his bones.

He looks up and Sandy sees the void within.

She is out of the car before the driver stops.

She runs to my dad.

The other occupants of the car fade away, Sandy's husband, my mom's brother and wife.

The barking dogs bring my mom and two sisters outside.

They form a circle on the lawn.

No beginning, no end, no sides, no corners.

Infinite misery.

Five stand together, as the absent one pulls them apart.

My dad speaks first.

He says, "I hope he knows what he has done to us."

He is so angry.

At life.

At me.

My sisters tell him that I didn't mean to die.

He breaks from the pack, but the pack follows.

He says, "I can't stay here. This was Jarett's farm and it still should be. Of four children, he is the one that would have stayed."

My mom says, "Jarett is here and I won't leave the parts of him he left behind."

The topics of conversation intensify.

The profundity of their misery spilling on the front lawn.

He blurts it out.

The subject the others are thinking about, but no one can articulate.

"I don't want Jarett's body rotting in the ground. I want him to be cremated."

I have no opinions about this.

We have never discussed death in terms of my parents, let alone me.

Son, should I bury you six feet deep or incinerate your remains to dust?

I am fine with whatever they decide.

My sudden death will assault and abuse them every day of their lives, and I have a front row seat.

My family lingers on the lawn, hoping that safety in numbers will thwart their thoughts.

It does not.

My dad heads for the quonset, his personal torture chamber now.

My mom longs for the supine position and the little prescription pills with her name on them.

Tricia follows my dad.

Bonny and Sandy enter the house with my mom.

On the mat at the front door sit my size twelve pair of work boots. Beneath them are mounds of mud that have fallen from the treads as they dried. It is the mud that I walked in at the creek bed yesterday when I helped my dad prime the pump. If you were to pick up those shoes, you would see a three-dimensional replica of the bottom of my soles, left in little piles on the floor. A clue about the life I lived. My soul haunting them, still disturbingly present. These seemingly meaningless bits of information are everywhere for my parents and sisters to find. There is the half-eaten sandwich that the dead teenager didn't finish. It will rot in the back of the fridge. There are my dirty clothes in the hamper. My mom will wash them and then put them back in the hamper to be washed again. The towel I used after I showered and hung on the back of the door in the bathroom. My toothbrush. The sweatshirt I left in the cab of my dad's truck. Those shoes at the front door will sit there for months. My parents and sisters are so afraid to move my things, because that might mean that I never existed.

Sandy will figuratively place her size seven feet in my dad's shoes now. She will stumble often, due to her inability to manage the gaping spaces she can't occupy. She will focus on Tricia's and her parents' needs.

She will care nothing of herself.

She will do many things wrong, but she will have the best of intentions. She is take charge, and Bonny will resent her for this.

THE FARM

My family walks hand in hand across the land.

They are extensions of one another.

Please don't let me be alone with this.

What courses through one, courses through the other.

The linking hands locking the torment within.

They walk along the creek bed and out to the grid and back. They walk through the alfalfa, the swaths of grass laying dormant, like me. They walk by the cluster of blue spruce that my mom and I planted last spring. The farmer is always adding to the stand of trees about him, as some will die each year. They pass by the bucket of grain that I left out yesterday morning and neglected to return to the wheat bin. My dad longs to scold me for my laziness. They see the tire on the old Minnie tractor that I pulled off on the weekend, the jack now holding the weight on the left side. The wind will push it over one day, as no one will complete the job that I started.

They walk as one.

There is an implicit sense of bidding goodbye.

Goodbye Jarett.

Goodbye farm.

THE VISITORS

And now come the visitors with lasagna in hand.

I don't get this visiting thing. Imagine your worst nightmare. Then imagine that everyone wants to talk to you about it over and over again. Imagine that everyone wants to come to your house and pretend that it is just another day. Think about how fucked up that is.

If you must visit, please understand that you are entering into a highly sensitive setting. The people you go to see are waging major battles against life inside their war-battered bodies from the onslaught of death. Really sit there and **think** about that. **Think** that almost anything you say will trigger some memory of their lost one. **Think** that however natural the opening phrase, "Hi, how are you?" is, logically, it is not appropriate in this quagmire where figures wander aimlessly, weary from death's wake. **Think** that some topics are just not appropriate. The wind chimes of life do not tinkle in the background softly anymore, they **GONG, GONG, GONG** inside their heads as you talk on about nothing. **Think** how hard it must be for them to look at you and see that your life is still intact and that you can go home to a normal life. They can never go home.

Sandy can't stay in the house with the stares she is trying to avoid. She wants to linger longer and steady her parents from the repetitious inquiry, but she leaves them in the capable hands of the eldest. Bonny excels at redirecting the conversation, and the stone cold statues of my parents flank her, leaning when they need to.
Tricia is hiding somewhere outside with her friends.

39

The dogs are by her side as they should be.
They are concerned for her.
Sandy takes refuge around the back of the house.
She carries paper and pen with her.
She walks around as a closed book.
Her tattered, tear stained pages hidden behind the covers.
Cloaking the darkness within.
She sits in the grass and leans against the wall separating her from the visitors.
She writes the words that ooze from her mind.

Come
Sit here with us
In our broken family room

Stay
As you are able
Laugh and talk and pretend with us

Death
Not in your house
Lives here in every room

Escape
We are not able
Your visit ends and you are whole again

DEATH

Death is pervasive.

It has taken my place in the house.

It sits in my chair at the table and it sleeps in my bed.

It has a physical presence when it comes for your youngest.

It is heavy and it is oppressive.

You can taste death in the spoken words of those who have gathered around my family — their exhalations hanging in the air — my parents breathe in the proclamations, *He has gone to a better place, God only takes the good ones, Time heals all wounds.* Their insides heave.

Teenage death.

You can smell death in the flowers that open and present themselves to my family. *We are here with our perfumes and colors arranged in baskets and vases to imprint upon you a feeling of sadness. You will never forget these smells.*

Death.

You can feel death as it slinks through the house. It presses its cold and clammy essence against my family's skin. It is in the shower where they stand alone — they can't escape it.

Sudden death.

You can see it in the eyes of the people who come to visit. There is relief in those averting lenses that fail to focus on why they are standing with my family and staring into their dead eyes.

Violent death.

My family can hear death in the last breath I took, the laborious inhalation, blood pooling in multiple organs, the rattle as the last air left my body, my expiration reverberating against their beings.

My death has consumed, covered, absorbed, encased, crushed, annihilated, swallowed, and regurgitated my family. Their bodies and minds are overtaken by this autocratic power, possessing unlimited knowledge of torture, distorting all that used to be real. People are near them, but they are alone. People speak to them, but their words mean nothing. With empty, cavernous eyes they stare back at those around them. They see nothing. They walk within a shell that is fragile and transparent. Any action is restricted and slowed by the sea of disbelief through which they wade.

My death has defined my life. It has taken the lead. It defines the lives of my family as well — *before Jarett died, before Jarett's accident, before we lost our son.* Death is personified at my house. Death has a face and it is bloody and smashed and the distortion hides the dimples. Death is tall and walks around with authority.

Death came for me, death didn't ask questions, and death took me away.

SNOW STORMS

Growing up in rural Saskatchewan (before cell phones), the first thing you learn about driving is that if you get stuck in the snow in a snowstorm, you never ever leave your car, even if you know what road you are on. The first thing you will underestimate, if you do, is the snow's ability to send you in circles. It winds across the flat land without anything to block or redirect it and so you think you are going north, but in fact you are headed east. And when the wind shifts and sends the snow spiraling in another direction, you will change course without knowing it, entranced with the hypnotic force of the fluttering flakes, your head down to keep the ice particles from pelting you in the face, your eyes following the movement across the snow drifts. The second thing you will sell short is the cold. You will think, *I am dressed warm enough*, but you won't be in minus forty degrees with the wind chill. Your eyelashes will freeze together, your lips will turn blue, and your toes and fingers will start to numb. Your movement will slow. The third thing that you will downplay is how deep the snow drifts will be and how tired you will get breaking through them with every step. Each forward motion that takes you farther and farther from your car, you will pray to your God that you will not break through the snow the next step, and when you do, you will long for the warmth of the car you abandoned. Your breathing will become labored and panicked. The final thing you will deny is how quickly your footsteps will be erased in the snow — the circling flakes covering the steps you took only moments prior — wiping away your route back to the car.

I feel like I must be lost in a snowstorm.
The ground is definitely swirling below me.

My steps deleted.
I am cold, but not on the inside, for my body has been voided.
I am shaking as a shadow, as the vapors move through me.

CHRIS

Chris — my best friend — comes to the farm the second night.

I see him stop his car before the turn into the yard.

I see him switch off the headlights long before the curve — the farm boy in him knowing that light in the country speaks volumes to those that wait.

He does not want to go to the house where I am not.

He sits with his head on the steering wheel, gathering the strength to face the parents who are his second family. Chris and I have been inseparable since kindergarten. Our homes and parents have been interchangeable. His mom would yell at me when she yelled at Chris if the chicken coop wasn't cleaned properly and I happened to be there. My mom would reprimand Chris and me equally when we walked across her clean floors with muddy work boots. I remember the scolding in the quonset when the two of us were lighting things on fire with my dad's torch. I remember the wrath of all four parents coming down on us when they found us marooned on the raft we built stranded in a dry creek bed. There was the time that I got frostbite on my wrists in minus thirty below weather, because neither one of us wanted to break from the fun of snowboarding behind the ski-do. My coat and my mittens didn't meet — I grew so much that year, so when I extended my arms to hold on to the towrope, a ring of flesh was exposed. My wrists blistered and I got yelled at a lot for that. We blew up dinky cars with firecrackers, and we played darts with Tricia's Ken doll as the target. Chris is the best friend I will ever have, and I doubt that even if I had lived to be one hundred, I would ever find another friend like him.

The memories keep coming. There is a bridge on Chris' road, the one that leads to the spot where I died. One winter when the wind carved the snow into a sea of rolling white banks, so deep that you couldn't walk without falling in up to your waist, Chris and I tried to trick the few cars that would pass by to stop. It was an elaborate setup and we thought it was ingenious. We brought an extra pair of boots that we found in his garage out to the bridge. We buried the boots in the snow, their soles facing upward, just beyond the railing that crossed over the creek. When a car finally approached, which was rare, I pushed Chris over the edge of the bridge and then he scrambled to hide beneath it. Our goal was to get the driver or the passengers to think that Chris had landed head first in the snow and that he was now buried, with only his feet sticking up. No one ever stopped, but we laughed our asses off every time we played out our roles. We eventually gave up on the cars and targeted Chris' brother with our prank. He is five years younger than us and so he seemed like someone who might fall for it all. He didn't. He just laughed and walked away.

Chris first heard about my car accident around 4 p.m. on the radio, roughly thirty-eight hours ago. The local news announcer stated that the accident was close to Richardson, so he stopped to think about whether he might know the people involved. He never thought of me. Chris had spent the day working construction at an offsite job in the city and was driving back to his home office to wrap up the day. Every Thursday night the guys he works with go out for a few beers. He knew something was up when his boss told him that he should probably go straight home that night. His parents had already called. He assumed it was one of his parents' friends, not his. When he saw his dad's face, he knew the accident would affect him directly in some way. He still didn't think it would be me.

Chris pulls up to the front of my house.
The dogs greet him as a member of the family.
There is no barking, no warning of a stranger approaching.
He knocks on the door when he would normally just walk in.
The lion knocker feels weighty and foreign in his hand.
The roles have changed already.

Death dictates that it is so.

The door opens.

Ten sad eyes are upon him.

Five pallid faces stare at my teenage friend.

There are tears and hugs while the ghost of me floats above them.

Chris is the touchstone to my life now.

A validation that I lived, told through the stories that only he can tell.

They gather round him like groupies.

Chris is the conduit that brings me to life.

His stories, the drug to the Jarett junkies before him.

Pulled from the gutter with the words of a boy who talks about motorbikes and cars and girls, getting stuck in the mud, getting lost in the city and laughing.

Good times that filled up the young lives of two boys from the country.

He talks openly and freely.

He is as funny as Chris always is.

The tales flow from his memory at rapid speed.

If the pace remains constant, the sallow faces regain some color.

When the words decelerate, the faces droop and the blood drains away.

He is the generator that sparks some life in their beaten down bodies.

His words bring them back to life.

I feel such gratitude for my friend Chris and all that he is trying to do for me.

Posthumously, he awards me with accolades, with laurels, with honors.

My gratitude will grow and grow from where I am now.

MY ELDEST SISTERS

Bonny came first. She was born in the sixties, and her personality was a good fit for the decade. She was a beauty of a baby, all plump and happy and the best first offspring anyone could ever have. She was filled with globs and globs of glee, her dimples lost in the chub of her cheeks, her legs and arms wrapped in the kind of pudge that is only adorable in infancy. My dad claims that as a baby Bonny literally never cried, as a toddler she never whined, and as a pre-teen she never sassed. I imagine that she let my mom and dad have a good head start at parenting, as she was just so darn perfect. She made motherhood look easy, I've been told.

Sandy came second, a little over a year later. She wasn't an easy baby from the start. I have seen the picture taken at the hospital and she is literally scowling, one eyebrow raised higher than the other, the right eye closed more than the left, indifference etched on the tiny face of a six-pound baby. She was the smallest of the four children born to my parents, but also the baby who delivered the most complicated birth.

If you look through the baby photos of my first two sisters, my parents developed rolls and rolls of film of the happy baby, but not so much of the grumpy one. It may have been the age-old excuse that says, *We have two kids now and so time is more limited,* but I think the happy subject simply offered an easier photo shoot than Sandy. We have had many a good family chuckle over the missing photos. *Bonny in the wagon, Bonny pushing the wagon, Bonny pulling the wagon... Where is Sandy?*

Bonny was the proud big sister from the start. As they grew into toddlers, Bonny played the little mother more and more. Sandy cried endlessly and Bonny would stand at the stroller, rocking it gently, whispering over and over, *Don't cry Sandy.* My dad always recounted these stories as they grew into teenagers and beyond, hoping as any father would, to bring the two back together, to stand as protector for the other, for who knows what the future will hold.

Bonny and Sandy shared a bedroom when they were younger. Two twin beds with matching handmade quilts. Bonny's bordered in yellow and Sandy's bordered in green. The hands that made them were my grandma's on my mom's side. I know those quilts, because they are wrapped in plastic and sit on the top shelf of the linen closet that Tricia and I shared.

Sandy started worrying at a very young age. I guess she was just wired that way. Bonny will tell you how Sandy needed to have my mom check the closet every night for bad people before she went to bed and how the door would then need to stay open. If Bonny happened to close it for some reason, the parental sweep of the closet would need to be done again. Sandy never asked my dad to do the check, and I would guess that had something to do with not wanting to appear weak in his eyes. She would have many opportunities for that in the future.

Bonny was more sure of herself as a youngster than Sandy. She could ride a two-wheeler at an earlier age, she wasn't afraid of the water like Sandy, and she didn't hide in her room when visitors came calling. *I'm going to my room*, Sandy would say. Sandy ate many a meal on her own, I am told, seated on her bed, her food on the TV tray, with her back to the closed door. You can still find those relics of the seventies out in the playhouse, the somber vision of a muted child eating a meal alone in her room.

Bonny was good at school and she had lots of friends. She could talk to adults with ease and everyone loved her can-do attitude. The roles would flip as the two girls became older. Sandy would find her way and Bonny would succumb to feelings of inadequacy. My death will flip them both on their asses and one will gain her footing much sooner than the other.

Bonny seemed to understand the depth of worry that surrounded Sandy at a young age — she was aware of it, but not until she was older did she understand its destructive capabilities. She had a genuine concern for her younger sister. She can tell you how Sandy could not sleep when our parents went out with friends. She would stand at the window searching the sky for the headlights that would bring them home. As a preschooler, if my mom left the house without telling her, Sandy would become panicked, screaming, *Mom, mom where are you?* Sandy cried every day at kindergarten. When my dad came in for supper and washed his hands at the kitchen sink and sang the song about "crying like a little whip pup," Bonny would be reminded that Sandy shed tears again at school and she would proudly announce it to my dad. He would be very displeased and Sandy would stutter, *I promise I won't cry in grade one.* And she didn't. As Sandy began to grow out of her fears, our family would still tease her well into her late teens and beyond. I remember once when I was quite young and Sandy was about 16, my dad left a note on the fridge when we went out for dinner last minute without her. It said, *We have moved. No forwarding address.* When we arrived home an hour or so later, Sandy was a good sport about it, but she said that when she read the words, the life in her body seized at the thought. A precursor for things to come.

My mom sewed most of Bonny and Sandy's clothes when they were younger, especially the fancy dresses they wore to weddings and on Christmas and birthday celebrations. You can see in the old photos that the fabric is always matching — the pink roses, the tiny dots, the white and blue check — but the sleeves on Sandy's dress were always different than Bonny's. Sandy would ask my mom to alter the sleeve in some way or add a different trim to make hers unique. Most people would ask my parents if they were twins, because their exterior appearances were similar, but their interior differences were opposite.

In high school, Sandy's personality began to shadow Bonny's. Sandy was not aware of the darkness she had cast in the direction of the eldest. They fought often, and as adults they would grow farther and farther apart. Their contrasting responses to my death will drive the wedge deeper still.

As an adult, Sandy is opinionated, take-charge, and very much like my dad. She is not tolerant of much and she is short on forgiveness. Bonny is calm and kind and will always give a person a second or third chance to win her over, more like my mom. Bonny is optimistic and Sandy is a pessimist.

I don't know when Bonny started keeping score, but I don't think Sandy was even aware of it. Sandy married first and moved far away to a life that Bonny imagined as something more than it was. Sandy was always in touch with us. She wrote letters, sent us gifts, called us regularly on the phone. She spent her summers with us when her university broke in June. Her husband typically had the summer months off as well, but he often stayed in the city with his parents due to his many allergies to the animals, the hay, and the grass. Sandy travelled to Montana and Mexico with us in the winters, because her husband always had a two-week road trip at that time. She lived farther away, but we often saw her more than Bonny.

I remember one December when Bonny used a holiday dinner as her soap box, the chairs filled with my family at home for the holidays, Bonny spoke openly of her dislike for the sister so unlike her. She was probably about twenty-seven, which would make Sandy twenty-six. Tricia was a teenager and I was a tween. I heard pieces of an earlier argument out in the yard when I was gassing up the John Deere mower, something about Sandy's old Mustang that she gave to Bonny and never having received payment. Everyone was dressed in their finest, trying their best to rival the beauty and bounty laid out on the table for ten. My mom used the pottery dishes from Mexico and they presented themselves in layers: large plate, salad plate, soup bowl. They sat on the plaid table cloth with the colors crossing over and under at ninety degree angles. Adorning the centre of the table were candles of varying shapes and sizes, acorns, dried fruit, and sheathes of wheat tied together with red ribbon, all the accoutrements made by the hands of the woman who sat in the chair nearest the kitchen.

The massive chandelier that hung at the middle of the interior court-yard, beside the dining room, cast a warm glow over the family that gathered to celebrate the end of another year.

Sandy sat there in disbelief, quizzically wondering why.

Bonny said, "You are too opinionated, you always think you are right, you are bossy, and I don't like you."

My dad was angry at the words that hung over the mashed potatoes, the turkey, and the apple pie.

He said, "Jealousy is not a feeling you should have for your sibling."

The eagerness for the meal stalled. Some of the spoken words fell into the potatoes, creating lumps that we all moved around in our mouths, not expecting them, chewing slower, not sure what to do. The passing of platters and pitchers halted, as the voracity for sustenance slowed. The fodder my mom worked so hard on cooled quickly on the table before us: casseroles, boats of gravy, tureens. Sandy sat upright in her chair, the black crinkling fabric of her skirt silenced like the rest of us, aware of her flaws, self conscious of her self. My dad stood and pushed back his chair abruptly, the wood legs scraping across the Mexican tile floor, catching on the lines of grout, falling back against the wall. My mom busied herself with dessert: blueberry, apple, pumpkin, à la mode? Sandy's husband broke the silence and the conversation picked up where it left off. Sandy helped my mom in the kitchen and Bonny stayed to converse with the men, Tricia, and me.

Bonny and Sandy each returned to their lives after the holidays — to the east and the west — and their sibling connection was further severed.

Bonny had two beautiful babies in her twenties.

Sandy had none.

Sandy endured needles and hormones and unnatural procedures in the name of procreation.

She longed for a child to fill the growing cavity in her heart.

Three years passed and still nothing.

Bonny had both of her children naturally and talked incessantly about the negative effects of drugs on the unborn. Sandy already knew that if she ever had the chance, she would not live up to her eldest sister's standards of childbirth. Bonny breastfed her kids until they walked, they only wore organic clothes, and they didn't play with plastic toys, which added to Sandy's feelings of how inadequate her uterus was.

When my death calls my eldest sisters home, they arrive with their baggage in tow — the characters from their past pushing hard against the characters of the present — clashing with the characters of the future. They will erect new walls and barriers in the house that I love, and they will tear down others in the name of hatred and loathing.

Sandy returns to the bedroom she shared with Tricia before she married. Bonny and her family are next door in my room. Tricia becomes Sandy's child in some ways; she comforts and croons the twenty-year-old who lived every day of her life with the boy they all mourn. There is an element of anger that Bonny and her family choose to sleep in my bedroom and that they are able to do it for that matter. Their clothes in my closet with mine, hanging silently, offering nothing. Sandy and Tricia stew in the bedroom next door.

There are family discussions about music and who will sit where and how will they celebrate me. Bonny and Sandy do not agree on anything.
Sandy pulls Tricia closer and gives Bonny a metaphorical shove.
My dad notices the two against one dynamic unfolding.
He says nothing, initially.

Sandy can't stand the yelling and the jumping.
Shouldn't kids be quiet when their uncle dies?, she wonders.
The noises from the second floor cause my parents to grimace and stare at the ceiling, willing it to stop.
Sandy enters the courtyard and yells up, "Bonny, you need to keep the kids from jumping and yelling so much."
The anger boils out of her.
Bonny matches that anger and trumps her a bit, allowing door slamming and jumping on the bed to the repertoire of noises coming from my room.
The gall of Sandy will push Bonny to ever-increasing leniency when it comes to restricting her kids' behavior. How dare Sandy

give advice on something she knows nothing about — *she isn't a mom.*

Sandy needs a purpose to propel her forward, and she will monitor the perceived needs of our parents and youngest sister. She limits too much alone time, she tracks food and fluid intake, medications, excessive noise, and any notice of calamitous behavior. Bonny will view her as dictatorial, her bitterness biting off more than it can chew.

Bonny has friends who will rally around her. She finds comfort in their words and their gestures. She appreciates them. Sandy has friends who call, but after two conversations, she chooses to "not be there" when the phone clangs to life, exposing the beasts that live inside, funeral directors, police officers, friends turned foe with their focus on the advice that enrages her. They call her husband instead, and he will instruct them to *give her some time,* and they will. Bonny likes people around her and Sandy only wants to sit in my tractor, alone. Bonny can find comfort in the words that people speak. Sandy despises the remarks that reaffirm her divergence. No one monitors Sandy's solitary tendencies but me.

Bonny feels removed from her sisters, but she would never let a description like "left out" define her. She busies and bustles about her children, using them as pawns to take down the queen.

Sandy and Tricia often find themselves sitting in the ditches up the road where I died. They walk there sometimes, their steps robotic, their words staccato. They don't consciously exclude Bonny from these walks, but they don't offer an invitation, either. The cleanup at the crash site has been completed, but there are still many small fragments of my red car remaining: silver trim, red body, black door handles, glass. The two walk through the fields searching for tiny pieces of their shattered lives to hide in their pockets. They pick up the pieces and carry them with them. They walk with their hands hidden — they feel the jagged edges — they feel the pieces of their lives and know that they will never fit together again.

The first time they go to the crash site, the tracks left by my braking tires are still visible — my car sliding across the dry dirt toward oblivion — brakes locked — a life passing by in an instant — the tire marks stopping on their westbound path and four tire marks scratching and clawing at the earth moving south — sideways — a body bashing about inside.

Tricia cries out, "Why didn't he turn away from it? Why did he let it hit him?"

I watch Sandy and Tricia sit for four hours at the crash site and not one car passes in any direction. They struggle with the knowledge that if I had stubbed my toe, kissed my mom a second time, or stopped to pet a dog, I would not have arrived at the intersection at the exact second the semi from the north passed through. I would have been just a little behind and would have driven safely through in the wake of his dust.

The things that Sandy and Tricia share out in those fields will add another layer to their already close relationship. Bonny exists outside of that bond. It is in this place of darkness that Sandy and Tricia will decide to make two plaques to honor me. One will sit where I died and the other will sit in the garden. They do not ask Bonny if she would like to help them. My dad cannot ignore his observations any further and he yells at Sandy for excluding Bonny from their tribute. He holds her responsible, because he expects more of her. Tricia is not at fault, because she would jump off a bridge if Sandy jumped first.

Sandy's obsession with having a child intensifies.

She knows that a tiny being will keep her from using alcohol to numb her thoughts.

Bonny and Sandy avoid each other. They can barely be in the same room.

Bonny resents Sandy's approach to everything and Sandy feels the same about her. Sandy will sever all ties to her personal life for over a year.

Bonny will return to hers in a week.

My family discusses who will sit in the front pews with them. Tricia states that Chris should be there, and Tyler, a city friend who spent many a weekend on the farm and loved it. Tyler has moved far away for university, but he will return for my memorial, because *Jarett was a big part of my childhood.* Another good friend. As my sisters discuss this with my mom and dad, Bonny states that she would like her friend Patty to sit with us as well. Sandy visibly quakes with confusion and says, "Patty has nothing to do with Jarett. She can sit in the front pew when you die."

Late that night, my two eldest sisters meet unintentionally at the bathroom door, their anger so tangible, it verges on physical, their auras circling their bodies, pushing back, indignation playing the puppeteer. What would become of the childhood they shared? Would their memories be deformed as they stared into each others pupils, combusting with rage? Would they forget about the matching white disco boots with white knee-highs and the homemade dresses with puff sleeves? I could see the spit and the veins in their necks coursing with hatred. The ghost of me stood in the shower, playing curator to their collection of disgraces. I know that my parents heard the sounds of their mutual loathing that night. I know that they rolled over, turning away from it, eyes open, staring into the void before them. They understood that two grown women who could not see eye to eye on a good day, could never see the same on a day that brought them all to their knees.

THE PLANS THEY MUST MAKE

Maybe it's morbid, but I think everyone should have a death plan. I wish I'd had one, and then I wouldn't have to watch my family flounder and flail through the details of how to honor me. I watch them drive to showrooms to purchase items they don't want to buy. They strive to present me and my short life to people who gather to 'celebrate' me. They do all of this while under the influence of grief, their thoughts and their actions impaired.

They discuss a church or a funeral home and quickly decide on the latter, as I have not been inside a church since I was a child.

They choose the one on Arcola that shares our last name — Speers.

Having an appointment with a funeral director is an unexpected position to be in when your son no longer fills your life with his presence. It is punishing to ponder the process while you drive to the city. I watch my parents as one of the husbands of my eldest sisters drives them. They sit like children staring out the window on a long road trip. *We aren't there yet, are we? I don't want to be there yet.*

The funeral director is a kindly man who wears a funereal black suit and a tie that is suitably somber. Appropriate, I know. One would think, however, that people dealing in death day to day would want to project a more positive first impression — a floral tie perhaps? The atmosphere is calm and quiet, and the people who work in the building move about as people sliding across the floor rather than walking, their words whispered instead of spoken, the doors closing soundlessly, the floors void of heels clacking against the wood. A respectful setting for discussions of the deceased — the dead lingering in the shadows like me — watching their families buy things they never thought they would need.

The process is well scripted. *We are so sorry and blah, blah, blah.* The first order of business deals with what will appear in the newspaper. Who should be mentioned that I 'left behind', that statement ringing with a suggestion of choice. In what order should the people I casually left behind be listed? Do you want to mention how he died or would you rather utilize the very convenient word suddenly? The funeral home will send the details to the newspaper, and my youth will lower the average age of the dead on the two days it runs in the obituaries. Tricia and Sandy are very upset that my parents sent in my graduation picture to accompany the details of whom I left behind. It may have something to do with never being able to look at that photo and see the smiling graduate, but honestly, it's because it's the face of the dead boy they love. They wish they didn't send a picture. Me too.

The subject of flowers is next, and whether or not they would prefer a donation to my favorite charity in lieu of the perfume-laden plants that will choke the air they breathe. They choose the donation.

The funeral director directs the details of death most efficiently; he tells my family where they will wait for the service to start, seating details, tables here and there, flower placement, etc. There will be a small table at the front where the urn holding my ashes will sit, and beside it will be an enlarged version of me in cap and gown. *I made it through this teenage milestone, but there will not be others*, the photo will say.

When you enter the funeral home, there will be two large tables containing as many photos of me as my family can fit. Me as an infant, me in a wagon, me on a horse, me playing baseball and skiing and snowboarding and laughing, me with the dimples. There will never be any new photos of me, and the sheer volume that my family chooses to display bellows deafeningly from the bowels of their beings. The pictures say, *Look at him, look at how handsome he is, look at the beautiful boy that was ours, look at how he lived, look at all that we lost.*

Before you take your seat, there will be a book to sign. The names listed there will say, *I travelled 40 kilometers to attend the memorial service of your child* and the names that are missing will say, *I was not willing to take the day off of work to celebrate your child's life with you.* The book was a stupid idea, but no one is really aware of what they are doing when they plan out the details of sudden teenage death.

I watch as they drive through the city picking out flowers, a casket, an urn.
Five ghosts sitting upright and silent.
Robotic.

At the flower shop, there is a young woman and two older women discussing in great detail floral options for a bouquet and table arrangements for an upcoming wedding. They do not notice that death has walked in the door in the shape of a mom, a dad, and three sisters. Sandy approaches the counter and the amorphous quietus falls in behind her.

"What can I help you with today?" says the perky petal pusher.

Sandy stutters out something along the lines of, "Memorial for a teenage boy."

The perk is replaced with pallor and death is led to a room with a door, so as not to interrupt the life affirming choices of corsages and boutonnieres, white roses, and calla lilies.

The floral designer presents options to my family and they all just stand there gawking in the direction of the voice. Sandy is good at details, so she steps forward to speed up the pace. She is like the quarterback laying out plays: she takes in the options, decides on one, and replays the plan to the muted and the maimed. The others are not capable of having an opinion. She will make certain that the arrangements are masculine and that they are large enough to fill the space behind the urn and photo. Bonny hates her for this, but sits quietly all the same. For the flowers Sandy picks sunflowers, golden rod, and other native plants — things that grow around the farm. My dad and mom stand wilted in the corner, and Sandy is aware of their need to exit the place of perfume and petals. Sandy directs the zombies to the car. Parents should never have to pick out flowers for their son, nor should they need to pay for them. Sandy will do both, and that will piss Bonny off even more.

And now for the box I will burn in.

The man selling caskets seems a little sleazy to me. I don't like his demeanor and neither does my dad. You are really leaning on a person's emotions when you present them with options to bury or burn their dead, the suggestion of, *Isn't your deceased worthy of the best we can offer?* He starts with the top of the line models. They are beautifully carved from expensive wood, they are silk lined, and there is a lace trim pillow for your dead head.

My dad speaks for the first time today. "You can stop right now."

They pick the cheapest, wooden casket, not because they can't afford the others, but because I would tell them to pick it.

They are true to me.

I could not look at myself lying in that ridiculous frilly box.

Finally, an urn.

The person there to help my family directs them away from the first section of urns, as they are too small and will not accommodate the ashes of a six-foot-six body.

They spend more time than they need to choosing the urn.

They decide on one that is again masculine, in neutral tones, and is engraved with sheaths of wheat. My dad takes the lead here.

It will never sit on the mantle above the fireplace, but it is where I will be, so it is important to them.

I thought that they would sprinkle my ashes throughout the farm eventually, but life will twist and turn away from that, and I will end up somewhere else.

I will have company.

MY TRACTOR

Sandy sits for hours in my tractor. When my dad leaves the house at night to find her, he looks there first. Sometimes she just sits and other times she screams and rages against the things that her mind tells her are true. It is a physical battle within her being, as she can't accept that I am gone. She comes to my tractor because she knows that if I was able to send her a sign, I would deliver it there. Sandy thinks that butterflies and rainbows are only coincidences, and that they are not signs from the dead.

She waits for me to show myself to her in some way that she would understand. She is not a religious person, but she has recently adopted the belief that the dead can and will leave you signs. She needs a gesture from the grave, a clue, a wave, a nod, to tell her that I am okay. She wants something concrete to take to my parents — a gift — he lives beyond the grave.

If only I could make the headlights on the tractor flicker off and on.

If only I could move my coveralls from the seat where Sandy put them to the steering wheel, then she would know I was there with her — for her.

People see what they want to see.
What they need to see.
Paranormal pandering.

Sandy knows that if I would expect anyone to look for signs, it would be her. I know that she is the one who lived with these fears and I was the one who made them come true.

Last night, as she did her ritualistic rounds, the harvest moon hanging in the sky bursting with melancholy, she noted the windows in the tractor were completely fogged over. She then ran obsessively to each and every vehicle parked in the yard and noted that none of the other windows were fogged. What she didn't notice was that my tractor still sat in the shade and the other vehicles all sat in the warmth of the sun. Her lamenting logic proved to her mournful mind that I had been there. This was her sign, and I was relieved that she had found what she needed. My dad came looking for her at the exact time she made this discovery, and as he listened to her recount the story, we both knew that she wasn't in her right mind. It was difficult for both of us to watch the sad, childless woman create these fantasies in her mind. My dad embraced her conclusion, knowing how much she needed others to believe in what she thought she saw. My death twisted and deformed her thoughts. She did not have control of her mind. And in the future, the despotic ruler will only offer tragic possibilities.

Sandy left the farm years ago, but on her returns, she has always sought some time in the fields with the power of the tractor beneath her. She has always needed some alone time with the farm-girl she left behind.

When she was home in the summer, she would ask my dad, "Do you have any summer fallowing that needs to get done?"

He would respond, "I can't trust some city slicker to drive my machinery."

They would laugh and then he always found a field in which she could find herself. I think he liked the idea that she actually missed the work of a farmer, the solitude and monotony of circling round and round, laying the weeds flat to wilt in the sun.

I taught Sandy how to drive the behemoth she sits in now. It is a bigger, more powerful version of anything she grew up driving, and she adjusted quickly to its immenseness and muscle. She was adept at maneuvering around the telephone poles pulling the thirty-seven foot cultivator, when she was accustomed to only twenty feet. She sat squarely in her seat, eyes forward, arms at ease, as she deftly adjusted the red levers to her right. A little forward on the controls where the land would slack and the shovels would need to dig deeper. A slight movement backwards when the land rose up to meet us, heaving, as her heart does now.

Bonny never spent as much time out in the fields as Sandy did. I guess that's why she isn't drawn to the places I was typically found. The fieldwork that Bonny did usually occurred when she needed money to pay for school. My dad would always find a field for her to plough, as he believes that if you pay your way with money you earned, you will be a better person for it. Bonny never looked back when she moved away, but for Sandy, there was always a sense of having left too much behind. She was always searching for what that might have been. And now she is just searching for me.

CATTLE

We had fifty head of cattle on the farm one year. This venture did not last long, as my dad quickly determined that, *Cows are the dumbest animals on earth.* We had horses that wouldn't cross a string of barbed wire lying on the ground, but the cows we had would throw themselves at four strings of wire, placed at varying heights across endless fence posts that defined our pastures. They would do anything to get to whatever lay beyond their confined space. Have you ever seen a calf trapped in barbed wire? If you approach it to help, it panics, and the wire tightens, causing the barbs to dig deeper. Huge saucer eyes bulge out at you, pleading for assistance, but they are too fearful to trust you.

It bawls and balks, twists and turns.

My mom reminds me of the calf I once tried to save.

The outcomes will be the same.

SANDY'S HUSBAND

Sandy's husband is a really smart guy. He is good with numbers and graphs and charts. He is a math/science geek. He strongly dislikes any kind of manual labor and would much rather pay someone to do any tasks requiring handiwork. He has never hung a picture or cut a lawn or built anything with his hands. He can talk endlessly about stocks and bonds and spreadsheets, and he can make money. He can't see the obvious, though. Sandy's husband is the type of person who can easily walk by you empty handed and keep walking, even when he sees that you hold a piano in one hand and an elephant in the other. I imagine what it must be like for my sister to hold grief in her arms every day and never have anyone to help her with it.

Her arms outstretched.
The muscles straining.
She tries to keep it all up in the air.
Her feet dance beneath her — side to side, back and forth.
Adjusting under the weight intent on crushing her.
She keeps looking around for her husband.
It's all falling.
Help me keep it up.
Help me catch it.
He isn't aware of all that she carries.
He is not capable of lightening her load.

HORSES

I hope there are horses where I am going. Horse and rider share a unique bond.

Horses have a distinct smell, and that scent lives forever in all the gear that they wear. When the horses are gone, like me, Tricia and Sandy will go often to where the saddles hang on two-by-fours secured to the ceiling with chains. They search for the smell that I speak of in the darkness where pieces of the farm are hidden. The oil and the sweat and the dander take them to the place they long for. They get lost in their minds on the phantom horses that carry them away.

The muscles and the power surging beneath them.

Leaning forward on the uphill.

Sitting back in the saddle going down.

They turn their heads to hear the sounds.

Hooves pounding the earth in quick succession.

The thrill of the race as they turn their mounts homeward.

The pace quickens.

They ease up on the reins and let the horses go.

The chargers dig deeper.

The movement — like floating.

The last quarter mile is the best.

Leaning into the curve, horse and rider as one, they are in the home stretch.

Equine nostrils snorting, the breathing faster and faster.

Hooves assaulting the earth.

The stampede to the edge of the corral.

Stopping only when their heaving chests touch the fence.

My sisters and I pulling back in the saddles, reins taut, grins effervescent. I can smell the horses too.

PLASTIC LETTERS

When I was young, my mom kept a big Tupperware container of magnetic letters in the kitchen. I can still see the clear, hexagonal canister with the yellow twist off lid. I would stand, teetering, at the metal front of the fridge and methodically pull one letter at a time from the bucket and place it haphazardly on the fridge door. There were no lower case letters, only capitals. Too young to spell, my letter choices and placement were more about color and my limited reach. When all of the letters clung to the metallic surface, my little hands would swat at them until they let go and fell to the floor. One by one I would pick them all up and then repeat, repeat, repeat. Today, I watch as Sandy and Tricia use those very same letters in a creative manner that could have never been predicted.

Some of the letters and numbers will serve their final purpose today and they will do so in my name.

The chosen letters will die a twisted death in honor of the child who stood at the fridge with them.

The letters that tell of loving memories.

The numbers that say when I was born and when I died.

The alphabetical characters that spell the name that my dad chose for me.

Each will be pulled and deformed from the drying cement that my sisters place them in.

Sandy and Tricia approach my dad about their idea. They find him in the quonset, with the gigantic door on the pulley closed tight, the sun streaming through the transom windows, and the man with the hands of a hero hiding in the shadows.

"Do you have any cement?" they ask him.

He is touched by their intentions.

He directs them to the sonoform, which will be the form that creates the circular shape they desire. He offers to cut through the heavy cardboard, but they prefer to tackle it themselves. He watches as they struggle to saw through the layers, but he hangs back. This is a process and it is theirs. He wants their distraction to last as long as possible.

They are intent upon doing something for me.

Even in my dead state it feels meaningful to them.

And it is.

I will watch them for many years to come, as they sit beside the memorials they create. They will sit with me in the rain, the snow, the wind, and the sunshine.

They both need a place to come to.

Tragedy will continue to choke the life from the two sisters intent upon self-torture.

My dad lays out a piece of particle board that will serve as the backing until the cement dries. My sisters place the two circular sonoforms on the board. They measure approximately seven inches deep and twenty-four inches across.

And now to mix the cement.

They search for a five-gallon pail. They clean it with the hose that sits by the power pole at the edge of the potato hills. They add the powder and slowly mix in the water with an old broom handle.

They pour so much love into that pail.

My dad feels it as he peeks through the crack in the door.

Purposefully left unlatched.

He can't stay in the quonset where two internally destructive sisters construct something special for me.

The weight of his body held upright by the door jam.

The sobbing silent within.

His shoulders rising and falling spasmodically, as the bile rises in his throat.

I feel the love where I rest in the rafters — the barn swallows about me.

The consistency of the cement is finally right.

Sandy and Tricia begin to experiment with the letters and numbers from my childhood.

They push the first three letters of my name into the cold, damp paste.

It responds to their touch.

Moving as a heart moves.

Like Jello.

A jiggle, a quiver, a shake.

The magnets will need to be removed.

And thus begins the dissection.

The obliteration of the toy that obeyed me, as it clung to its place on the fridge.

My sisters see me standing there.

My mom at the counter chopping onions.

They search for the needle nose pliers and then they pry each magnet from each shape.

The plastic, colorful letters.

Their purpose ripped free.

My sisters obsess about the placement and the spacing.

They trowel the cement over and over, wiping the slate clean on the letters and numbers that tell of the short life I lived.

The blank slate appeals to them and they relish in the process of wiping away the words.

But they try again.

My name screaming at them.

I am dead and you are not.

To the older sister, it says — *I am nineteen and you are over thirty. You live two thousand three hundred miles away, and I live here on this farm where I was content to live forever.*

To the youngest sister it speaks loudest — *I was the perfect son and you are not the perfect daughter. You should have been sitting in the passenger seat and your body should have absorbed all of the impact and left me alive. You should have lain broken and bloody on the hood of my car, not me.*

My dad busies himself at his workbench.

The work has changed.

He struggles to stand upright.
He watches over his girls as they watch over him.
He allows them only so much alone time and then he reappears.

The layout finally works and they have two identical, home-made memorials.

JARETT MICHAEL SPEERS
IN LOVING MEMORY
MARCH 10ᵀᴴ, 1979 - SEPTEMBER 17ᵀᴴ, 1998

My sisters leave the cement to dry and return to the house to tell my mom.
She is detached and uninterested in the telling of memorials made for her son.
She rarely leaves the house.
She can't enter the quonset where I am not.
She can't stand to see the purposeless man hiding in the silhouettes that the memories of me cast across the walls.
She prefers to feel the heaviness of her eyelids pressing down on her, drug induced, suppressing the visions of me.

My dad leaves the shadows and approaches the circular cement forms drying in the sun.
He was not aware of how my sisters were forming the letters and numbers.
He sees the container that used to sit on the counter in the kitchen by the fridge.
He moves closer.
He sinks slowly to the cold cement.
He reaches out his hands and pulls the jug of letters to his chest.
He sobs as he cradles the letters that spelled out fun on a fridge for a child.
His child.
The same letters sunk into the cement before him.
Their colors wailing, *We don't belong here.*

My sisters return to pull the letters free with pliers.
My dad retreats to the darkness.

The cement is dry enough to hold the shapes, but not so dry as to bury the shapes within.

One memorial will stay forever in the ditch where I died.

The farmer who owns the land will respectfully maneuver his farm equipment around it.

The second identical version will be placed in the garden for my mom, on the east side of a sloping hill at its centre.

She will plant bleeding hearts and daffodils around it.

The daffodils for my March birthday.

The bleeding hearts for her hemorrhaging organ.

My mom will be able to see the memorial from every vantage point.

Standing at the strawberry raised planters.

Kneeling in the dirt.

Hoeing and rototilling.

Picking raspberries.

Good intentions.

But the shapes from the little plastic letters will haunt her in that garden.

She will try to continue on with pulling the weeds from her life, but they will grow too fast and too big for her to keep up with.

Weeds will not grow around the circular monument.

I watch as the people left on the farm secretively tend to the small patch of land where I am memorialized.

My dad goes mostly in the dark of the night.

My mom sees the beam of the flashlight from their bathroom window and cries at the shadow of the broken man crouching in the dirt.

My sisters tactfully pull one weed at a time on their way to the horse barn.

They do not tarry there, for they are not the keepers of the garden.

My mom is, and for all intents and purposes, she still is.

At least in the eyes of those that need her to be.

FIRE

The funeral home calls and asks if anyone from the family would like to accompany me to the crematorium.

I am waiting in a refrigerator to halt the rot.

Funny story about my sister Bonny. She once put two dead cats in her freezer after they died in the winter, and these were two of the biggest cats I have ever seen, Wes and Jesse. She recounted this fact in a calm manner at the dinner table one summer night, her sisters and their families gathered around the picnic table outside. One of the cats was her son's and the other was her niece's. She wanted to preserve their bodies for burial until spring. I can't help but think of this story and how my family all stared at her in disbelief. Just imagine if she asked you to go out to the freezer to get some frozen peas and you happened on the frozen feline corpses. Imagine if you were one of the cats' owners. It makes me laugh every time I think about it.

But back to my refrigeration and the incoming inquiry that will slow physical and mental movement, similar to what happens when your body is refrigerated.

Sandy takes the call.

The funeral director is straight forward, but sensitive.

Sandy recounts the conversation to my family in a bumbling manner, unable to find the words.

They all listen, eyes cast downward, hands wringing hands, as she speaks the unspeakable, the words like insurgent soldiers — invading — uncaring of the harm they inflict.

Sandy and Tricia won't let me go alone.

They are the first to volunteer, which lets the others off the hook.

They accept the torture that they will feel as they follow me in a hearse through the streets of the city, but they each feel that they deserve it, so they will go.

Partners in the crime of self-torture.

My parents are relieved that they will accompany me.

I am off on a journey to a new place.

I should not go alone.

I think of my first day of kindergarten and how Tricia was there with me on the bus and how she showed me to my class. All the teachers in the hall knew her, and she walked with pride and certainty while introducing me to her independence.

Tricia wishes that we were taking this new voyage together.

Bonny is occupied with her kids.

The fact that she doesn't offer to go further separates her from the two sisters who have become one.

My mom retreats to her room and rages about the date I should be going on, the round of golf I should be playing, but instead I have an appointment with a furnace that will reduce my body to ashes. The body she grew inside of her, the body she gave birth to, the body she watched grow into a nineteen-year-old. She imagines my hair, my skin, my bones, the dimpled smile on the face with the patches of stubble I shaved. She cries out for the boy who will lie naked in a pine box and burn.

There is much tension in the house as Sandy and Tricia prepare to leave.

There are no words for the two who will convoy with me to my body's extermination.

There are no discussions about the elephant in the room who sits with all his weight on their beings.

Sandy and Tricia leave the farm and take the longest route to the city, the rocks on the grid road pinging off the hubcaps, the dust behind the car — like a parachute — pulling them back.

Sandy drives.

The city looms in the distance.

They stop at a flower shop to buy a bouquet — something pretty to offset the ugliness — something to leave for me as I journey on.

The flowers are wrapped in orange paper and tied with raffia.

They say, *We are here. You are not alone. We love you.*

They smell like spring on the prairies — rose hips and goldenrod.

My sisters arrive at the funeral home.

A man in a suit with his tie tied too high, greets them and asks, "Is there anything you would like me to place in the coffin with your brother?"

There are — letters from Sandy and Tricia, a special t-shirt, and family photos.

A part of my family will burn in that box with me today, the edges of their lives curling up, turning to ash, crumbling.

My mom lies alone in her bed and imagines the smells.

She can't stop herself.

She can picture the hair on my body igniting first.

She knows of the odor from when she scorched her hair while taking something from the oven one day.

She can feel the heat.

She envisions my youthful skin melting from my form, like wax sliding down, erasing my face and my scars and my birthmarks.

Deleting me.

She lies in her bed and screams.

My dad walks the wheat fields alone.

He follows the lines of the swaths, like a maze, leading him deeper into the abyss. He yearns for the six-foot-six child who walked these fields beside him.

Bonny sits at the kitchen counter, her youngest playing with Play-dough on the plastic mat and her son building Lego at her feet. She thinks of me and knows she made the right choice by not going. She is detached but present. She looks at her kids and sees the future. She thinks of me and knows I am from the past. Bonny's strength is her ability to see the truth.

Tricia and Sandy are both grey in color.

The hearse appears from behind the building and turns onto Arcola Avenue.

Sandy pulls in behind.

We are here Jarett. We are here.

They bawl in unison, their sobs filling the space like noxious gases.

Their minds screaming, *How can we be doing this?*

Two sisters escorting a brother.

Tears dig trenches in their faces as they drive, eyes forward.

They follow their dead brother who lies in a box, in a black car with curtains.

Sandy almost misses the light turning left onto Broad St.

She panics and accelerates aggressively — she can't lose the brother in the box.

The driver of the hearse proceeds slower now, reminding himself of the importance of the car that follows. The gaunt faces of the two young women in the car say, *Help us. Don't let our brother's body be in that car.* And everywhere around them people are going for groceries, meeting friends, buying houses, driving in cars that aren't following hearses, living life, while they live in their Halloween-inspired lives of coffins, cremation, and crypts.

The crematorium sits within a graveyard.

There are winding roads and trees as big as houses.

The ground is filled with rot and decay.

The hearse pulls up and stops in the carport attached to the front entrance.

The man with the short tie is there. He approaches the driver's side window. He asks if the two despondent sisters would like to stay while I am cremated. Tricia is inconsolable, but Sandy finds the strength to answer with a shake of her head.

"Do you want to see the coffin at all?" Another head shake.

The guy with the short tie informs them of the next steps, "We are going to remove the coffin now and I will return to tell you when it is placed inside behind the curtain. Please stay as long as you want. We will not begin the process until you have driven away."

I watch as Sandy leans on the steering wheel, face hidden, and Tricia collapses on the dashboard, body convulsing. Their eyes are closed and yet the visions are crystal clear. I weep for my two sisters who sit in a car and wait for an invitation to my torching.

A tap on the window.

They jump.

"Your brother is inside."

The two exit the car and enter the building with hesitation.

Such uncharted territory.

Such awkwardness.

So movie horror picture show — let me go in this room where people scream bloodcurdling screams — where someone is chasing me with a chainsaw, so I think I will hide in this shower where there is no escape.

They advance cautiously.

Walking with great trepidation.

Each of them worried about seeing a glimpse of a coffin, of me, of a furnace, of a fire burning brightly.

Straight ahead there is an expansive curtain across the entire width of the room. It is navy and hangs heavy, like a wall. There are chairs in front of it like a small theatre. I wonder if some people actually choose to stay and watch the coffin be placed in the furnace? Is that an option? Coming from the dead guy in the coffin, that sounds sadistic.

My sisters take a seat. They sit side-by-side and lean into each other, their shoulders acting as braces to keep the other steady. They are dumbfounded as to what they should do next. So they sit and they stare at the curtain and they imagine the horror that goes on back there. Their visions are accurate.

They share a mutual goal. They want me to know that they didn't let me go alone. And I do. *Can he see us? He isn't actually in the body that will burn when we leave, is he?* The silence constricts about them, each of them waiting for a sound that will speak of the process behind the curtain. Familiar sounds in an unfamiliar place. The sound of an oven door opening, the sound of wood crackling, the sound of a heavy object sliding across metal, like a cookie sheet being pushed into an oven. They sit there as long as they can, each wanting the other to leave, begging for this splice in time to end. They leave the flowers on a chair and the man with the short tie kindly picks them up and places them on my coffin while I wait for my turn.

My sisters run to the car, like children fleeing from the haunted house at the fair.
It is just the body that I lived in.
It is nothing.
But it is.
It is the body that my mom hugged and loved and cherished.
I mourn it for her and for the mom that she will never be again.

Hansel and Gretel come to my mind. I don't know why.
My mom read me that story when I was young, but always with the disclaimer of, *Parents don't leave their children in the woods and women who live in candy houses don't bake children in their ovens,* but teenage boys who drive carelessly can end up in a grim fairytale.

It takes over two and a-half hours to reduce my body to ashes.
The temperature in the crematorium reaches 1,400 degrees Fahrenheit and maxes out at 1,800.
My body arrives on a gurney type pushcart with wheels, the height in line with the door that leads to the inferno. It opens exactly like the door at the back of a grain truck — push the bar up and the door slides up at the same time — the grain racing to the exit where it falls to the auger.
My body is pushed flat through the open door, the heat bursting from within, escaping as I wish I could command my body to do.
The flame encircles my casket, fueling it as it rises higher.
I think of all the bonfires we had at the farm, the flames intensifying when my dad threw on the biggest fallen branches.
I think about stoking the furnace in the basement. Feeding the fire. I am the fuel this time.
The casket disappears first, exposing an outline of a mummified body.
I am engulfed.
My body dries quickly.
The heat and the flame burn off my hair and my skin first.
My muscles contract and char.
The features that define me vanishing.

The peach fuzz on my upper lip; my dimples; my closely set Speers eyes as Tricia and I refer to them; the ears that seemed too big when I was eight; my farmer tan; the muscles that ripple across my back and my shoulders; the calluses on my hands that speak to the man I longed to be; my wounds and my scars; the two-inch jagged seam of skin on my left shin where I walked into the cutting table on the combine; the indentation on my right thumb where I accidently caught it in the tire jack; the generator belt burn on my right pointer finger.

My soft tissues vaporize.

My bones calcify.

The goal is to get the bones to crumble.

Unfortunately, young bones are harder to break down, so they require some extra work.

I see the outline of my skull, my thighbones, and my hip sockets — defiant to the process.

The man responsible for reducing my bones to ashes pokes at my remains with a long metal pole.

Remnants of the me I once lived in.

I break easily now.

With a flattened rake, they pull my reduced remains to the front of the furnace, where the ash falls into a rectangular metal container. They pull the larger pieces to the side and let them cool. These parts of me will be further reduced in the bone blender. It is hard to watch bones from my body flying around in a big container, whizzing past the sides, getting smaller and smaller with each pass. I have heard about phantom pain when someone loses a limb, but this feels much worse than that.

When I am completely reduced to ash, I weigh a little over seven pounds.

I watch as they siphon the tiny particles of me, the tiniest hanging in the air, not wanting to enter the tomb.

I fit nicely in the oversized urn that my family bought for me.

CHRIS' GRANDPA'S BARN

Most barns in Saskatchewan are painted bright red. Some are bigger and better than others, and Chris' Grandpa's farm has one of the best barns I have ever seen. It is massive. The enormity of their barn has to do with the loft where hay is stored for the animals who live below. It is a gambrel style roof with a hay hood, and the hay sling still hangs on the outside. The sling is how the farmer transfers the hay to the loft, a system of ropes and pulleys that hoists the bales into the upper portion of the building to feed the cows and horses through the winter. There are holes in the floor of the loft where the farmer can easily throw down the bales into the stalls. Barn lofts aren't really used much any more, but Chris' Grandpa still uses his.

The ceiling in the loft is very high and there are hay bales stacked along the front and back walls that create a staircase of sorts. At the centre, the highest point, is a rope attached to the ceiling and beneath that rope is a huge pile of broken bales. This is the hay that gets pushed down the holes to the animals below. Chris and I made the pile in the middle as big as we could and then we grabbed the rope, climbed the stacked bales, and swung into the soft pile of hay, screaming like Tarzan.
I remember pulling the rope tight,
jumping straight up and then moving forward.
I remember the momentum.
Purposeful.
Feeling like a pendulum.
The gradual slowing at the furthest point and then moving backward.
I remember stopping mid air when I let go,

then falling.
Landing lightly.
Going again.

THE OTHER DRIVER

I am curious, but I don't ever go to see the driver of the semi that killed me. He was a teenager like me, and he was driving a massive vehicle at a speed that he never should have been. We can probably divvy up the blame evenly. Both stupid.

Both immortal in our teenage minds.

But only one of us is dead.

I think what I am afraid of seeing is a person unaffected by what he did and saw. I want him to have suffered in some way. I want him to refuse to ever drive a car again and to wait around in the snow and rain for people to pick him up, and I want the people to be late, and if he takes the bus I want it to be full, and I want him to have to stand the entire ride hanging onto the pole above his head. I want him to at least be inconvenienced by my death. I want him to think about me, and my family too. I want him to wake every morning and be bothered by the vision of me. I want him to think about the part he played in that one act and what it did to the lives of others. I don't want to see him living the life I am not.

His dad came to the crash site shortly after Tricia was taken away to the loony bin of her life. I hated that he came there to see the carnage. I hated that he could walk amid the gore, while his teenage son sat upright in a hospital bed and I lay covered beneath a sheet, my face hidden and unrecognizable. My parents heard about the other driver's father's visit to the crash site and they recoiled from life further at the thought of someone else choosing to view their wreckage.

The dirt road to the city where I died no longer exists for my family — it became a bridge out, a man down, a train derailed — it is one of the many detours and roadblocks that they face every day, as the sun rises and as it sets.

DAY FIVE

It's been five days since my death and the skies are layered in grey — the ominous colors streaking across the Heavens from the east to the west — my woebegone family unable to find shelter from its wrath. It rains daggers and swords and Sandy sits alone in the tractor again. Very few people will come to the farm for Sandy, as she moved away from here over ten years ago. There is just one who braves the weather outdoors and the storm that rages in our home. Her name is Candace. They have known each other since kindergarten, they grew up together, and their friendship is real. When the two were younger it was Candy and Sandy. She is the only friend who comes from Sandy's childhood. I watch as she walks with determination and focus through the mud that consumes her feet with each step. She wears flat, expensive shoes that coordinate effortlessly with her trousers and her blouse. She does not tiptoe through the sludge, but rather, she assaults it with each step. She climbs the ladder that leads to the tractor cab, a city girl not at ease on the farm. She sits and she listens. She doesn't offer advice on things she knows nothing about. She doesn't tell Sandy that *everything will be alright.* Candace doesn't draw attention to the fact that she sits in grease, her trousers have gas stains, and her make-up runs down her face. There is a genuineness about her that I like. I was a child when I knew her, and as a dead nineteen year old, I respect her.

MONTANA

Just two weeks ago, my family gathered amid the ponderosa pines of Montana. We went to the small cabin outside Whitefish where we have gone many times before, the tiny house with one bathroom and two bedrooms for ten. No luxury, no frills, no concierge, just family. Montana has always offered us experiences as a family that were wrinkle-forming from laughter. We could simply be sitting outside on the deck, and that could turn into an exercise in hilarity with songs, or skits, or charades. Siblings and ski slopes, great tee drives and greens. It is here that we had snowball fights in the winter with the snow falling heavy, but soundless, in great puffs of fluff from the sky. The snow falls differently there than in Saskatchewan. It descends from the Heavens as if suspended on a line. I can visualize my sisters and I catching soft marshmallow flakes on our tongues. It feels like bobbing for apples, but in the reverse.

Montana is all about trees and how you feel beneath them. We all left the Rocky Mountain Juniper, the Douglas-fir, and the Lodgepole pine behind that August day. For a family born and raised on the bald prairies, trees are something to respect. In the winter, the heavy snow covers the trees and they emerge as snow ghosts. Their eyes, noses, and mouths appear haphazardly where the snow pulls the branches apart. In the summer, they are the shade and the movement in the breeze. They are the cracking in a gust of wind and the shelter in a storm.

Montana exists for the dead in their hearts now.
It is not a place to make memories, but to bury them.

Montana has always been our vacation destination in the winter, as we all love to ski. During the past few years from time to time, we have also traveled there in the summer months. During our last family gathering at the end of August, we spent the days golfing — we putted, we birdied, we bogied, we did the back nine, the front nine, the bunkers. The fairways stretched before us providing runways to the world. The greens were lush and the endless opportunities to get the little white ball in the cup mesmerized us. At night we swam in the lake, played cards, and laughed.

The little house will sit empty now for many years.
The white painted cabinets with the wallpaper-lined shelves will hold captive the laughter that fueled our family.
The inviting warmth of the front furnace will not entice them to return to the shadows that lurk and loom.
The scab-covered memories are left bleeding in the corners.
It will be a sad day when my family sells the little house in the woods that sits at the base of a mountain.

We all left and went our separate ways after we said our goodbyes on the circle drive two weeks ago. My mom took her obligatory photo, with me in the centre and everyone else leaning in on the sides. There are smiles on all of our faces, and we are optimistic about returning here in a few short months for ski season.

This was the last time that we were all together as a family. Bonny, her husband, and kids piled into their van and hit the road for Alberta. My mom, dad, Tricia, and I left next for the ten-hour ride home, and Sandy and her husband headed to the airport. Sandy's last words to me were:
"Be careful. Drive safely. I love you."

I keep seeing a snow globe.
We all are standing in it and the white flakes rest at our feet.
Someone shakes the globe.
The snow flies.
When it settles,
I disappear.

THE HOUSE MY DAD BUILT

The original house on the farm was nothing like the house my dad built. It was a two-story stucco structure that was minimalistic, generic, and functional. I was only a baby when my dad started construction on the new house. It is a Spanish style home that sits proudly at the centre of our 320 acres. It is not the typical farmhouse with its clay roof tiles, stucco arches, indoor and outdoor courtyards, and wrought iron balconies. It stands in stark contrast to the farm equipment, the garden, and the quonset — the grandness living beside the utilitarian. My dad built the house over the course of a couple of years with minimal help. He is a Jack-of-all-trades and believes that *if you want something done right, do it yourself.* He mixed and poured cement, he built floors and walls, he laid tiles and carpet, he shingled and hammered and nailed. He built our home sturdy and skimped on nothing. Anyone who knows anything about construction, knows that 2x6, double-studded, staggered walls will produce a structure to withstand the weather and keep the family safe.

When a house is first built, it has yet to settle on its foundation, and some would say that it is lacking in character. Over time, a house speaks to the inhabitants that walk on its floors and climb its stairs; they establish a relationship of sorts from their continual interactions. The people who live in our house know how to get the house to speak to them, how to welcome them home; the floor responds with a squeak when they walk across the threshold into the bathroom upstairs; the third stair to the basement gives way and dips down on their descent and ascent; the door to the pantry whines on its hinges when they open the double door on their right. Little signs of a house's personality build through time, and the noises it emits soothe the people who live there.

My parents have a love of Spanish architecture and collected books through the years with house plans from Spain and Mexico. My older sisters remember them leaning over the kitchen counter with rulers and pencils, making changes to their favorites. The original plans for our home had six sliding glass doors leading to patios and courtyards, bringing outdoor spaces indoors. The Saskatchewan prairies dictated that they cut way back on the indoor/outdoor theme, due to the harsh temperatures in the winter, but they maintained all the other details.

We traveled to Mexico to buy authentic furniture, dishes, and finishing touches for our casa on the prairie. My dad built a fifth wheel trailer to pull behind his big diesel truck, and then my mom, my dad, Tricia, and I made the trip to Mexico to purchase the furniture that would fill our home. We would be gone for quite a while, and so Sandy needed to stay at home to take care of the animals. After travelling for over three weeks, we arrived home at 2:45 a.m. — my dad can really drive like a truck driver when he sets his mind on a destination. Sandy woke easily to the noises filling the house and helped us unload our treasures. I remember how my dad left his truck running and how my mom and Sandy lined up their cars beside his to help us see, the six headlights casting giant shadows of mammoth tarp covered shapes against the stucco of the house. The sun was rising before we were done, and inside were the pieces of furniture that my mom would use to make our house a home.

My dad scoured endless auctions to find the appropriate sconces, lights, and the centre courtyard chandelier — each was stylistically inline with the Spanish theme. The tiles on the floor are Spanish red clay to match the red tile shingles on the roof. In the outdoor courtyard, twelve metal lanterns light up the space and the patio cushions are covered with authentic serapes — the stripes so festive and inviting — the feel so authentic. Tricia had a piñata party in the courtyard for her eighth birthday, my dad hoisting the donkey up and down on the rope while the kids fumbled to find it with the stick they swung, blind to its whereabouts, blind to the future. My parents played mariachi music on the stereo just inside the screen door on warm summer nights, the festive sounds reverberating to the barn and back, leaving impressions on the people who lived there, impressions that will be hard to leave behind.

The front door is massive mahogany, set back on the porch and placed in line with the first arch that leads you into our home. Two additional arches rise and fall the length of the porch to the left. There are four chairs and a table — prime seating to witness the start of the day — the view straight east, where you can watch the sun cresting the horizon. My mom always planted flowers that filled the beds in the summer, the blooms reaching up and on to the outdoor space. At the highest point of each arch she hung a basket, filling the porch with the perfume and colors she loved.

When you enter the Spanish style home that my dad built, the first thing you see is the room with the balcony that looks out over the interior courtyard below. It sits at the centre of the house and your eye is drawn to it when you enter. Tricia's bedroom is behind that door. When I read *Romeo and Juliet* in high school, I always thought of my sister's bedroom, the turquoise stained glass flanking the opening that sits in the archway, two sconce lights sitting to the left and the right of it.

To the right of the front door is a game room of sorts. There is a pool table that also adapts to a ping-pong table. We had mini tournaments all the time, and I was typically the champion at ping-pong and my dad the winner at pool. Tricia, Sandy, and I sang the blues in that room. We lounged on the two love seats, me accompanying on the guitar, playing the same lick over and over as we took turns singing out a line.

Tricia: *My baby she left me.*
Sandy: *I don't want to be free.*
Jarett: *I'm so sad and blue.*
Tricia: *The rent is past due.*
And so on…

The staircase is to your left and it turns right at the landing and crosses over you like a bridge when you walk through to the family room. The space is open and big, yet unassuming. As you continue on, the dining room is on your right. The table and ten chairs are impressive. The backs of each of the chairs are intricately carved from pine, the lattice and the spindles suggestive of their origin. Leather hides are stretched taught, forming seats, which are secured with massive grommets the size of silver dollars. When you sit in the chairs at our dining room table, they move and creak like the leather saddles that hang out in the tack barn.

The family room sits at the back of the house and opens to the kitchen and the exterior courtyard. This was the most used area of the house before I died. Now no one wants to sit in a room called the *family room*.

If you stand in the courtyard and look up to your right, you will see an arched interior window, like the ones in a church. It is placed beside the door of the master bedroom and it looks out on the staircase and courtyard below. My dad added the opening with the intention of having a stained glass window installed. As the ultimate do it yourselfer, he took a stained glass class and constructed a studio for himself in the basement. He painstakingly searched for patterns and decided on a flamenco dancer with all of the vivid colors he loves.
To date he is about two-thirds done.
The tiny pieces of glass laid out on the table he made.
Taking shape.
His vision visible.
But not complete.

My dad will never finish the flamenco dancer.
It will sit beneath Sandy's guest bedroom bed for years.
Until she finds the courage to do the work for him.

We all played a part in the assembly of that house. I remember laying the bricks in the outdoor courtyard the weekend before Bonny was married. She wanted a small affair in the intimacy of our home on the farm. I was only seven and my mom forced me to stay in those fancy clothes for photos. I am so glad that she did. One more photo with me in it.

The house still speaks to my family, but in an eerie kind of way. The branches at the back scratching across the eaves trough, the metal gate in the courtyard neglectfully banging, because someone forgot to close it. The wind howling in through the fireplace, whipping the ashes about in the hearth, toying with the burnt remains. The snow and the leaves and the weeds surrounding the house, moving in for the kill.

My empty chair at the dining room table will push them to eat elsewhere. No one will sit at the table for ten and stare at the black hole my chair represents. Those left behind will disperse throughout the house so as not to call attention to my absence. They will keep my bedroom as I left it until the world devours them at last.

This is the house that love built, and death will tear it down.

THE FARMER'S WIFE

The farmer's wife: the benevolent. She serves the greater good and spends less time thinking about herself than most would be capable of. She is in charge of every meat and potatoes meal. She cooks and she cleans and she shops for groceries that she hopes to last for at least a week, always preferring to stay on the farm instead of making endless trips to the city. She can make a great meal from leftovers and what she finds in the pantry. She also needs to be able to drive a three-ton truck beside a combine that is unloading the wheat into the back bed — go too fast and your summer crop ends up on the ground — go too slow and the wheat covers the cab. The farmer's wife needs to have a calmness about her, an ebb and flow if you will. She needs to be able to drop everything she is doing and drive to the city for a part if one of the large machinery breaks down. She needs to know her crescent wrenches and her screwdrivers, so that she can pass them to the man who lies beneath a motor and requests the necessary tools from her.

The farmer's wife is master planner of the gardens. She will order her seeds in February and look forward to the day that they arrive in the mail. She will yearn for the warmth of spring so that she can dig in the dirt. She is a miniature farmer, and she lives her life as he.
Optimistically.
She's the Jill to his Jack.

Let me tell you about the minutiae of my mom. She was born and raised on a wheat farm, went to teachers college and then married a man who lived a town away on another farm. My mom was a schoolteacher before she was a mom. She is kind and caring, and I imagine that she was the recipient of many "#1 Teacher" coffee mugs. I have never liked to read, and she struggled with that as an educator. She would do almost anything to get me to absorb the information in the novels we read at school. She read many books in their entirety out loud and recorded herself so that I could listen to them when I was getting ready for school, doing fieldwork, or lying in bed. I don't know many moms that would have taken the time to do that for their growing boy through high school.

My mom hates confrontation. She hates returning anything to a store, she hates asking someone to do more, and she will not fight over the belongings of the dead. When her parents died, she let the brother who put his name on everything take it all without a fight. I remember how mad my dad and older sisters were, but it was her fight to fight and nobody else's. She did go back into the old homestead and take the electric floor polisher, hoping it would simplify the polishing of the Spanish tiles in our home. This caused great agitation for the brother who had literally taped his name to the undersides of chairs and tables and bureaus before their parents were dead.

The brother said, "How dare you take things from the house without telling me."

She took one thing — an obsolete polisher — with absolutely no monetary value, or of any use to him, with his lavender shag rug from the seventies. Meanwhile, the brother 'bought' the family farm without telling the eldest sister. My mom just walked away from it all.

Before I died, my mom was the quintessential mom. Every morning before school, she rose early to make a hearty farm breakfast for her kids — eggs, bacon, and toast with homemade strawberry jam. At the end of the school day, there was always a snack waiting for us before we did our chores — homemade cookies on the counter with a cold glass of milk, cinnamon buns, fresh bread, or a bowl of fruit with a sprinkle of sugar to release the juices. My mom cared for the animals in the same way. Whenever one of our horses succumbed to the ravages of old age and had trouble eating hay, she mixed up a daily batch of some concoction she found in an Equine magazine. She swore by it and the horses loved it. She started by separating the ailing beneficiary from the others and placed the handpicked mount in a separate corral. The chosen horse understood the ritual and watched as she picked up one of the feed pails and carried it back to the house with her. The horse made noises that can only be described as purring like a big cat, knowing of the warmth forthcoming. My mom measured out the bran, molasses, corn, and alfalfa and then added warm water. She mixed it all together into a consistency that was easy to digest, and then exited the front door to the sound of a whinnying horse. She was smiling the entire time — so at ease with the task of providing for others.

My mom made numerous scrapbooks for each of her four kids. She cut and pasted and decorated with stickers and colorful paper. She spent countless hours with our photos laid out across the pool table and on the piano bench. At the front of each of our books she wrote, "You may have tangible wealth untold, caskets of jewels and coffers of gold. Richer than I can ever be, I have a mother who made a scrapbook for me!" — Adapted from the Reading Mother by Strickland Gillian

There is nothing forceful or authoritarian about my mom, but she has some intense willpower for someone her size. I remember a day when Tricia and I were quite small. Sandy had just returned from a long ride on her beloved Pal, and my mom sat in the shade of the willows by the corral fence holding the lead rope, while Sandy unsaddled him. Tricia and I were playing in the tall grass beside Pal, feeding him grain and combing his mane. He was such a calm horse with kids underfoot. Of any of our horses, Pal was beyond trustworthy.

There are two straps on a western saddle that go under a horse's belly. One is behind the front legs, and is fastened tightly to hold the saddle in place, while the other is looser and hangs beyond the mid-point of the belly. Sandy unfastened the cinch belt at the front, but forgot to unbuckle the back belt. When she went to lift the saddle off of Pal, the back belt hit him forcefully underneath and startled him. He leapt forward as a reaction to the snap on his underbelly, which caused Sandy to let go of the saddle, which then slipped sideways and backward toward his rear, the belt tightening as the weight of the saddle spun it up-side-down. Pal was in a full twisting buck by then, scared out of his mind and intent upon removing the tightening force. My mom held steadfast to the rope to steer the powerful Pal away from her children. Sandy could do nothing, as Pal was crazed and intent upon freeing himself from the saddle that had now moved to hobble his two back legs. Pal was insane with fear, and still my mom held on. Pal kicked the saddle to pieces and dragged my mom through the dirt. She finally let go when the danger was removed from the vicinity of her children. Pal ran, shaken to stand at the corral gate. Sandy was running to put Pal back in the pasture, but turned around when Tricia and I started screaming. My mom stood up and her hands were bloody and raw. She had wrapped the rope around both of her hands and fingers to gain a stronger hold, and all of the skin was literally ripped off. My mom's biggest concern was calming Tricia and me. She tried to hide her hands from our view. Sandy ran to get my dad, and he took her to the hospital in the city. When they returned, her hands were wrapped in gauze like Michelin man hands. They reminded me of paws, like those of the dogs and the cats. It was months before she regained the use of her hands, but she never complained once. Especially not to Sandy, who knew the blame was hers to own.

Before I died, if you couldn't find my mom in the garden on a summer day, she was probably standing at the sink in the kitchen. When you entered, her back would be to you and her petite frame would be at the centre of the large window that looks out on her crab apple trees and chokecherry bushes. She always loved the view from this window. The light in the afternoon bouncing off of the produce placed in piles on the counter. As the sun set, the colors danced between the trees and the leaves. She loved the produce she pulled from the ground and pulled off of plants. If you stood and watched her, you would see a familiarity, a love, a joy that she found in each shape and size.

Shucking the corn was a ritual of discovery — she pulled back the corn husk to reveal the silk and the yellow beneath — the plump, juicy kernels presenting themselves to her. She dried the husks and made angels that hung on our Christmas tree. The peas were her favorite. Each pod *popped* when she pressed lightly on the seams, revealing the uniform, circular morsels inside. She slid her thumb down the centre and the peas gently succumbed to her touch. They fell to the bowl on the counter in the kitchen the farmer built for her. She snouted green beans until her fingertips were sore. She peeled carrots and beets and washed lettuce leaves and berries. She spent so much time simply washing the dirt off of carrots and potatoes. The soil in the garden is rich and black and sticks like gumbo to the produce that grows under the ground. The horses loved the carrot tops and peels, so my mom took great care in dividing those into plastic bags that she took out to the mammals with the flowing manes and tails, the ones that called to her each time she left the house. They pawed at the earth and whinnied to the woman who used to bring them scraps from her kitchen sink. She left and entered the house each time with pails and bowls and bags. Food for her family when she entered, food for her furry friends when she left. Her hands are empty now.

Fall on the Saskatchewan prairies is a short season; the wind and the frost come suddenly. In order to protect the produce that still lay in her garden, my mom would cover the plants with blankets at night. If you watched her, you would see a kind of tenderness that not many possess. She endeavored to save every tomato and every cucumber, pulling on the corners to stretch the fabric more, tucking each colorful shape that she planted and tended, safely beneath the blanket's cover.

My mom was not the disciplinarian at our house. It was my dad that we all feared when we made a mistake. Shortly after moving into the new house, Tricia placed a hot pot on the counter where she should not have. The result was a circular burn mark the size of the pot. It sits to the left of the double sink. My dad was madder than a hornet, but my mom simply solved the problem by hiding the mistake with a glass cutting board.

Always able to see beyond the blunder.

Until now.

Before I died, my mom cared deeply about the footprint our family left on the earth. She recycled everything: she washed Ziploc plastic bags and bottles, she used both sides of every piece of paper, glass jars were filled again and again, tinfoil was wiped off and folded neatly in a drawer, any animal carcass was used for the base of a soup. *Waste not, want not,* she said.

The farmer's wife struggles with the black, nocturnal rodents that build molehills throughout the farmer's yard. She is especially concerned with the moles that reside in her gardens, with their velvety fur and cylindrical bodies. She sets traps in the hopes of catching them. They live beneath the earth and move about through tunnels they dig with their powerful forelimbs and large paws. They construct their subterranean passageways beneath the green beans, the cabbages, the lettuce, and the zucchini. At night, the produce disappears. They approach the carrots from underground and pull their prizes into the darkness below.

My mom sits alone in the garden and cries for me.
The moles come for her every time.
Pulled under.
Buried alive.

GUNS

In my dad's office, through the double doors, is a gun rack. There is a .22, a shotgun, and an automatic rifle. My dad is not a hunter, but most farmers in these parts will have weapons to combat the gophers in the wheat fields and the raccoons in the corn patch. I recall one summer when the raccoons were rampant and each morning we found piles of cobs stripped clean amongst the carrots and the cucumbers. The black-eyed, nocturnal bandits were feasting on our produce and their dexterous front paws allowed them to peel the corncobs with ease. I remember the night my dad sat on the round grainery beside the garden, gun in hand, intent upon killing the varmints that were stealing our kernels of corn. I remember how I wanted to sit out there with him in my footsie pajamas, but he wouldn't let me. Morning came and he told us of his inability to kill the creatures with the black rings decorating their tails. He told us how the cleverness of these animals had saved them from death and that he marveled at their ingenuity and nimble hand-like paws.

I have held and shot a gun, but I don't find pleasure in ripping bullets through the flesh of innocent animals in order to make sausage or hang a head above the fireplace. I am responsible, though, for having created some intense carnage. I can see each of the five that I left behind, and I can visualize my accident hunting them down and taking aim. I have committed a mass murder of sorts.

The first impact sends them staggering backwards, falling, hearing only the echo of the blast that was impaled upon them.
Accident.

Oblivious, shaken, certain there has been an error, screaming, "No, not Jarett," they stumble to their feet.

They must fight against this information and make it untrue.

A second blast, with as much force as the first, sends them cowering to the floor. *Dead.*

They are lost.

They cry out for help, to no avail.

Now the blasts are being fired repeatedly as they lay immobile on the floor.

Died instantly, no hope, at the morgue, hurry home.

I can feel their bodies buckle against each blow, but they are unable to redirect the words meant for them.

They lay in a pool of agony battling mind and body in an onslaught of feelings that they have never known or can accurately describe.

They are helpless.

They try to purge their minds and bodies of the words, in hopes of purifying themselves and returning to who they were before.

Shot down.

Gone.

Forever.

TRICIA AND ME

Tricia was born one and a half years before me. Bonny and Sandy were fourteen and twelve years old and already in middle school. All of the kids at school told them that my mom was going to die giving birth — *She is too old,* they whispered. Bonny didn't dwell much on these statements, but Sandy did.

Tricia was a similar baby to Bonny, content as can be and the apple of my dad's eye. She was a towhead, with flaxen blond framing blubbery cheeks, a smile that she employed to her advantage, and eyes that held the eyes of the observer captive. When I think of that smile from our childhood beaming back at me, I think effervescence, unmitigated jubilation.

Tricia never complained and she very rarely cried as an infant or a toddler. She was not ruled by the temper tantrum, nor did she proclaim, *I want, I want, I want.* Tricia spent her childhood in contentment, as there were not many things that could get her worked up. We got snowed in on the farm quite often in the winter. We would use the ski-dos to get out to the main road where we parked my dad's truck and my mom's car. The snow in those days came in drifts that would require a bulldozer to clear our road. As a testament to Tricia's cheerfulness as a baby, my dad would often tell the story about when she was bundled up in numerous layers of blankets and somehow my mom picked her up the wrong way and held her upside down on the ski-do ride bouncing across the fields. Tricia never made a sound. When they opened the swaddling in the warmth of the car, her feet were where her face should have been. When my mom righted the child in her arms, the toothless smile that we as a family would feed on was liberated through the layers.

Tricia was the perfect 'little big' sister for a baby brother to come home to from the hospital. I can imagine her standing at the front window, the curtains billowing behind her as she waited for the sound of my dad's diesel truck bringing me home. I was bird-like in appearance and had more skin than my body could fill. Bonny and Sandy actually called me a bird — my mouth always open, crying for food, crying for someone to pick me up. There is an adorable photo of Tricia holding me immediately after my mom and I arrived home. She is wearing a navy and yellow baseball shirt, her hair is curled in a pageboy haircut, and she is sitting on a turquoise knitted blanket that my grandma made for me. Her legs are placed straight out in front of her and I am told that she just kept saying, *Me knee, me knee.*
She wanted desperately to hold me and of course my mom obliged. I stole her heart right then, and nineteen years later I handed it back to her — obliterated.

I understand that as a child I was about as stubborn as a kid could be. I had very strong ideas about what a little boy growing up on a farm should wear, never sweatpants or shorts or corduroys. In every single picture of me between the ages of two and eight, I am wearing cowboy boots, jean overalls, and a shirt. My mom explained that even on the hottest days in the summer, the only piece of clothing that she could negotiate away from me was the t-shirt. Sure enough, there are photos of me bare-chested beneath the bib of my overalls. I was the kid that embarrassed my mom at the mall with fits of rage. I was the kid that she held under the cold shower, holding me up by the straps of my overalls, to get me to cool off. I was the kid that my two older sisters would walk away from in public when my mom couldn't control me.

Tricia is the sister with whom I shared the most. We grew up in the bedrooms at the end of the hall. We grew up playing in the dirt that grows the grain that we harvested. There are photos that hang throughout the house — the ones they avoid with their eyes now — where we have dirty faces and dirty clothes, but in a cute farm-kid kind of way, nothing neglected looking. Tricia and I loved the dirt that surrounded us in every form: sandy dirt, muddy dirt, dirt mixed with clay, blowing dirt, dirt clumps, and dirt piles. Our toys were somewhat limited and we were always encouraged to be outdoors. We had the sky and the clouds, the wind and the rain. We had each other.

Tricia and I shared some of our friends growing up. She had a good pal from the city named Tyler and she would let me play with them when we were younger. As we grew older, there were times when Tricia would cry to my mom, "Tyler is my friend and Jarett is stealing him from me," but such is the dynamic with boys as they grow, girls get "icky" before they become appealing again. Tricia was by no means a girly girl. She never played with Barbies or babies and she never baked brownies in an Easy Bake Oven. She did dissect dead gophers on my dad's work-bench in the quonset, though. Chris and Tyler and I would recoil in disgust as Tricia cut through their bellies with an olfa knife and then proceeded to identify each organ and disembowel them. Chris was the friend that Tricia treated as another little brother in a bigger sister sort of way.

She would answer the phone when he called for me, "Is Jarett there?" Chris would ask.

"No, Chris, he isn't," but meanwhile, I was standing right there.

When I would call him back she would pick up the phone in my dad's office and listen in on our conversations, making strange noises into the receiver.

Chris will try very hard to fill the void of me in Tricia's life. He will not succeed, but he will put in a valiant effort.

In the winter we skated on the winding creek bed up to the culvert and back. Tricia wore a New York Islanders jersey and I wore a Bruins jersey. We built snow caves in the huge drifts in the yard — only one of us was allowed in the cave at a time and we were told to always enter feet first and leave our heads beyond the interior. My mom was always afraid of the caves collapsing.

We played in the old machinery that sat on the neighboring land down by the creek. There was an old combine and my friend Chris and I locked Tricia in there one time. She was never so naive to enter a small, cramped space when we asked her to again. We laughed so hard as we ran away. We could hear the banging all the way up to the house.

Tricia and I both drove tractors, combines, and other vehicles at early ages. We were adept at automatics and standards before we were twelve. On warm summer nights, we would push the old '68 green GMC truck silently through the yard with our friends leaning into the weight with us — giggling at the mischief — loving the darkness. When we hit the bend in the lane, Tricia would jump in and pop the clutch, revving the motor, as the rest of us climbed in the truck bed, or jumped as I did onto the running board, holding tight to the mirror. We needed to start the motor before we reached the bend, as the road climbed upward at that point. The '68 model was a standard, a three on the tree, and Tricia would drive us the mile and a half to the neighboring yard in second gear, far enough from the house that our parents couldn't hear the motor. No one lived at the old Swenson farm anymore, the tree-lined lane thinning as the years passed by, but they had an amazing garden that we frequented. Our raids consisted of pulling a carrot here and there from the earth, wiping the dirt off on our pants, munching loudly in the light of the moon. We sat in the dirt as all farm kids do, the smell of tomatoes on the vines beside us. We sat among the potato hills, the fragrance of the dill from our mom's potato salad strong in our nostrils. Farm kids appreciate all things that come from the earth and can differentiate between a radish plant, a bean plant, and a pumpkin patch. Farm kids respect the food that the earth grows. These trips were never about vandalizing — all of our moms planted huge gardens and we understood the work behind it all. We only ate a few peas, maybe a cucumber and the odd crab apple from their tree. These trips were about friendship and memories. I know that now. I think of the group of us rolling into the yard a few hours later, Tricia cutting the motor at the bend where the momentum of the incline would bring us almost to the tire swing, the silent movement of the truck slicing through the night. I think of myself, the carefree me. I think of how I stole Tricia's carefree from her by dying and how I left her forlorn and fretful with just our memories. I hate what I did to her.

Tricia and I shared secrets. We had a horse named Summer who was a bit skittish. Summer made Tricia the good rider she is today, but she hit the ground often on that young mare. She would beg me not to tell my parents what Summer had done that day: four feet off the ground bucking, slammed her into a barbed wire fence, bit her back while she saddled her. The horse was a menace. I never wanted to ride that damn beast, but Tricia would saddle her back up again and again. She was a very determined rider, more so than me.

We solved problems together: flat tires, grain accidentally dumped on the ground when one of us hoisted the lift on the truck too far, pasture gates that wouldn't close. We covered for each other — *Who left the bikes out? Who didn't finish sweeping out the grainery? Who left the gas cap off the diesel barrel?* We traded weekends at home on Friday and Saturday nights to keep my mom company when my dad left her alone in the country, seeking the company of others over her.

Tricia had stitches twice, and once, I was the cause. The golf club I swung hit her in the forehead and required five stitches. I was also with her when the neighbor's dog bit her in the face, hung on, and wouldn't let go. We were a mile and a half away from home, feeding the dogs while the neighbors were away on vacation. I watched as the blood ran down her face. She was calmer than me. I ran all the way home to get my mom. I remember being scared to leave Tricia alone with the dog, but I had to get help. I ran as the crow flies, trying to shorten the distance, straight through our wheat fields, parting the tall standing wheat with my legs, stumbling over the uneven ground, my feet foundering to find a footing. I found my mom in the strawberry patch, a basket half full, the knees of her jeans dirty with mud. We raced back in the car and found Tricia sitting on a picnic table away from the dogs. She was crying and her shirt was covered with blood. My mom made some good time on the way to the city. I watched Tricia get seventeen stitches on her right cheek. She was braver than I would have been. The marks on her face are still visible, but she has never complained about that.

The amazing thing to me about Tricia is that she never had a fear of dogs, even after being bit on the face by a pet she had played with and fed for years. The dog's owners were not concerned with the possibility of future attacks and chose to do nothing. This made my parents exceptionally angry. The farmyard where the dog lived was very close to the main grid and this particular dog would run out to the road, barking and chasing whenever a car passed by. My dad never said anything, but when I drove with him, I witnessed him speeding up and veering toward the dog whenever we passed by, which was daily. I wanted him to get that damn dog for my sister. He never did, but that dog bit their own kid the next year; it never chased our car again.

Tricia and I did chores together, which weren't as easy as taking the garbage barrel to the curb. We chopped wood and carried it each fall into the basement, stacking it meticulously; we watered the livestock through the frozen months of winter; we cut the grass each week in our eight-acre farmyard; and we battled a fire in the field near the house one year. Tricia and I were twelve and ten years old, respectively, and our mom was in Boston with Sandy, so Tricia was driving the grain truck for harvest that year. We were working in the field that hugs the farmyard on two sides — the stubble and the wheat as dry as kindling. My dad was driving the combine and was not aware of the bird's nest that was apparently stuck in the exhaust, which was heated up and shot out in the form of a flaming ball behind him. The whole field went up like millions of matchsticks. Tricia and I raced after him in the three-ton truck — the engine screaming — our child-like bodies bouncing over the ruts like hot popcorn seeds in a pan — Tricia as calm and as capable as Tricia always was. We caught up with him before the flames reached the bank of dried-out trees surrounding the house, the quonset, and all the other buildings. He told us to get to the yard and start spraying down the house with the garden hoses. We were scared, but Tricia never showed it and so I followed her lead. My dad raced to start up our tractor and connect an implement to dig up the earth. His efforts would have never made it in time. Two things saved the farm that day. First, a municipal grader was grading the road nearby, saw the smoke, and rushed to the field, scraping up all of the stubble. Secondly, a fast acting neighbor working in an adjoining field summer-fallowed a swath around the yard, so the fire could not reach the trees. We burned off the weeds in the ditches, we helped my mom in the garden, and we assisted my dad with motor re-hauls and anything else mechanical. We worked hard. We were farm kids. Big distinction from the city kids we knew.

But we laughed too. We lightened menial tasks by doing impersonations. Tricia could do an Arnold Schwarzenegger that would render me speechless and guffawing. Once when we were going out of town, Chris volunteered to take care of the animals. I left him a paper bag and drew a funny face on it. I instructed him to wear it so the animals would think he was Tricia. She laughed her ass off when we got back and Chris had left it with a note. Tricia doesn't take herself too seriously, and I like that about her.

I protected Tricia on the school bus. At almost six foot six, no one would really mess with me. Not that I was ever a violent person — more of a gentle giant — but assholes understood the potential harm I could inflict. Tricia struggled socially in middle school and through areas of high school as well. She let a group of mean girls dictate to her who she was and who she wasn't. She lost every bit of her self-esteem wandering around the halls of grades seven through ten. She was the girl who ate alone in the bathroom and didn't tell anyone until she was an adult.

Tricia protected me too. My parents love to tell this story, and I have always loved hearing it, as I don't remember it happening. When we were quite small — Tricia was probably five and I would have been three — we were playing in a culvert in the yard. My dad was building a road to cross the creek and so the culvert was waiting in the yard to be placed. The height of the culvert was taller than both Tricia and me at the time, so we would run through it and out the other side. Our screams of glee bounced off the walls that encircled us, sending us on a continual loop through the metal cylinder. Whenever the grass needed mowing, the culvert would of course be moved to a new position. With little regard for its placement, my dad and Sandy had rolled it to a point where the farthest end lined up exactly with a large badger hole. I ran through first this time, with Tricia close behind. When I reached the end of the culvert, I fell into the badger hole, leaving just my arms and head exposed. Tricia dove for me and bear hugged me around my chest. She obviously thought that I was going to keep going down the hole if she dared to let go. My parents don't know how long she hung onto me like that, but when they arrived, after having heard her screams, she was crying hysterically and I was just sitting there in the hole. She thought she was going to lose me.

Through the years, the two of us buried sixteen felines in the pet cemetery in the trees behind the house. We conducted the same number of cat funerals and even read from an old Bible we found. We dug the graves as deep as we could, which varied in summer and winter. We placed the dead corpses in a box and marked each grave with a tree branch and tied on a popsicle stick. *Here lies Fluffy.*

We hid a cat for six months in Tricia's bedroom without my dad even knowing it was there. His name was Jake and he was a tiny kitten when we got him, so he couldn't be outside with the other animals. I bought her that cat for her birthday. She is an avid animal lover to begin with, but she has a natural affinity for cats. I always joked with her that one day she will be one of those old women who live in a tiny house, litter boxes everywhere, cat toys hanging from chairs, her furniture covered with plastic to simplify the fur maintenance, with cats everywhere. Jake was the last cat she thought she would ever love.

I rode across the prairies with Tricia on the backs of the great chargers we owned.

The last dog we loved together will die on her living room floor and she will lose another piece of me. Anything I had touched, brands her with the finality of my gone-ness.

SANDY AND TRICIA

Tricia and Sandy shared much more as sisters than Bonny and Sandy did. They shared the bedroom with the balcony in the new house before Sandy moved away. Bonny had already moved out before we moved in, so she never had a bedroom to call her own. The balcony room will be the vacant room soon and Sandy and Tricia will impale themselves again and again with the daggers of death they find next door in my room.

Tricia imprinted herself on Sandy at an early age and Sandy welcomed it. Sandy loved fashion, and when she moved away, she would send enormous parcels with unique clothes that you couldn't find on the prairies of Saskatchewan. They shared an undying love of horseflesh, and when life takes even more then it should in a short time from now, I will rarely see them smile, except when they ride.

Our horses will be gone by then, but there is a woman out at McLean with well trained quarter mile competitors and she knows their riding ability, so she will let them go as fast as they need to in order to run from the memories.

They enter the tack room — the smell so familiar.
The saddles hanging on pegs with name plates.
Tricia rides Knight.
Sandy rides Whinny.

Knight is actually a slower horse than Whinny, but Tricia chooses him because of his personality, his spirit, his ability to go the extra mile.

The owner of the horses mentions that more speed exists in Whinny's legs, but Tricia can ask a horse to show her its guts, and that horse will run for her because she is not afraid to show her fearlessness to the titan she rides. She beats Sandy every time.

There is comfort in the ritual.
The blanket is first — plaid with leather knee patches — like the ones we had at the farm.
The horses blowing air past their massive lips — *Let's go!*
The saddle is next — the weight of the western version at home in their hands.
The right stirrup is hooked on the horn.
Up and up, then placed just so on the blanket.
The horses lifting their feet up and down — settling into it — accepting it.
The horses bloat their bellies in anticipation of the cinch belt.
Tricia knees Knight in the gut, teasing him, playfully scolding him.
Sandy steps Whinny forward to release the air.
Gently, they tighten the straps that sit just behind their front legs.
The anticipation grows.
The bit in the mouth — metal clanking on teeth.
The bridle placed high on their heads — bending of ears to place it behind.
Left foot in left stirrup, right leg reaching up and over.
The horses circling, giving their riders time to collect the reins in their hands.
The squeak of leather on leather as the weight of their bodies distributes.
Standing high in the saddle at first — adjusting.
Settling in — sitting back.
Smiling.

MY MEMORIAL

My dad never wears a suit. He does have one, though, and he looks handsome in the navy blazer and pants. I watch him as he tries five or six different ties. In his mind, none of them are right. I want him to know that I see him and tell him that the tie doesn't matter, but it matters to him at this moment, on this day, in honor of me.

My mom wears navy too — a smart looking suit she bought in Boston with Sandy. She keeps sitting down on the side of the bed to catch her breath. She does not want to go and pretend to be the strong mom who will sit in the front row, all eyes upon her, as she stares at the urn and my picture.

My sisters all wear black.

How do you prepare for your child's funeral? My mom stares at herself in the bathroom mirror, her typical primping and prepping feeling inappropriate for this outing. She ritualistically puts on lipstick and then smears it from her face — leaving the look of a clown from a horror movie. She stares at herself in the mirror and then rubs her skin red with a washcloth. *I don't care what I look like.* None of the women in my family wear make-up today. They will not be described as appearing to possess great fortitude. People will not say — *Did you see Joan? She looks so strong.* You will hear their names in the whispers that speak of anguish, tragedy, and hopelessness. *Joan is withering away.* Devoid of color, my family longs to blend in to the funeral home décor of pigmented pallor. *Please do not look at us as we languish in loss.*

Bonny and her husband take their own car, and the rest of my family piles into my dad's new Chevy Silverado extend-a-cab. The new car smell, along with the dead boy silence, squelches the air they breathe.

The gas gauge flirts with "E." The farmer who went to the city six days ago did not fill up with diesel, because the blue sky from every corner of the earth folded in on him like colossal dominoes, trapping him in the skin that crawls over him now.

Tricia, Sandy, and my mom sit together on the back bench, eyes forward, arms linked in a state of unity against the slayer of their lives.

They arrive at the funeral home and are taken to a separate room where extended family will gather and greet.

My parents and my sisters move together as one. There is a sense of protectiveness, of shielding, of deflecting — the inquiries, the eyes, the pity, the shame of having outlived the youngest.

Bonny is crawling up the wall, Tricia isn't acknowledging anyone, and Sandy sits motionless except for her bouncing right leg.

It bounces nonstop.

A movement from her heel to her hip.

Only the knee rising and falling in rapid succession.

She can't halt it.

It is time to enter the memorial space and see the urn for the first time.

Filled to the brim with blended bone, skin, and hair.

The photo front and centre for all to see.

The urn thoughtfully placed to the right, and behind.

The flowers blooming — cascading — their petals opening to the new world — emitting their odor of death.

The funeral director asks my family to line up.

My older sisters and their husbands take up the front and the rear.

Tricia, my mom and dad are lovingly sandwiched in the middle.

Chris and Tyler are with them in the front row.

They all seem so small to me.

Today my family walks in the valley of death following my footsteps.

They are not aware of those around them.

Their lives were dismembered on that morning of September 17th, 1998. Death broke the door down and stormed into their lives with such magnitude of force, that none of them were left standing. Their walk through life has been reduced to a crawl. Like the elephants in a row at a circus, trunk to tail, they move slowly along, slouching, eyes to the ground.

They take their seats in the front row and join hands.

The view from behind shows heaving shoulders, slumping spines, lowered faces.

The sounds are muffled, but come with clarity from deep within — from the gutter, the trenches, the sewer.

The service proceeds as services tend to.

They sit on a wooden bench — eyes forward — staring into un-moving eyes behind the glass frame — encased in walnut.

I look left and right across the front bench.

I see twisting hands, crumpled Kleenex, hands locking hands, hands crying, "Help."

Sandy's leg is still bouncing.

My dad places his hand on it — gently — to calm it.

But it won't stop.

It can't.

Sandy's husband reads the words she wrote.

My guitar teacher plays the music we played together.

It ends and my family moves again as a unit.

Like the paper chains we made at Christmas and laid on the out-stretched boughs.

Three remaining children linked to my parents.

The chain appears intact, but it is broken.

My guitar teacher keeps playing. My family is drawn to the sounds that are familiar to them — the sounds that I played in the front room, sitting on the high stool beside the pool table. They are pulled to the music like magnets. An elderly woman approaches Sandy and tells her to believe in God's plan.

It was Jarett's time.

I want to scream at her and say, *She can't hear you old lady with your crow's feet and your bunions, because life has put her in a death grip and it keeps squeezing.*

I want to ask her, *When will you be a part of God's plan, by the way?*

Do people even think about what they say?

Do they think it is a compliment when they utter the words *God only takes the good ones?*

It has been six days since I died. Six days since I have been home and slept in my bed, ate my mom's meals, and felt warmed by her love. She misses me so. She walks to the front of the funeral home — resolutely — she picks up my urn. Her body language saying, *He is mine and I will not be away from him for another second.*

On the way back to the farm, my mom holds me on her lap like she did when I was a child. The vessel I am contained in is rigid and cold, but she holds me tenderly just the same.

There is a gathering at the farm following the ceremony. The community of Kronau has made sandwiches and desserts. I don't understand why my family has to endure hosting a reception right now.

Many people are there.

The house is full, but they are alone.

My parents stand stoically and greet their guests — the inquiry endless — the repetition relentless. One woman brings five copies of the *Leaderpost* with a photo of my accident — in color — as well as five copies of my obituary.

"Here Joan, I thought you might want extra copies," the woman says.

My mom winces as she accepts this offering, and above her I scream, *It's not like I made the fucking all star football team and my mom wants to make a scrapbook of my accomplishments and cut out little newspaper clippings to place in the Christmas cards she sends out — Look at what Jarett is doing. I am fucking dead, woman, and you think she wants multiple copies of that?*

Tricia has changed into jeans and a t-shirt from my closet. Her friends are there and they rally around her. They understand the bond that we shared and what my absence has done to her and what it will do to her in the future. Chris and Tyler are among them — conjuring up memories — making her smile. They hide in the trees in the darkest of shadows.

Habits forming.

Destruction building.

Bonny has endless patience with people. She is able to stay in the house and answer questions and smile and act thankful for the efforts of others. Her younger sisters do not share this talent. Bonny can stand tall and erect when the well-meaning people make comments like, *I know how you feel.* Well how the hell could anyone other than someone who has lost a teenager in a car accident ever utter the words, *I know how you feel,* to my parents? I watch as my family lives in a re-run of a bad horror movie day after day. They are so devoid of any comprehension of what their minds and bodies are encountering. Every morning, teenage death gong, gong, gongs an alarm, and their fitful slumber ceases as the totality of all things fixed, permanent and immovable slam into their consciousness again and again. They are so isolated from others that they don't even see them — they see only the carcasses that used to be them. They move about in a daze not knowing what to do, where to go or what to say. They don't know themselves anymore. How the fuck could anyone else know what they are feeling? Bonny responds with a labored smile and pulls her stunned parents closer.

Neither Sandy or Tricia can take the advice or the commiserating. They both know their potential for lashing out in destructive ways, while Bonny can let the words pass through her mind, leaving no traces behind. More people than I care to mention will compare my death to their ninety-eight-year-old grandmother's passing and one will go so far as to mention their dog. That person will receive a call from Sandy late one night when she is extremely drunk — she will yell at her for her transgression. Anger rules Sandy now.

Sandy is bereft of the gift of gab.

She follows the tree line out to my tractor.

Camouflaged in the shadows like Tricia.

Wanting to hide, but not wanting attention for wanting to hide.

Most comfortable on her own — consumed by the grief that only a few share.

The fragrances wafting through the air from the flowers are choking my mom. She needs to lie down and she needs her pills.

I want the people to leave.

My dad stands as a part of the tripod — Mom, Bonny, Dad. He wonders where Sandy and Tricia are. He wants the people that offer him nothing to go home.

The people should leave.

A SHELF FOR ME

I live in a walk-in closet now. My mom's to be precise. Her closet sits on the same wall as my dad's and mirrors it in size and layout. They are both U-shaped, with hanging space, as well as floor to ceiling shelving. I do not know why my urn was placed in my mom's closet and not my dad's.

There was never any discussion about its placement.

Oh it will look so good on the bureau beside the window.

They never argued about who would keep it safe.

I want it.

No I do.

Well you can't have it, it's mine.

Following my memorial, my mom walked from the truck to her room, clutching me in her arms. She opened the closet door, placed me on a shelf, and then closed the door quickly. She leaned against it like a woman intent on not letting what is behind the door out. My dad sat on the edge of the bed, thankful that my mom took ownership of my remains. My mom walked down the stairs to greet the people who came to mourn my death, and my dad followed.

That was the last time she ever held me.

My presence will be felt every time my mom enters her closet in search of a sweater to warm her, or some work jeans to propel her into productivity. She never looks at the urn, but it controls her just the same with its mastery and dominance of motherly love. The closet is large enough that there are actually photos of my younger sister and me hanging on the wall across from the shoe rack. You know the photos that are from kindergarten, but your mom can't put them away in a box, because you are missing teeth and you are smiling like you really love school and so she moves your younger self to the only free wall space she can find. So there you are in your navy sweater with the grey polo shirt and your hair has a cow-lick, your smile is lopsided, and you are the embodiment of the perfect child.

And now you sit and you stare at your ashes.

Behind the safety of the glass.

Sitting in the frame that your dad made from the old barn door.

In a closet.

And you watch your mom crumple to the floor like dirty laundry.

But you can't help her.

So the child that you were simply watches.

You can't close your eyes and you can't turn your head away.

You are trapped on a wall.

Hanging from a hook.

LIFE MOVES ON

Bonny and her family left today.

They stayed for a week.

She said to my parents from her passenger side car window, "I need to get back to my life in Lethbridge and get on with living. I have two small children that need me, a husband, a home, and a business to run."

My parents were pleased that she had the strength to do so.

She also said, "You need to tell Sandy to get back to her life in Boston. If you don't, she will never leave."

Bonny was right.

Sandy will stay a long time on the farm.

She will never return to the job that she loved.

Bonny holds more power than she is aware of. She does not let my death become her world, while Sandy and Tricia define themselves by it. Their feelings, their reactions, and their life philosophies are borne of the blood that I shed up the road. Bonny holds the power now.

My family is acutely aware of the world that ceased to spin on its axis when I died.

They know that life moved on for others when theirs did not.

Full stop.

The revolutions altering the sure-footedness from before.

The movement dizzying.

The realization nauseating.

My dad makes the short drive to Kronau to get the mail.
He is aware that he did the same drive on the day I died.
The bills will speak volumes to him about life to come.
The pity on the face of the postmaster too much for him to bear.
He quickly returns to the farm.
My dad sits in his office and pulls the cheque-book from the metal drawer to the right of his chair.
The large white stallion framed in oak stares down on him.
A Father's Day gift from his kids.
Behind him is the family computer where I sat every afternoon after school.
He feels me in the room.
I watch as he lifts the pen from the onyx holder — the weight of it intolerable.
His hand shakes.
He writes the numbers.
He struggles to fill in the Pay to the Order of…
Speers Funeral Home.

My mom returns to the church.
She returns to the girl growing up who played the organ in small town Sceptre every Sunday morning.
She asks for someone to go with her, and Sandy says yes.
She will go for our mom, but not for herself.
I see Sandy's rigid body tense as she enters the house of God.
She does not belong there among the elderly seeking comfort for their impending death. Everyone singing, *When you call me great Lord, I shall come.*
She wishes they had gone, because her brother wasn't ready.
I see what she writes in her diary.

If you came to my home and I was never there
Would you come again?
If I offered you hope through faith and then left you
Would you still believe?
If I promised to combat evil and then took your pride and joy
Would you praise me?
If I was almighty and I allowed the poor to starve

Would you follow me?
If I murdered the innocent and let the wretched live
Would you pray to me?
If you were a good person and I punished you
Would you curse me?
If I stole your brother from you
Would you see like me?

Sandy can't stop reading about death. She is voracious for knowledge, of what specifically, I am not sure. She reads books written by rabbis, by mothers, by psychiatry/psychology experts, by siblings, by doctors of this and that. She rarely finds what she is looking for, but she keeps reading.

Tricia is lethargic, withdrawn, and angry. There is a part of her that will never forgive me for dying at nineteen. She spends most of her time in my bedroom. Sandy, who is equally as poisoned inside, makes Tricia her special project.

Sandy is so desperate to be someone else. She cuts her hair very short — seeking to be unrecognizable.

Bonny is at her home now and the routine of daily life pushes teenage death aside.
The positive-minded, the, *I must make this work for me,* finds sleep necessary to deal with her two young children.
She mourns me — she does — but in a very competent manner.

Night comes again and again and again.
Sandy — the one who plays the helper — is still not able to stay in the house.
When she attempts to sleep, she is in my room with Tricia.
Her husband, back in Boston, is tying loose strings into neat little bows.
Sandy exits through the front door.
She tries diligently to suppress the creak of the door that screams, *Help me.*
Some are aware of her leaving.
She runs through the yard crying.

She is so completely lost.

She runs from place to place.

To the gas shed, the old chicken coop, the horse barn, the tire swing, the playhouse.

She keeps running and searching.

Searching for some sign of herself.

Tricia lies quietly in my bed.

She can't stand for it to be empty.

She lies motionless amidst my golf clubs, my water skis, my clothing, all things me.

Her unblinking eyes tell me of the anguish within.

The destruction.

Cataclysmic to the core.

My dad will eventually leave the house to search for the daughter who can't still her mind or her heart.

He does not always find her, as her ability to hide all things is uncanny.

She is to others as they need her to be, but to herself she is nothing.

The sister that roams outside in the dark will eventually return to the house where I lived and seek solace in the space that was mine.

These two sisters will lie awake in the dark together.

They are inseparable.

Bonny feels a kind of guilt for having left the farm. She wonders if anyone thinks that she loved me less.

My mom tries so hard to help herself, her husband, her daughters, but she can't.

Chris solidifies his friendship with Tricia and becomes her surrogate brother. He watches out for her, like any brother would do.

CRASH SITE

Sandy and Tricia still scour the earth for fragments of my car that were smashed to smithereens — carrying the pieces of fiberglass in their pockets — weighing heavy on their splintered lives. I find this a little disturbing. The bits of their dead brother's car reminding them of all the gory details — another form of torture.

Tricia and Sandy come to sit with me in the grass and the snow all the time. They think that if I am anywhere, I am at the place where I died. The plaque they made in the quonset, with the plastic letters of a child, sits between them like an anchor, pulling them under. They made the plaque for me, but mostly it is for them. They meticulously maintain the circle of stones where their handmade memorial sits. Weeds are snuffed out, leaves brushed away, and snow shoveled off.

They dig a hole to the right of the plaque and place a Tupperware container in the opening. Like a coffin for their thoughts. They cover the hole with a board and then roll the grass back over it, hiding it beneath the earth. Over the years they will leave me many things in that box: letters written on paper warped by salty tears, ticket stubs from amusement park rides they rode in my name, newborn baby pictures, a diploma, and birthday cards. They make a collection of the fragments of their lives and they bring them to me like gifts on a platter.

Bonny never comes to see the plaque with my name on it that sits half a mile north of Chris' house.

My mom came once. She squatted in the grass, placed her cold hand on the cold stone, and cried.

She brought with her a present.

She pulled a hammer from the trunk of her car and drove a curved metal spike into the ground at the top of the plaque.

On it she hung a wind chime — an exact replica of the wind chime that hangs on the porch at home.

Sounds of the farm for me.

My dad came once too.

He carried nothing with him, but the weight of a man with no son.

He stood in the grass — not wanting to come too close — not wanting to read the words that the plastic letters made.

Chris can see the crash site from his farm a half-mile up the road.

The proximity is unnerving to him.

He can see the two that sit in the dirt and cry.

He thinks about going to sit with them, but never does.

He feels uncomfortable with their inability to control their feelings.

Chris is a huge Bruins fan and has been since he was in kindergarten. He wears a baseball hat every day — always a Bruins logo. His favorite hat is soft and worn out, fraying on the edges. The peak is curved just so, the colors faded, the fit loose. He leaves me that hat one day when the sun shines bright in his eyes. I watch him walk away, his appearance unfamiliar to me with his bare head.

Tricia and Sandy find the hat the next day.

They are touched by the gesture and place it in the hidden box for safe-keeping.

People love to bring gifts to the dead. It's not that we don't appreciate them, we do, it's just that the anguish it takes seems colossal in comparison to what the dead person gets — the offerings are emotional and wracked with such misery that they are hard to witness.

CHRIS AND ME

Chris would tell you that I was the mastermind of most of the crazy things we did and he would be right. I was kind of inventive and good at repurposing. One day, I invented a game called Fat Man. I took the wooden shish kabob skewers from the drawer in the kitchen and broke them in half. Chris and I used them as arrows, shooting them at each other with fat elastic bands. I called the game Fat Man because we stuffed pillows under our shirts to protect us — not sure why we didn't wear goggles, too.

I had some kind of obsession with fire and explosions when I was younger. I remember once when my dad was in town, Chris and I were out in the quonset experimenting with my dad's torch. I came up with the idea of spraying the WD40 can in front of the torch, which made a huge fireball. Keep in mind we were doing all of this inside a wooden building filled with wooden things. Tricia happened to be spying on us through the windows in the big white door. She ran and told my mom who then told Chris' mom. We both got in a lot of trouble, and we deserved it.

Chris and I also tried to make a bomb. We took an old paint can, siphoned some gasoline from the gas shed, cut open some shot gun shells, and put the gun powder in the pail. We attempted to make a wick with some twine from the hay bales, soaking it in the gas to use as the fuse. When we tried to light it, the fuse just burned out because of the plastic coating on the twine. We never did get any kind of explosion like we were hoping for.

Chris and I shared our first beer at my house when we were thirteen. We had a cold storage room in the basement, and I came up with the idea of sneaking one out of the house. I was certain that my dad would notice if we took two. It was a Miller Highlife — my dad's favorite. We snuck out behind the old chicken coop, giggling at our mischievousness, liking the bubbles and the taste, belching as loud as we could.

Chores on the farm never stop. There aren't many kids who would tell you that they love doing chores. They just happen to be necessary evils in order to keep a large farmyard looking good and to keep the fields producing. There is always something to fix or build or adjust. There were many times when Chris was over at my house that my dad would make me do chores he needed done right away. Having company was never an excuse for sitting idle on the farm. I always felt bad, but Chris volunteered to help every time and then we were done sooner. I did the same at his house, but his dad wasn't as demanding as mine. I never complained when my dad asked me to do a job. My sisters complained all the time. I just did it. Chris was always impressed by my positive attitude, and now that I am dead, he tries to live up to the standard I set. He gets annoyed with people who complain about stupid things. He idolizes my actions and I appreciate the fact that he noticed.

MY SHOES

Other than my wallet, the only thing that comes back to my family are my shoes. I was wearing my favorite Tower of Terror t-shirt when I died and they were hopeful that it would come back to them. The obvious statement the shoes make is, *Jarett's feet were the only part of him that were not mangled and deformed.* The shoes arrive solemnly and without fanfare. My family doesn't want the shoes. People can live without feet. They can't live with their internal organs bleeding and their brain matter smashed against their skull. The shoes should have stayed away. Sandy takes them and hides them under my bed, but first she examines them for signs of the trauma I endured. Nothing. Perfectly good shoes. The shoelaces are not frayed, the heels are not worn and the toes are not scuffed. My mom will find them one day while vacuuming in the shrine they create for me.

Those shoes — my shoes — will haunt my mom on the farm and beyond.
Hidden beneath the bed where my sisters lie.
The double long bed for the six foot six boy.
No one can fill my shoes.
No one will walk in them.
My deserted death shoes fill my mom's with cement.

HIDING AND HELPLESSNESS

I sit in the tree with the tire swing and watch the sun come up. I wait for the seemingly old man of fifty-nine to exit the house that he built and I tore down. The sun has already reached a point in the sky above the tree line, which tells of the lateness of the day. No respectable farmer could justify such a late start to the work that needs to be done.

Weeks have passed and Sandy is still at the farm.
She won't leave.
She can't.
Her husband has returned to Boston on a more permanent basis. He needs to get back to his job.
Sandy's boss keeps calling her and asking if she has changed her mind about returning.
She says, "No."
And she means it.

Sandy takes on the gruesome tasks that need to get done when someone vanishes from life.
She goes to the city to get the autopsy report.
After she picks it up in the building across from City Hall, she enters a phone booth and calls a friend for the first time. There is so much emotion released in that glass enclosure — she is a fish in a bowl — immersed in her watery grave.

My parents don't want to see the autopsy report, but they want Sandy to read it to them. She can't get through it and neither can they. My mom pleads with her to stop. My dad leaves the house, slamming the door on the broken jaw, the internal bleeding, the head trauma, the smashed pelvis and legs.

Sandy goes to the university to withdraw me from my classes. Tricia goes with her. The woman behind the counter says, "Oh, I guess he won't be needing anymore classes then."

Tricia starts to cry. Sandy escorts her out of the Admin building, tries to calm her in the car, starts to drive away and then parks again, ramming the stick shift forward.

That fucking bitch.

Sandy tells Tricia to stay in the car and she obeys like a child.

She goes back to the counter and yells at the woman for her lack of decorum.

"What the hell is wrong with you? Our brother died for Christ's sake. He didn't decide to become a plumber or move to Vancouver. He's fucking dead you idiot."

The woman just stands there — mouth gaping.

She doesn't speak.

Additional employees behind the counter stop midstride and stare.

The people standing in the rope path behind Sandy don't react either.

They are dumbfounded.

I stress the word dumb.

Sandy is protective of her little sister.

She makes a scene and she doesn't care.

She is my avenger.

I chuckle when she unintentionally burns rubber out of the parking lot.

Sandy obsesses about whether or not I died instantly. She arranges to speak with the nurse of the pathologist who examined me. She needs to know that everything that could have been done was done. She needs to know that I did not lie there alone writhing in pain. The nurse consults with the doctor before the meeting and she assures Sandy that even if a medical staff had been standing in the wheat field, scrubbed, gloves on, faces masked, and they watched as the cars hit, operating music filling the air, they still could not have saved me.

"Your brother died instantly," says the definitive nurse.

Which is almost true.

Sandy and Tricia meet with the police officers that were at the scene of my accident.

Sandy asks that they meet them at the corner field.

She does not want another police car in the yard for my parents to see. They oblige.

Standing in a cornfield with my crazy sister Sandy firing questions at them.

Tricia kicking the dirt with her feet.

Sandy drills them with questions about the skid marks in the dirt: Do they think I would have lived if I was wearing my seatbelt? What if I had rolled the car? Was the other driver drunk? Were there any signs of life in me that they saw? How long did it take the ambulance to get to me? Did they cover me with a sheet so no one could see me? How long did I lie there? How was my body positioned? Sandy tries feverishly to solve the mystery of how and why I died. Could I have lived? Can others share in the blame? Sandy needs to point her finger at someone other than me.

Sandy takes Tricia and my mom to see my car at the impound in the city. I don't understand why they want to go. I don't want them to see it.

They notice the red of the car when they enter the chain link fence.

They form a blob of sobbing as they approach.

My mom stands at the front passenger side rocking back and forth — the first point of impact within her touch.

She thinks to herself — *I should not have come.*

I should not have come here to see this.

She chants the same words over and over in her head.

Tricia crawls through the wreckage seeking pieces of my life that might have been overlooked.

She searches for the gold chain I wore on my neck and never took off.

Its absence speaks to the trauma I endured.

She won't find it in my car.

It is lying in the dirt where I died, hidden in the sunflowers.

Tricia just keeps saying, "Why? Why Jarett? Why?"

Sandy can't open the driver side door, so she hoists herself through the window and sits in the driver's seat. My mom screams for her to get out. For whatever reason, Sandy needs to sit where I sat and know that my space was fully intact.

She responds with unfounded optimism, "His seat wasn't destroyed, Mom. He should have been okay. He didn't get squished. He should have been okay."

Death, like a sponge, has sopped up all of the sanity from their minds.

Inside the claims office, people watch the circus unfolding.

One of the claims officers says, "A kid died in that car out by Kronau. That's his mom and sisters. Poor people."

The juggernaut of information sends the three back to the farm posthaste.

Bonny's life is back in full swing mother motion. She works full time, preps lunches in the early morning hours, plans out dinners for the week on Sundays, has date night with her husband on Fridays, does laundry, cleans her house, and reads to her kids every night at bedtime. She lives six hours away from the farm and she is able to pretend that I am still there. She is getting on with life appropriately. I spend less time watching over her than I do the others. I need to be with the people who need me most and I get to make that choice. I only wish they knew of my presence.

Bonny and Tricia pull their friends nearer, while Sandy pushes everyone aside.

My dad wants Tricia to return to university, to continue on with her classes. He feels strongly about creating a structure, a schedule, a routine that will keep her moving forward. I understand what he is trying to do, but I am not sure that she can focus on learning when she waited there for me and I never came.

He wants her to go and to invest in her future.

He will lose the money he spent on my tuition and then spend even more to exterminate the me that lived in his house.

The me that idolized him.

There will be no return on his money there.

No investment in the future, just ashes.

Sandy will take Tricia to school. She is Tricia's death maze partner. She is like the kindergarten friend you hold hands with when you walk to the library and the gym, the kid who helps you find your school bus at the end of the day, the kid you eat lunch with. My buddy when

I started school was Chris. I lucked out there. Tricia drops three of her five courses and Sandy talks to the two remaining professors, she will attend classes with her. Tricia will not go without her. The two of them drive to the university every morning and their bond binds ever tighter about them. They walk through the hall where my locker was and they imagine the janitor cutting off the lock and placing my things in a plastic bag from Safeway. They walk by the place where Tricia and I met for maple bagels in the morning. They avoid the parking lot where my absence agitated Tricia on the day I died and her nerves tied nooses about her. Those nooses will tighten further still in a couple of months from now.

People avoid my parents.
Perhaps they think they can catch teenage death like a cold.
Or maybe it is just too hard to look directly into the eyes of the sonless.

Sandy writes more and more.
She writes the best when she is drunk.
A fog encases her, allowing the demons to introduce themselves in the murk of her mind.
She can't push them away.
The alcohol frees them.
She addresses them not as herself, but as someone who lives outside of herself.
In the morning, she reads what she wrote as if for the first time.

Sandy's interactions with people are minimal, but she still encounters people that say things she will never forget. I watch as a woman who should know better tells Sandy of a family whose son was recently in a car accident and is now crippled. The person tells her how the family wishes that he had died, as his injuries will require extensive twenty-four hour care and he will never walk again.
Like my family won some fucking lottery.
People talk menacingly about searching for something positive within the confining walls of tragedy. As a first hand observer who is deeply invested in the people trapped behind those walls, I am not sure I can buy this pronouncement. The walls encircling my family are so high, that when they look up, all they see are the outer edges

converging together into a point. They cannot scale the walls, there is no light at the top of their enclosure and the floor has dropped out from below them. And still the wise and the unaffected want them, the misunderstood and the afflicted, to forge on against their adversities. I watch as the words of those most willing to offer advice are spoken by people who have never experienced the kind of hell I am putting my family through. Their words fall on deaf ears. Stop preaching to them.

SANDY'S FIRST HORSE

Sandy's first horse came with a name: Pal. He was a sizeable Palomino who stood seventeen hands tall. He was big and beautiful with his long white mane and tail flowing in the breeze. Sandy didn't love the name Pal. She favored the likes of Dakota or Pasqua. But Pal had grown up with the name, and she thought it would be too confusing to rename him and to bring him to a new home at the same time. Pal was a cow pony. Sit in the saddle, release the reins, and upon command, he would commence to round up the cattle before you. Sandy would tell you that Pal was too much horse for her when she first got him. Her riding skills didn't match his training. He was feisty and smart as hell. Just lift your leg in the direction of the stirrup and he would begin circling, ready to go. This horse never stood still when he had a saddle on his back. In the beginning, Sandy got bucked off many times. Pal was testing her. After she hit the ground, Pal would stop, turn around, and stare at her. *Do you want to go again?* Taunting her with the eyes of a docile doe.

My dad would say, "Get back up on that horse. You never walk away and let the horse win."

Pal and my dad taught Sandy so many lessons when she was learning how to handle a more challenging steed.

Sandy eventually grew into that horse named Pal. She loved him with all of her farm girl being. We were away when Pal died. Sandy beat herself up about that. She wouldn't eat or talk on the long two-day drive home. My dad let her live in the quiet of her sorrow.

He said to us, "Leave her alone, Tricia and Jarett. She will eat if she needs to."

I remember that the people looking after Pal had put him in the shed by the tire swing with the door that slid sideways on rollers. My dad told Tricia and me to *leave Sandy alone with her horse*. We stood at the garden in snowsuits and snow boots. We watched as she pulled on the door that slid open to reveal the frozen corpse within. Tricia and I snuck closer and watched as Sandy lay her body across the best friend she ever had. She stayed with Pal a long time and then she asked the two of us to go to the house and bring her some scissors and a ribbon from my mom's sewing kit. We were obedient little children of four and six, so we did what we were told. She cried giant tears that froze like puddles, pooling on Pal's fur where she sat in the saddle, where she stroked his face. She cut a section of his mane and then she tied the ribbon around his tail, cut it off, and placed them both in a bag. She still has that mane and tail.

I wish Sandy could draw upon some of the lessons she learned from Pal long ago.

I wish I could whisper them to her.

Get back on that horse, Sandy.

Get back on and ride.

LETHBRIDGE

My mom and dad try a change of scenery. They travel to Bonny's house in Lethbridge to spend a few days with her and her family.

Bonny's life depicts a watercolor image of what moving forward looks like: her children playing in the yard on the swings; delicious, organic meals; positive visions of me dripping with nostalgia.

My parents pop out of the painting like 3-D characters on springs. They can't blend in.

Sandy and Tricia stay on the farm.
It is fall on the prairies.
The air turns cool and the leaves fall quickly from the trees.
The green now brown.
The crunch underfoot reminding them of death.
They walk aimlessly through the pastures.
Sometimes silent, sometimes talking.
The horses following forlornly behind.

Sandy and Tricia try to be productive. They try to please my parents. *If only we can beautify the yard in some way, they will smile at our efforts.*

They tear down an old shed. Physical work that absorbs their anger, sledge hammers deconstructing feelings, manual labor releasing tears from every pore in their bodies, the suffering released in their sweat. They work like ten men — not stopping to eat or drink — intent on tearing down the walls that they all live behind.

MIRAGES

In the summer, on the country grid roads that divide this land into a patchwork quilt from the sky, the heat hangs heavy in a haze just above the ground. I have walked the grid roads that outline our property on days when the dry summer heat was oppressive. The roads are in a straight line that end in a pinpoint at the edge of the earth as I see it. I know these roads, and I know that there are not any bodies of water looming in the distance. But the prairie will play tricks on your mind. It will offer you things that are not there. Light that heated air refracts causes hallucinations. Like watering holes "seen" in the desert, mirages on the prairie are real.

My mom sees visions of me wherever she goes. Like a mirage, the young men she glimpses offer her the possibility of me. I have watched her leave a full grocery cart and follow tall teenagers through Safeway. Mesmerized. The young men wear baseball caps, jeans, and t-shirts like me. They are tall. I have watched her stand back by the deli counter and wait for the young men to turn and exit with their cheese and salami. There is a willingness to believe in the possibility that I am alive — I went to school one day and she never saw me again — perhaps there was a huge error. Perhaps someone else sits in the urn in her closet. She believes I could be alive, because she never saw me dead. Her face always tells of the disappointment at seeing a young man that she does not know. She leaves the grocery cart abandoned in the aisle by the tuna and walks robotically to the car. She returns to the farm and her bed. Watching other people live pains her greatly. She questions why one tall teenager should live when the one she gave birth to could not.

FARMING

A large portion of all farming responsibilities had begun to pass to me in the last couple of years. My dad became less involved, and I liked how it all felt on my shoulders. I watch now as my family struggles to continue with the many tasks that are required on the farm. They see me everywhere. I am in the cab of the combine, changing a tire, petting the dogs, cutting the grass with the Minnie tractor, pulling weeds with my mom.

Farming will never feel the same to my dad again. He will act as if he is cultivating me into the ground each time he enters the field to work the land. Each swath of the wheat will render him powerless to my absence. Every furrow closer to the demise he secretly longs for. The seeding in the spring will not bring promise and new growth, but rather drudgery and resentment. The fields will soon be filled with weeds. Fast growing, unwanted plants that will suck the life from the farm, as I have done to my family.

In the spring, the farmer plants the wheat kernels below the earth. On our farm, we use a discer to open up the ground and place the seeds beneath its cover. The tractor pulls the discer through the fields of fertile soil. The circular discs are set at an angle, and as they turn and slice through the ground, the seeds and the fertilizer are released from their boxes, travelling down tubes that drop the tiny grains in the earth. As the discs continue turning, and the tractor pulls them forward, the earth rises up in a small wave and lays itself down in a blanket of warmth and protection.
Burying the seeds.

Entombing bits of me.
Laying the future to rest.

Farmers always take note of their neighbouring farmer's land. As they drive by, they note the color of the earth turned over on itself — the blackest color of freshly worked soil — *The Speers' finished seeding early this year.* My dad used to make the same notations when we drove by our neighbours' land. As the short farming season progresses, the farmer finds much to be proud of — a ploughed field, a thick stand of wheat swaying in the breeze, wide swathes laying in the sun to dry, and then only stubble remaining, with the grain in the yard in the bins.

Under the most favorable conditions, a wheat seedling will emerge from the ground within seven days. In order to germinate and grow, the seeds need warm temperatures and water from the soil. As the first leaf emerges from the ground, a protective leaf like structure will cover and protect it as it exits the earth. As the seedling sends the leaves to reach for the sun, beneath the ground, the fibrous root system anchors the wheat.

I am the wheat that grows on the farm.
My roots branching out beneath the soil.
My family has lost their anchor.
I was ripped from this earth.
I took the roots that branched beneath the soil too.

Farming requires an optimistic mentality. A good crop depends so much on the weather, that many farmers insure the costs they incur in order to offset their risks. Farmers are subject to the hands of nature or fate or God or whatever you assign as that higher force. And right now, my family doesn't have faith in anything, so farming has become too much of a gamble for them.

The farm is slowing to the machinations of mournfulness.
The movements of the people left to keep the gears in motion have slowed.
The engine stopping abruptly.
Ceasing.
My family lurching forward, as the laws of physics dictate.

HARVEST

The harvest moon fills the sky with orange, hanging close to the horizon, as the farmers bring in their crops. Look as far as you can see on a September night on the prairies, and in the glow of the giant ball of gold and yellow, you will see the lights and the dust, as the farmers scramble to get their crops out of the fields and into their granaries.

Chris' family has already started to pull the grain from their fields. I witness the process and long to be a part of the coming together. His mom in the kitchen cooking homemade soup and stew, transporting the food to the fields, so that when the weather allows, there is no stopping. If the wheat stays dry, they will go all night. Chris is swathing, his brother drives the truck, and their dad is combining. They are thick with dust and beyond tired, but I still feel pangs of jealousy as I watch them accept their individual lunch pails from their mom and wife and then dip the homemade bread in the warmth of the broth. The dust swirls about them in the calm of a peaceful night, the combine spitting chaff out the back, the wheel on the swather turning and laying to rest the tall stand of wheat, the noise of the truck moving from the combine to the yard to unload and then back again — the sounds of a life I lived.

There are no sounds on my farm.
Just silence.
Dead silence.

My dad walks to each of our fields to check on the wheat and its progress. I watch as he pulls one stalk of wheat from the ground.

He places the head of wheat in his hand and swirls it while pushing downward. The kernels are quickly freed from their covering. Meticulously, he picks the chaff from his hand. Twenty to thirty wheat kernels remain. He cups his hand and delivers the kernels to his mouth. He begins to chew. Any farmer worthy of the designation knows how the kernels should break down and become gummy in texture. They stick together in his mouth. The wheat is ready, but my dad can't bring it down. I planted this wheat. It is my crop to slay and he will not drive the swather that cuts my crop below the knees and lays it in the sun to dry. He will not drive the combine that scoops up the swaths and then beats it from its protective covering to rest in the hopper. He will not transport it to the granaries in the yard and use it for seed in the spring. He will not get a fair price for my wheat, because he is already over his quota. He will not look at a granary filled with my wheat in the yard. He will pay a neighbour to bring in my wheat and take it directly to town.

The weather is dry and hot. Perfect for leveling a crop. The neighbour and his two sons start early in the morning. My dad stays in the house, trying to block out the sounds of harvest. The combine whirling, and spewing the chaff out the back. The air heavy with dust and straw and sweat. The trucks in low gear, transporting my wheat away. The roar of first gear and the weight of the load pitching back and forth across the furrows. The engine revving, straining to increase its speed, screaming now as the farmer's son grinds it into second gear — he is at the "S" curve and the engine noises waft away in the heat of the day.

When the harvest moon shines bright, lighting the sky with a radiance that every farmer knows and marvels at, my dad sits in his office with the shades pulled down.

MY DAD PLANTS A SEED

My dad and Sandy walk out to the grid and back, to pass the time and to simply keep moving. One step in front of the other — left, right, left, right, left, right. Mindless chatter with mindless motion. There is one comment my dad makes that disturbs me. He says, "I knew things were going too good. I had a feeling that something bad was coming." For whatever reason, this man, this good, honest man, chose to think of the unbearable loss of me as something he should have seen barreling down the road to our family farm. *The fortuitous farmers on this land will pay!* This man who worked the land, who had the heart of a workhorse, who demanded respect from his children, who never did an extravagant thing in his life, who believed in right and wrong, didn't owe the universe anything, but for some reason he thought he did. He planted a seed in Sandy's mind. The rotting, putrid, maggot-filled seed.

CHORES

I had many chores on the farm and Tricia and Sandy try so hard to keep up with everything I would normally be doing, offering the illusion that I am still there. They find comfort in the monotony of day-to-day tasks that keep them moving. They are silent a lot of the time, but always together. Weeks have passed since my death and they are lost in the routine of covering for me.

The one chore that I think all farm kids detest is dealing with the garbage. The metal, plastic, and glass are recycled; the food scraps are composted; and the paper is burned. Proud farmers (like my dad) organize an area behind the graineries where the recycling, composting, and burning are efficiently laid out. I watch Tricia and Sandy stretch a one day a week chore into a nightly ritual. In the name of depression, grief, and life loathing, the two of them embrace the monotony, while at the same time escaping the longing eyes of my parents that scream, *Help Me*.

After the sun sets behind the trees, the leaves no longer filtering the colors but lying crumpled and forgotten on the frozen ground, the garage door opener engages with a *BANG* and the wooden panels lift slowly. Sandy and Tricia flitter about like bats in the old horse barn — seeing best in the darkness — most at home in their solitude.

They begin the transportation of the different categories of trash from the garage. They save the burning until last. They light the three burn barrels and then recede into the dark shadows of the surrounding buildings. My parents' bedroom has a direct view from their window, so they hide the harm that they are trying to inflict upon themselves, wanting their own chance to escape, but not wanting to be cause for concern.

One has smoked before and one has not. They don't talk about it, but they know what the other is thinking. *Smoking can lead to cancer and then death.* All is fair game when a teenager goes to school and never comes back. It's a nightly ceremony, following days of suffering. It is sad and it is theirs. They ask no questions and tell no lies. I watch them light up — loving the sound of the hard stick matches against an old metal tire ring — the sulphur popping to life. I look down on them as they puff away, dragging deeply to capitalize on the tar and nicotine contained in the little white sticks. I feel the love that they have for me. I feel it with each inhalation and each exhalation. Tricia, the experienced smoker, blows rings in the air up to me — throwing life preservers of sorts to the Heavens — *Please come back to me.* The older, less experienced smoker holds the toxins in as long as she can. Tricia has smoked off and on for a few years, and so Sandy feels the need to catch up to her. They tarry a while in the dark, the smoke hanging heavy in the air, the two figures lost in the haze that helps them to hide.

I see the rundown ruin the farm has become.
My sisters, the shells that life left behind.
Staring into the fire.
No hopes and no dreams.
Two red dots in the night.
The tips burning vibrant in the darkness.
The harder they puff, the bigger the burn.
The life of the cigarette shrinking.
The ashes cool and fall to the ground.

GRIEF GROUP

Six weeks following my death, my mom asks Tricia and Sandy if they will take her to a grief group that meets bi-weekly in the basement of an old church in the city. They both agree to go, in the hopes of finding people they can relate to.

They sit in a circle and everyone holds Styrofoam cups with lukewarm coffee. Something to occupy the fidgeting hands. Each person — mostly women — takes turns telling their stories.

My mom is next in the circle.

She tries to begin, but quickly falters.

"My son" — is all she can say.

Shoulders forward, eyes down, body thrashing in shame on the cold, metal folding chair.

Your mom trying to explain your death to complete strangers is fucked up!

Sandy's body mimics my mom's.

Tricia takes over and delivers the gory details. She struggles through. She is compelled to tell the story that may connect her to others.

I find the gathering difficult to watch, but it isn't about me, it's about my family finding people that hurt like they do, and there are plenty. There are parents who have endured multiple miscarriages and stillborn babies, a fifty-something year old woman who lost her sister, there is a couple who lost a ten year old child to cancer. The woman who leads the group, her young son died while crossing the Ring Road. She worked in the cafeteria at the high school nearby and people whispered about her and blamed her. It wasn't her fault. And people say children are mean.

The stories continue. There is a couple who also lost a teenage boy — a car, speed, and a country road involved. I see my mom and sisters immediately charged by their story, bodies instinctually turning towards them, backs straightening.
There are others.
We are not alone.

The factor that binds the people, who sit in the metal chairs, is loss.
There is no sadness meter that computes the most tragic bereavement and neither is there any attempt to decipher loss A from loss B and categorize one as more worthy of unbearable pain and suffering. Each loss is equally respected, but there appears to be some alignment by age that seems predictable. My mom and sisters connect immediately with the parents of the dead teenage boy. They speak the same language. They establish an immediate kinship — relatives connected by blood on cars driven by teenage boys.

I went to university one morning and I never came back. This couple's son went to a neighboring town with friends, for ice-cream one summer night, and never came back. Our leaving was so unexpected, so 'in your face' violent and life altering. We were not expected to die. It was assumed we would continue with our higher education, find a sweetheart, build a home, live a life, raise some kids, work long hours, grow old.

My mom and sisters attend the grief group every second week. My dad has no interest in going. A strong friendship develops with the couple who lost a teenage boy. They are Sandy's age. Although my mom and the other mom are at different stages in life, they share something that lifelong friendships cannot. They share death anniversaries, lonely holidays, birthdays without aging, marriages and babies of their son's friends. They share hearts exploding when trucks roll and semis crash into cars on country roads.

FRUGAL

I would guess that the average farmer is as frugal as my dad and despises waste and gluttony in anything. At our house, we have electric heat in each room, but the main source of warmth came from the old coal furnace that had been in the original farmhouse. My dad was ingenious at adapting the old to work in the new.

We always waited as long as we could to turn the heat on in the house, and it became a game of sorts: How long can we make it this year? I recall with fondness the smell and the sounds in the house when the heat came on for the first time. The dust on the registers heating up and the clanking in the walls as it all came to life; the fine, dry particles cooking on the tops of the metal baseboard heaters, speaking of the time spent outdoors in the sun, neglecting the chores inside. The heat coming on evokes a sense of hunkering down, of coming together, of beef stew on Sundays, of family.

We burned mostly wood in the old coal furnace, and we spent hours as a family chopping and hauling the fallen, dead trees. My dad was in charge of the chain saw, and the rest of us were sorters and stackers and wheelbarrow drivers. I came up with the idea of dropping the wood through an open window in the basement, instead of climbing the stairs with bulging armfuls. We took turns at the stations, all of us preferring to be outside where the sun and the chill in the air reminded us how lucky we were to be kids growing up on a farm. We piled the wood meticulously, starting along the west wall, moving outward from there to fill the room from floor to ceiling. When the line of wood reached the door, we were done — such a feeling of accomplishment, of togetherness, of seeing a job well done. My parents taught my sisters and me about hard work and the pride that comes with it.

What we learned on our farm means something to the four of us.

Those memories will keep my sisters moving forward in the cold, lonely days that are to come.

My dad can't adapt to this new life. He is nothing like the old furnace in the new house.

The cellar will be empty next year.

LAST NIGHT OUT

The weekend before I died, Chris and I went into the city to shoot pool and have a couple of beers at Boston Pizza in the south end. There were some girls who were flirting with us and I really liked the attention, so did Chris. I was just getting to the point where I actually had an interest in girls — now I am dead and have never been kissed — sucks, I know.

The alcohol loosened up my inhibitions and I told Chris how I didn't really like university. In fact I hated it. I was only two weeks in, but I could already tell that it wasn't for me. I liked being outside, working with my hands like my dad. I also told Chris that I had some interest in being in the Air-force, I would have liked to be a pilot. I had never told anyone that before, and I didn't want to disappoint my dad who thought I should study computers — the way of the future. Oddly enough, I will never have one.

A couple of beers turned into multiple beers.

Chris' cousin drove us back out to his farm because we drank too much. I puked a couple of times before I fell asleep. I had to get up early to get back home, a deal I made with my dad in order to gain his permission to go to the city the night before. I never saw Chris again. My dad took one look at me when I arrived home at 6:30 a.m. and knew that I had had too much to drink. He chose a special chore for me that day. It was hot as hell outside and my instructions were to take the torch and the propane tank and burn off all the weeds on both sides of our quarter mile road that leads to the yard. Farmers do this in September in order to eliminate anything for the coming snow to build banks against. Tricia knew that I was hung over and she brought me a big jug of water on her bike. She laughed her ass off knowing firsthand how I felt.

When the snow flies in a couple of months from now, and it skims across the road with nothing for it to catch on, eliminating the snow banks, my dad will feel guilty. Burning off the weeds was my last chore, and he did it to teach me a lesson.

ANGER

There is so much anger.

Debilitating anger, uncontrollable anger, indescribable anger.

Anger at the senselessness of my death.

Always swimming just beneath the surface.

Anger at the drivers for not looking.

Climb the next hill and anger meets you at the top.

Anger lurks just around the next corner.

Anger at the people around them whose lives are day dreams, when theirs is possessed by such horrific, unimaginable demons.

The pitiful faces they see when they open the door.

Anger at the people who try with meaningless and inappropriate words to deafen the sound of death that rings in their ears.

TORTURE THYSELF

Tricia and Sandy are both prone to feelings of guilt. My dad does have a way of letting you think you could have done more, which can leave an impression of never having done enough. Bonny gave up on the idea of coveting his praise a long time ago. Sandy and Tricia never have.

My dad and I — being his only son — had a relationship unique to that of his daughters. My mom and I had a special bond as well. My sisters call me the favorite, and they are right. The great thing about our family dynamic is that my three sisters would say that I am deserving of that favoritism from both of our parents. There are no grudges, but they still teased me relentlessly.

So now enter into the world without the sibling that pleased both parents and you might begin to understand the need to self-torture. Tricia is the daughter that sleeps down the hall in the bed of the boy who could do no wrong. She should have been with me on the day I died. She blames herself for my death. She imagines our parents lying awake in their bed, wishing that it was her in the urn in the closet. She dreams of me — lying awake in her bed.

Sandy would sacrifice her life for mine in a second. She moved away from the farm a long time ago and our lives have moved forward without her — she is dispensable in her mind. Sandy is fourteen years older than me. She lies awake at night and wonders what might have happened if she had stayed. Would she somehow have averted the harm that barreled into me that September morning? She feels guilty because she left.

Bonny is not ruled by guilt or regret or *what if.* She does not let the fantastical control her thoughts. She is too sensible for that.

THE LEADER POST

In the past, my dad never came home from the city without buying the local newspaper, *The Regina Leader Post*. He would return with a copy rolled and left on the dashboard of his truck, "Jarett, go and get me my newspaper. It's in the truck." He still buys the odd copy, to project an air of ordinariness, but he never seems to read it. My mom, Tricia, and Sandy have a newfound interest in the newspaper though, and their inquisitiveness is in the obituaries. Caring nothing for land sales and grain prices or Canadian politics, they search the list of dead names and photos for young faces and small digits between *Born...* and *Died...* They are not heartless or coldblooded, but they are always looking for others — seeking the kind of company that they are unable to find in the people from their past.

I watch as Tricia's finger slides down the columns.
Slowly.
Stopping briefly.
Doing the math when there is no photo.
Not close enough to my age.

Moving on.
Tricia talks out loud, "One hundred and two years old. Lucky bastard."
The white hair, the dentures, the wrinkles.
Next.
A baby born at twenty-one weeks.
Horrific — but not what she needs to find.

Searching on.

Thirty-seven.

Much too young to die, but not quite a match.

Next.

The photo with the cap and gown, like mine.

Tricia shares her find out loud. "John Doe. Born 1979. Died suddenly September 1998. Loving parents and sisters left behind."

They silently evaluate the chances that this boy was also in a car accident and that a policeman knocked on their door as they knocked on ours and how these parents were completely devastated and how two of the sisters wished it had been them and now they knew that there were people out there like them and it felt comforting in an odd sort of way and they kept looking for more...

As time passes, Tricia and Sandy will occasionally peruse the obits, but for different reasons. It becomes a way to make sure they don't forget — the searing pain and me. It's like a touchstone. We lost the same. We loved him too.

The pain so real that they can feel it in the numbers and the photo. They imagine the parents and the siblings and the teenage body that will never lie in the bed down the hall. They wonder what choices the families made about viewing the dead corpse, about burial, about memorializing them. Only two or three days have passed since they lost their teen. It is all so new for them right now and people keep coming and they wonder if they find comfort in that. My sisters live through the families who are forced to join the teenage death club — it allows them to keep me present. The siblings I left behind are far too familiar with each laborious step these strangers will take and how life will pull their feet to the earth like magnets. My sisters mourn for the anguish of others who will walk in their shoes. They talk about these families and debate the possibilities of what the sudden death they live with now might have entailed. Sandy and Tricia let the deaths of other teenagers gnaw away at bits and pieces of themselves. It is so sad to watch.

A LETTER FOR SANDY

Sandy's husband's brother is the only person to try to reach her.
He writes her a touching letter.
It comes to her on the farm.
Sandy cries when she receives it and places it in her diary.
She is not able to contact him immediately, but one day she will,
when the darkness eclipses the light.

Oct .21/98
Dear Sandy,

From time to time, especially while at work, my mind has a ten-dency to wander. Lately, I've been thinking about you and how you are doing. So I wanted to let you know that you are in my thoughts. Even though we haven't had the opportunity over the years to spend much time together, I feel very close to you.

There are many things I would like to tell you in an attempt to ease your pain, but who am I to give advice? Nevertheless, I am going to say one thing to you. Forgive me if you don't appreciate this:

If Jarett could tell you himself, I'm sure he'd want to thank you for being such a great sister and more importantly, he would want you to be happy again.

I also want you to be happy again.
P.S. If you want somebody (else) to talk to, I'm a pretty good listener

BIRTH AND DEATH

Being born is a miracle of course, but none of us have any memories of that journey. Dying and being dead are different. I imagine that as a child enters the world, the process occurs in slow motion, the contractions of the mother's body pushing the baby forward, helping them to enter this new space. It is a forward moving process.

Death and dying for the young are the opposite.
You are being pulled back.
Frantically.
Like being stuck in a vacuum hose that won't let you go.
Life is all you know.
The people who love you grab on and won't let go.
And so you hover above them, straddling life and death because they need you to.

Time does not exist on the other side of life. I will never be older than nineteen.

But time passes differently for the living. Every day is another day without me, every holiday marking years they have moved through my nonexistence. The milestones dive bomb them daily. There is a sense of panic when the snow falls in November, and they know that the first holiday without me threatens to materialize.

How can we have Christmas without Jarett?

So they keep their heads down, concentrating on placing one foot in front of the other, they move through the days like slowed animation, successive poses that create the illusion of life when shown in a sequence.

DEALING WITH DEATH

Each of my sisters deals with my death in three very different ways.
One is outwardly destructive; one regroups, refocuses, and continues; and one lets it eat her from the inside out.

Two of them need therapy and only one goes, pulled eagerly by the "numb her mind" husband. The one who acquiesces does not benefit from the bearded, bespeckled man that sits across from her and asks, "So tell me about your brother." She hates that fucking guy.

My mom partners with death.
She invites it into her body.
Come to me, she says.
Take me to my son.

My dad duels with death.
In the light of day he holds it back with his strong hands — death flailing in his face.
You took my son you bastard.
At night, death keeps my dad from sleeping.
He wanders through wheat fields, death following in his footsteps — knowing it has won.

CHRISTMAS

Christmas passes like any other day. There are no decorations or presents. There are no shortbread cookies with cherries and there is no fruitcake — with or without nuts. My mom's baking traditions will not come alive from the pages of her mom's cookbooks, the smears of butter and the dapples of vanilla extract clouding the directions. She will not smile at the notes she wrote in the margins: *Jarett's favorite, Best damn cookie,* in his words. My mom will not sit at the piano and play "Silent Night."

The nights in this house are neither calm nor bright.

My dad will not walk through the stand of evergreens, pick from the best, and then place a tree in the family room without me. The ornaments, made by my sisters' and my hands, will rest in their boxes for many years.

My mom will not decorate the house with lights as she usually does. Every December and January she places three candles in three vertically oblong windows that face south. When you enter the farmyard at night, you will be struck by the welcoming presence of the three beacons that bring you home in the blackness of the prairie sky. I felt that every time I saw them — the New England tradition passed to my mom from Sandy. Those three lights shine bright in those windows every night now. They shine for me. Throughout the year, my parents always left the centre yard light on until each of their kids was home. My mom struggles with shutting it off now. I won't be driving into the yard again, and I won't need the light to help me open the gate on the front porch. Leaving the three candle lights in the south facing windows solves the problem for her.

She whispers to me in the night, *I'll always leave a light on for you Jarett.*

The warmth and the glow lighting the sky for me.

Bringing me home to her.

INFERTILITY

Sandy flies back to Boston for the first time at the end of January. Almost five months have passed since my accident. She only plans to be gone for two weeks, but she struggles to leave the sister whom she feels solely responsible for. The sister she knows carries so much potential for darkness. The sister whom our parents are unable to pull from the undercurrents of grief that drag her away from them. Tricia circles a drain that leads to a level of harm that Sandy knows she is capable of.

Sandy married her high-school sweetheart at twenty and moved away from here. Opposites attracted — the Rebecca of SunnyBrook Farm girl married the professional athlete. Things were good for them — both driven and focused — able to build their separate identities, while at the same time respecting the goals of the other. They decided at thirty to have a baby. Three years later, I am dead and there's still no baby.

Sandy's husband has come to the farm as his work allows. He travels back and forth over two thousand miles, hoping to see glimpses of the wife he married. He calls daily, but has seemingly overlooked the obvious — 'to have and to hold, for better, for worse, in sickness and in health'. My death and what it did to his wife, my sister, does not fit into any cell on a spreadsheet.

Sandy flies through Winnipeg, Toronto, then Boston, in search of the thing that will keep her moving forward — a child. She gets smashed at an airport bar when her flight is delayed for hours. I watch her sit alone at the bar, drinking rum and coke like my dad. There is a stack of napkins to her right, and she keeps taking another and then another off the pile that twists upward, each napkin on top angled further right, creating a staircase of sorts. She cries silently — the tears streaming softly down her face. She brushes them away discreetly when they reach her jaw line and then places the napkins in her purse to hide her desolation. She feels so alone without Tricia, my mom and dad. She goes to the pay phone three times — reaching out to the others who cling to the capsized raft of gloom. She needs to keep checking in with them.

Are you still hanging on?
If you let go, I will let go too.

For the first thirteen years of marriage, Sandy and her husband were like-minded. People change when young people die though. Sandy is one of them.

Sandy doesn't want to leave the farm. All she wants to do is hide and avoid the normalcy of life that exists beyond it. Her husband has never questioned the time she has spent on the farm, but he doesn't understand her need to be there either. Sandy never asked if he was okay with her staying. They are two cogs in the wheel of their marriage and they both turn independently. She needs to be with people in the same state of mind as her. She feels so out of place anywhere else.

Sandy's husband wants to move past the horror.
He wants his wife to live at home again.
He wants her to be happy.
But he never verbalizes any of it.
She needed to hear those words.

Sandy is obsessed with having a baby.
She thinks a baby will save her.
And she is right.

Sandy drinks when she is alone. She knows that her days of swimming around in the warmth of inebriation are numbered. She likes how the alcohol takes a hold of her, how it wraps its capable arms about her being and holds her up, how it rewires the thoughts in her head and makes them feel distant, how it dilutes the memories, how it gives her a strength. She likes how it feels to place one foot in front of the other and not have a memory of placing it there. A baby will change all of that. She will have a new drug.

Sandy is alone most of the time in Boston. Even when she hears the bang of the garage door opening, she knows that the man who enters their home will do nothing to fill the vacuity within her. She spends her days devoured by despair. She talks endlessly on the phone to Tricia and my mom. It is then and only then that she feels steadied.

Her husband goes to work in the morning and returns in the evening to the shell of the woman he married.

He never speaks of me — he just hopes that one day she can leave me behind.

When she is able, Sandy sits at her desk in the room with the blue toile curtains she made, and she writes the words that cry out to be read. She writes about me, about missing me, about loneliness. She writes to refute what she has read, she writes about 'how to' and 'how not to,' she writes non-fiction, and she writes poetry. She writes to her husband about things he will never understand.

Oh such power and strength has he
Leaving me alone with me

Reached out my hand for him to hold
No words, no tears to negate the cold

Speaks to me of time and hope
Never shows me how to cope

Alone I stand with all my fear
He is there and I am here

Sandy loves when the night moves in through the slats in the blinds — how it swallows the light and creeps like molasses around her. Standing at the kitchen window, she watches as it makes its approach through the trees.

The darkness comes down like a hood before a hanging.
Hiding the outside world and the terror on the face beneath.

Sandy weeps away in the king size bed where they lay.
Drops of salty water hollowing out rock.
Boring holes in their marriage.
Her husband, so at peace.
She, so close to drowning.
The tears forming a moat between them.
Her grief fortified within.

Sandy does not call any of her friends while she is in town. She lets the days move through her like fiction — characters and feelings that are not real — she ignores them. She does not long for the company of others, nor does she need to hear the words that they speak. The phone goes unanswered and no one knocks on the door. Her days are focused on injections and ultrasounds. Her nights are filled with wakefulness.

Her husband's snoring saws away at the life they built.
Her whimpers, unnoticed, whittle away at all they had.

Sandy lives in her war-battered armor of grief and her husband lives in his optimistic, forget what you cannot change, business suit. Some would describe his actions as fortitude; I see them as cold and uncaring. Sandy left her life and her husband to do what had to be done, and she will leave them both again and again in the future — she will not have a choice.

Sandy's grief-soaked body absorbs the hormone shots, resulting in a cocktail that fuels her depression. She waits for the day when they will place the potential for the tiny being inside of her.

TRICIA

Tricia hates being the only child in the house with the parents who are both so sad. There is insurmountable pressure to be all that she can be — to be something for me as well — to be everything for our parents. She looks forward to going to school every morning and escaping the stares that ask so much of her. She drives alone in a car for the first time since Sandy left. She is scared, but she does it anyway.

Tricia does not spend as much time with the horses as she used to. She doesn't seem to have the energy, nor does she want to ride alone. As the two of us raced up and over ditches, down in the creek bed, across the fields of summer fallow, I was always on her right or her left side, a little behind, pushing my horsemanship skills to match hers, always chasing her.

Something else chases her now.

Tricia's life is limited to my bedroom and her classes at the University of Regina. She does not socialize with friends beyond the farm, but in time, the city will be all that she craves.

SECRETS

My mom is sick. She and I know the death that is growing within her before the doctors confirm it. She lets it grow and take hold of her before she seeks medical attention — there were signs worth exploring immediately following my accident. She is pulled between two places — the place where I exist and the world where my sisters live.

My mom makes an appointment with her doctor and disguises it as a need for more pills to help her cope. Tricia drives her into the city, the purpose of the appointment unknown to her. She sits in the waiting room. Unaware of the next collision course careening towards her.

My mom is host to a concerning mass and she is referred to a surgeon.
A surgical biopsy is necessary — possible breast cancer.
My mom is silent on the ride home.
She thinks mostly about the twenty-one year old daughter sitting next to her — the one who wears my clothes every day and barely leaves my bedroom.

My mom tells my dad first. He is quiet, but concerned. He does not make any promises to her about how they will combat the cancer together.

My mom sits Tricia down in the big green chair.
It sits in the family room where you will not find any kinfolk gathered.
Embers in the fireplace revealing reds and oranges — the colors of heartache.

The river rock from the creek bed framing the fireplace — the colors of the farm.

The mantle, the focal point in the room, filled with my face at varying ages, a testament to my physical absence.

My mom speaks calmly and explains the situation — she whispers the word biopsy. Tricia begins another transformation away from the sister I know.

The peeling layers exposing raw flesh.

She weeps uncontrollably — the thought insurmountable.

My mom squeezes into the green chair beside Tricia and calls her two eldest. Bonny is in shock, but as a teacher, it will be hard for her to take any more time off from work. Her husband also has a business that is failing, so money is tight. Bonny talks to her husband and he calms her with promising words like *benign, caught it early, she will be fine.*

Sandy is distraught and plans to return to the farm before they cut a piece of flesh from my mom. She knows she cannot be far away and hear bad news again. She would not have the strength to board another plane and fly through the skies with the oppressing weight of doom pushing her back in her seat. The fertility procedure will be completed tomorrow, and she will find out if she is pregnant or not on the prairies that define her and slice through her. Sandy sits alone in a chair in front of her fireplace in Boston and stares at the mantle — the same photos staring back at her that stare at Tricia and my mom on the farm. Sandy thinks of words like *malignant, metastasized, death sentence.*

I watch as my mom tries to comfort her daughters, while at the same time hoping she has an out.

I have been dead for one hundred and twenty-seven days.

My family hasn't even come up for air since teenage death crashed over them.

And **SLAM**.

A new cancer wave plows into them.

What the hell is happening?

I don't understand this cruel burden that life has placed on my family. Wounds so deep they will never heal and now salt is rubbed in them,

life pummeling the innocent with an onslaught of new information.
What The Fuck?

My mom stands at the middle of a tug of war between her two youngest.
Tricia on one side.
Me on the other.

Tricia will ratchet down another notch without her.
The destruction she is drawn to pulling her away.
Never letting up.
Winning her at last.
I let up on the rope, hoping Tricia will pull my mom away from me.

ACROSS THE CREEK

The soil across the creek is sandy and has never produced a bumper crop; the wheat standing tall in the wind, the kernels hard and ready for harvest, yielding a high return per acre, causing any farmer to whistle on the way to the grain elevator.

The horse pasture follows the banks of the creek bed and runs kitty corner to kitty corner across our land. The horses love to congregate at the highest point along the fence line when the wind blows summer breezes across their backs. You can see them from my mom's garden and from the big white door on the pulley chain that locks my dad in the quonset now. In the past, he would always open the mammoth door that is big enough for a three-ton grain truck to drive through.
Jarett, get the door.
I would unlatch the chain from the lock position and then I would jump and grab it as high as I could reach, riding the rattling chain down as the door raised slowly upward, revealing the pasture before me in steps — again and again I jumped and I pulled.

The horses stand with their faces into the wind and turn themselves as the gusts approach from different directions — the movement of the air not allowing the flies to land. The sun breaks warm on their short coats and the moving air pushes their mane and tails into photogenic poses. It reminds me of a model on a photo-shoot with fans positioned to produce the perfect wind blown image. The horses are majestic and from the farmyard below, even the nags resemble stallions.

Tricia and I spent many a peaceful summer afternoon on that rise with the horses.

We lay in the tall grass across the winding flow of water.
My sister and I.
Lying back — looking up.
The horses munched on the blades about us.
Noisily, greedily.
Their tails and mane swatted at the flies that buzzed about.
The dogs nestled beside us, knowing that they belonged.
The farmyard lay like a mirage below us.
Is it really there?
Overhead, the clouds passed like great beasts moving across the prairie.
We took turns calling out what we saw — *Elephant, approaching from the west. Giraffe, straight ahead.*

Sandy and Tricia lie in the grasses without me now. This is no longer a place of childhood comfort, but rather, a place where the moving grasses conceal the sadness on the face of the one who lies in the blades beside you.

When it rains or snows, the horses come in from the high ground and seek the lowest land. The barn is always open for them, but sometimes they choose to stay outside in the weather. With the changing precipitation, they stand with their backsides to the brunt of the elements, the rain and the snow slanting in at an angle, pelting them with the force from the skies. This approach to dealing with the elements has always struck me as clever. As grief rains down on my family, I wish that they could find some tactics to aid them in the onslaught — adjust and adapt to the impending forces that rule their world — stand and face it or turn their backsides to it and wait it out.

COMING HOME AGAIN

Sandy boards the plane alone. She doesn't drink — she would like to — but she hopes that she harbors a tiny being within her, so the days of letting her mind slosh about in her brain are gone. She flies home to the potential of another storm, and she has yet to emerge from the last. She talks to me in the clouds as she did when she traveled home the last time, my death and my mom's tumor bouncing her across the skies like the worst kind of turbulence one can endure. She makes more promises, and she will keep them all, improving her average from the last trip home.

Bonny pushes aside the guilt she feels for not being able to go to the farm and focuses on the positive — her adorable kids, her supportive husband.

Tricia started a new semester two weeks ago. She takes a reduced workload, but she makes me proud just the same. My parents urge her to hold her course and keep on with her studies. She agrees to try, but promises nothing. She knows that everything depends on the biopsy results. Tricia's life will become one of starts and stops.
One step forward.
Pull the earth out from under her.
Three back.

Tricia picks up Sandy at the airport. She stands directly in line with the outward swinging doors from Customs. She wants to be the smile that Sandy sees when she exits. And she is. They rush to each other and embrace — daughters of a mom with a tumor, adding darker dimension to the fucked up sisters with a dead brother.

The farm quickly pulls Sandy back into its fold. She returns to my bedroom where Tricia prefers to be. They talk long into the night — lying like mummies in the blackness — inseparable again — bound together by loss.

My mom is outwardly optimistic to my sisters about the upcoming results from the biopsy, while inwardly confident that she let the tumor fester long enough to do some real harm.

My dad is happy to have Sandy back on the farm. She is take-charge and she gets things done. She also guides Tricia in a way that projects competence, and focus — it is actually the blind leading the blind, but Sandy makes it seem otherwise.

ELEVATOR

The biopsy results are back. Sandy takes my mom to the city, where the effectiveness of waiting to seek medical advice, when your body puckers and pulls and deforms itself, will be confirmed. My dad does not go with them. He is not the best at comforting and calming the woman who sleeps in his bed. Tricia wants to prolong the news as long as possible, so she stays at home with my dad. The ride to the city is filled with chatter about the possibility of Sandy being pregnant. She will have a blood test in three days to see if the trip to Boston was fruitful. My mom prays that Sandy will have a baby soon.

The elevator ride to the fourth floor of General Hospital seems longer than it should. My mom standing culpably in the corner, while her second eldest hangs nervously at her elbow. The waiting room is filled with people looking at magazines, not reading, just flipping pages to occupy their minds and to create some sound in the still space.

They call my mom's name, "Joan Speers."

The female surgeon enters the small room and wastes no time with pleasantries.

She says, "I am sorry, Joan. The cancer is stage IV, it has metastasized, you will need surgery to start, then chemotherapy and then radiation. I have scheduled your surgery for the day after tomorrow."

My mom embraces her sentence. Sandy rifles off her questions and then gathers the added weight of the news and piles it on top of everything else. My mom stands quickly, knowing the part she played in the news. Sandy's rise to upright is slow, the heaviness coaxing her to stay for a while in the chair.

They stand in the elevator — one playing host to something that will kill her — the other playing host to something that will save her. The ride down is even longer than the ascending trip. The doors close, coming together in a seam that binds the news of cancer into the lives of my mom and my sister. The ding of the door closing speaks audibly — *life moves on* — to those who hear nothing. People enter and exit the square box that hangs suspended in a shaft, on a wire, moving up and moving down, moving through words like cancer, stage IV, metastasized. The music, so named for its ability to calm and not offend, softly pipes in through the speakers in the walls. The numbered buttons light up and offer destinations in the minds of the two that stand and stare up at them.

Next floor for my mom.
Heaven.
Next floor for Sandy.
Black hole.

In a parked car, in the General Hospital parking lot, Sandy fails to keep her emotions in check. She says, "I guess it isn't the greatest time to try and have a baby."

My mom consoles her with her mom voice, her tender ways and says, "It's always a good time to have a baby."

HOME WITH THE NEWS

Tricia is sitting on the bottom stair when my mom and Sandy enter the house. She sits with her knees folded against her chest, her arms pulling the bit of self that is left into the smallest space possible. She is braced for the news. My dad sits in his office, his back to the door, to news about cancer, to life.

Tricia reads the message on my mom's face before the door closes on the February squall outside. She wraps her twenty-one year old body around the women who will now take up arms against a new foe. Like grief, cancer makes you fight alone.

My dad walks slowly from his office to the front door. He knows by Tricia's guttural noises that cancer has entered our home. It was there on the front door mat that father, mother, and sister — the first to know of my accident — melded together against teenage death. Greeting this new unwanted guest plays out differently.

My mom is outwardly resolute and inwardly confident cancer will win. "I need to lie down."

The baby of the family, Tricia, needs her mom and will not leave her side.

Sandy and my dad stand and stare at each other.

The front door mat speaking to them of past encounters with Satan. He comes again for my family.

Sandy says, "She can fight this and she will fight hard." Taking up the battle on her behalf — acting before asking — filling another role.

My dad picks up the additional weight placed in front of him, as any man with his competent hands would do, and turns back to his office.

He will carry it, but he can't fix it.

My mom calls Bonny. Tricia lies curled beside her beneath the covers, burrowing beneath the cancer and the grief intent on burying her. Bonny offers words that ring poetically across the miles — unable to think the worst even after all that they have endured.

"The surgery will get it all, Mom. You will beat this," says the eldest child.

My family is pulling away from each other. This new journey changes them all; Tricia returns to infancy, Sandy becomes a revolutionary, Bonny sees only the flowers through the weeds, and my dad is the silent partner — "Your mom needs to decide what she wants to do."

The day before surgery, my dad and Sandy walk out to the main road and back two times. They have words — tense words.

Sandy's voice is agitated, "Mom needs to be in an aggressive treatment plan and I am not sure I trust that she can get that type of treatment here."

My dad's voice is equally as heated, "Don't be ridiculous Sandy. Every plan will be the same."

Sandy takes the big city stance, "You are being naive Dad. Regina isn't exactly where medical minds gather."

My dad hits back with motherhood, "Your mom needs to stay here for Tricia."

Sandy counters with reality, "But the doctor thinks it has already spread to her lymph nodes, so we need to hit it hard or she won't be here at all."

They break away from each other where the field on the right side of the road meets the edge of the yard. My dad walks on to the quonset and Sandy makes a u-turn to my tractor. They both sit and stew for a while.

Two hours later, my dad climbs into the cab of my tractor and sits on the dash directly across from Sandy. They continue to discuss my mom's cancer. Sandy doesn't think my dad is taking the situation seriously enough. She spent some time researching clinical trials out of Boston and talking to some doctors whom her husband knows. They urged Sandy to get our mom into the most aggressive program and to get her in quick. There is a trial through a Boston hospital that could be offered in Saskatoon — a two-hour and forty-five minute drive from the farm. Sandy and Tricia are willing to take on the task of getting my mom there and back for every treatment. My dad thinks that my mom should drive the twenty minutes to Regina for her treatments. The medical minds in Boston think the approach there will not be able to combat the advanced stage of cancer my mom has.

"What part of stage IV cancer are you not understanding, Dad?" Sandy asks.

"I think you are overreacting," my dad says calmly.

Sandy has the last word, "And I think you are underestimating how serious this is."

Sandy leaves my dad in the tractor and gets in the old pickup truck. The ruts of snow on the road from the storm last night toss the old Ford from side to side, the ice scrapes the undercarriage, digging away at her thoughts. Sandy is going to the place where she always goes if she isn't sitting in my tractor — the place where I died. The roads are packed in with drifting snow that not even a four-wheel drive can ram through. The municipality does not clear the side roads where she is headed.

She stays on the grid as long as she can, and then loops around, coming in on Chris's road. She exits the truck and bundles up against the cold. The wind has whipped up some thigh high drifts, and she breaks through the crust often, her emotions zapping her energy as much as stepping straight up and down does. Eventually, she succumbs to the snow and crawls. I watch her scramble through the white to the place where I died. Her emotions spill out of her onto the snow, her tears freezing as they fall toward the crystals she squirms across. I see the tiny being that was planted in her belly at the fertility clinic and I understand before she does that there is hope within her. The child growing inside of her will begin to allow her to leave parts of me behind.

My mom's cancer is aggressive. She has let it fester long enough to require invasive and grueling procedures. My sisters are by her side for every pinch, examination, and changing prognoses. Three are divided in two. The added strains of having a sick parent, who already moves through life as if suspended in a Jello mold, will pull Sandy and Tricia closer, and ostracize Bonny further from their clique. Bonny's ability to move forward and through her grief handicaps her in the game of sibling synergy. She maintains her personal life, and so the fury of the farm does not feed on her like it does the other two — gnawing away on two broken-down women in order to fuel itself. Bonny lives as normal people do, and her sisters live in reclusion, choosing phantoms of me as their companions over people. Sandy and Tricia search for wormholes in my mom's garden, and Bonny gets on with life on earth.

Bonny is unable to be present for every pinprick and treatment that my mom endures — she lives too far away. It is hard for her not to be able to stand by her bedside and hold the hands with the veins that run and hide from the needles now. No one is blaming Bonny for her absence, but Sandy and Tricia are logging hours that time will not replay.

My mom is in surgery. Tricia and Sandy pace and sit, sit and pace around the room with the sallow yellow walls. They pull the curtain that divides the space in two — another frail woman with cancer lying so tiny in a bed that dwarfs her. I find it odd that hospitals line up sick people together and then doctors come in to discuss some of the most personal shit with their patients with just a mere wall of fabric offered for privacy.

My sisters prep their space for optimal containment.

Pulling on the corners, wanting them to touch, wanting to close the gaping holes.

This is our space and that is yours and we will not listen to your whispers of worrisome woes and please don't listen to ours.

Wanting to hide everything ugly — the news — the frail mother — behind a drape that doesn't even reach the ceiling.

When my sisters enter and exit the room, their eyes tunnel forward, never gazing upon the other sick woman.

Don't worry, we didn't hear or see anything — her family gathered round — the doctors speaking softly.

Two women dressed in blue scrubs and long blue robes — super hero-like capes open and flowing as the air pushes back on them — their demeanor saying, *We can cut her and we can make her bleed, and then we can bring her back to you* — wheel my mom into the room. She lies there in her unknowing state, the Betadine still visible at her neck and peeking out of her sleeve on the left. My sisters flank her on the left and the right, and wait for her to come around. My dad enters just when she begins to pull herself from the lure of the drugs. He squirms and struggles to stay in the room with a view of his withering wife. My sisters plead for his attention to be directed toward the shrinking woman beneath the sheets. I watch as he quickly leaves. He steadies himself outside in the hall — no one sees his agony but me. He has left her many times in the past, and one day soon, he will long to secure the final exit ahead of her, but he will not.

Following the surgery, the lab will test the cells taken from my mom and they will determine that a large enough swath was not taken. The tissue that was thought to be healthy is cancerous and so back to the table and the bright lights and the knife.

Sandy goes alone to a lab for a blood test. On a cold but sunny February day, she learns of the child that she harbors within her.
The knowledge lifts her.
The purpose calms her.
The hope casts an anchor in her future.

GARDENING 101

In Saskatchewan, you should ideally have your garden in the ground before May 15th. My mom always prepped the soil with the rototiller twice — turning the land over from north to south and then plowing it under again from east to west. She has always taken her garden planning seriously, laying everything out on a grid with colorful hand-painted markers indicating what is planted in each row.

Vegetable gardens are made up of mostly fruits and vegetables that need to be planted every year. The only two plants that return each spring in my mom's garden are rhubarb and asparagus. We all used to fight over the asparagus and now it just goes to seed, the thin green stalks with the tender tips that we cut off at ground level were seven inches tall. Now, they wave in the wind at three feet, tough and chewy and tasteless.

My mom always went to great lengths to insure straight rows of produce in her garden. She used a plumb line tied to two sticks to guide her — so determined as she dug out each row with her hoe — following the line from stick to stick.

The first signs of green emerging from the earth were always the most exciting for my mom.

She would update us at the dinner table, "The cucumbers and the carrots are up first this year. I think they will be happier now that I moved them out of the shade beside the horse corral."

My mom watered her garden diligently, donning her rubber boots to move the sprinkler hoses around through the mud. She crawled in the dirt on sunny days, pulling any signs of weeds that dared to grow in her garden. As the plants grew and grew, my mom would bring out the trellises my dad and I built for her and place them beside the natural climbers — the peas and the beans. This created a simplicity when picking the produce, the plants stretching upward instead of folding over on themselves. My mom loved to harvest the food she grew. She displayed a profound sense of pride as she transported her overflowing buckets and baskets and bags into the house.

The growing season in Saskatchewan is quite short and the first signs of that are evident at the beginning of August; production slows and the plants produce fewer and fewer blooms. You start to notice the edges of the leaves yellowing and the roots pulling away from the dirt, the plants programmed to last for only one season.

The potatoes, the carrots, the onions, the radishes, and the turnips stay in the garden the longest. They grow underneath the ground and can tolerate the dip in temperature, as August ends and September begins. My mom would scurry about pulling tomatoes off the vines, saving every cucumber that hid beneath the leaves and every bean camouflaged between the many tendrils before the heaviest frost arrived. She listened every day to the forecast, intent on saving every morsel from the cold.

Something else grows in the garden now with the rhubarb and the asparagus — it arrives in the form of a scarecrow — dressed like me. My dad has a recurring nightmare where a flock of crows comes to pick at my body propped on a stick in the garden. Every time he runs to get his shotgun and then shoots wildly at the crows picking away at my scarecrow corpse. The crows won't leave. The dream always ends with him not being able to save my dead body from being picked to pieces.

CHEMOTHERAPY

Chemotherapy starts shortly after my mom's second surgery. She opts for the more aggressive treatment in the name of daughters and babies and grandkids.

Her thoughts fleetingly reaching for the future.

I want to meet more grandchildren!

I need to see Tricia graduate!

The more combative choice will send as much poison coursing through her body as she can take. My sisters approach my mom's cancer like greedy, new-time farmers — *kill all of the weeds that grow in the fields with pesticides and who cares what long-term damage there is.* Life revolves around white and red blood cell counts. *Can she take more? Can we give her more?* **Give her more!**

There are over five hours of driving on chemotherapy days, so they start early in the morning and end late in the day. My mom is always tired. Her grief drags her to the bottom of her life and dredges up so much shit.

My dad never offers to take my mom to Saskatoon for her treatments, and Bonny lives too far away, so Tricia and Sandy divide the time driving the woman who sits in the passenger seat.

She stares to her right out the window.

Portraying obedience in her mind.

I will do what you tell me, but that is all I can do.

Relinquishing control.

Retreating from life.

The recliner chair cancer club is where the nasty drugs get pumped into the veins of the sick. I look around the room and see the same stoic faces week after week: luscious locks lingering here and there; head-wear prolific among all ages; pallid faces; deep set eyes looking into deep set eyes. I hate the damn scarves and the wigs that my mom wears — she looks like a wax figure with the wig on, an ancient genie with the turban on and a sixties crack-head with the scarf on. I hate that people suggest she looks good — *Joan, you are looking stronger.* There seems to be an allowable amount of bullshit when you sit with people who are willingly getting poison pumped into their veins. There is a camaraderie in that room — a sisterhood — a brotherhood — of those who have fought in the same war. People come here from the many farming communities throughout Saskatchewan. They talk of their wounded, their brave, and their fatalities — *it spread to his lungs; her children are only four and six; he fought long and hard.*

My mom is a puppet to the cancer and her daughters. My sisters pull all the strings that move the cancer puppet. She is dutiful to the manipulation of her body. She stands upright because they hold her there. When they don't keep the lines taut, she crumples quickly to the floor in a heap.

The puppeteers create the illusion of life in the puppet.

They are masters at hiding the strings from onlookers.

When the nausea rides in on the wave of despair, my sisters are there with the buckets and washcloths, clean nightgowns and breath mints. Two of them can change the bedding in two minutes flat, fluff the pillows, and hide the wilting woman quickly beneath the sheets.

My dad finds ways to busy himself out in the quonset.

Unable to help his wife.

Unable to help himself.

When my mom is able to eat, she asks for the same thing every time: mashed potatoes and peas.

My sisters bring her petite green morsels cascading down a mountain of mash.

They create works of art out of green and white vegetables.

Enticing her to give something back to her body, when the chemo takes so much.

My mom attempts to stir the peas into the potatoes.

Chasing the bits of green with the fork that trembles in her hand.

Peas fall off the edge of the plate.

Repeatedly, my sisters say, "You need to sit up to eat Mom. You can't lie down."

They hoist her upward — propping pillows behind.

My sisters watch to see how many bites she takes.

One.

Sometimes two.

Again and again, my mom pleads with my sisters,

"I can't eat anymore. Please take it away."

My mom surrenders to the venom.

My sisters beat wildly at the serpent that wraps itself about her.

My dad moves machinery about in the yard.

My mom's hair is falling out in patches, leaving tufts of wiry clumps. Her cheekbones protrude too much, her eye sockets sink too much, and there is no color in the crayon box for this shade of skin. When I look at her, I think derangement, escaped from a mental institution or living at a concentration camp. I do not think mom. The ever-increasing expanse of scalp makes her look older than her dad who lived to be ninety-nine. She is fifty-eight. The look is war-torn and haggard — not exactly something for my sisters to rally around. The worse my mom looks, the more Sandy and Bonny fight — the two of them feed on their frenzied feelings — *We are the eldest daughters and we need to hold it all together, but we can't because we don't see things the same way.*

When I see black she sees white.

When I see white she sees black.

One day my mom asks Tricia to cut off her remaining hair. My sisters are relieved. This was her request to own and they patiently waited until she was ready. Tricia sets up a chair in the kitchen with a sheet beneath it and goes to get my mom, "I am ready for you Mom. Let me help you to the kitchen."

My mom replies emphatically, "Oh, I don't want to do it in the kitchen. I want to go outside on the grass. Can you get me a lawn chair from the garage?"

"Okay, but why outside?" asks Tricia.

My mom predictably says, "I like the thought of a mother robin finding my hair on the lawn while foraging for worms and then using it to build a nest for her babies. When we are done, I would like to sit on the porch for a while and watch to see if one of them flies away with the pieces in their mouth. Can you get me a blanket?"

My dad can't stand to see my mom's bald head.

Grief and my ghost and the cancer push him farther and farther from the farm.

SOME HOPE FOR SANDY

There are two babies growing inside of Sandy. She learns this on a trip back to Boston for an ultrasound. She is ecstatic.

She attends the appointment on her own.

Sitting solo amid the fawning couples.

The anticipation palpable.

Families about to bloom singling her out.

Still alone.

But not as much as before.

Sandy's husband gets on with what he is good at — making money. The shift from pro athlete to business man years ago was seamless — work hard — work harder — don't lose.

His wife's emotions and her sadness are not entities that he can manipulate or understand.

Sandy loosens her hold on her newfound strength and even speaks with a friend.

Bad choice for her.

The friend tells her how thrilled she is that she is pregnant, but she doesn't stop there and she should have.

"Jarett is coming back to you through the baby. How beautiful. What a miracle."

Sandy loses her grip on her newfound strength.

"Don't you dare tell me that I had to lose my brother so that I could get pregnant. You still have your brother, plus you have three kids. Don't fucking tell me that."

Back to the farm she goes.

Sandy's expanding midriff grows around her like a life preserver — the buoyancy allowing her to float for a while in the calm waters of expecting — the promise of the tiny beings keeping her head above the grief and the cancer.

SUCCESSFUL DAY

A successful day on the farm is gauged in part by how low the sun is on the eastern horizon in the morning and how much dirt is piled in the shower at the end. A farmer works hard and isn't afraid to get dirty. The farmer's wife does more laundry than most — choosing to hang a portion to dry in the sun on the clothesline — a relic from the past, but still in existence on the farm. The framer's wife goes to great lengths to air dry the farmer's clothes and the bedding. It would be much easier to simply pull the items from the large washing machine and place them directly into the matching white drying machine. But the farmer's wife is not lazy. She will place the heavy, wet items in the large wicker basket, leave the house through the sliding patio door in the family room, walk around to the back to hang the trousers and the pillowcases on the line, and clip them in place with wooden clothespins. The farmer loves when the clean bedding transports the smell of the outdoors inside to rest beneath. The farmer's wife likes when the farmer is happy, so when the sun is still high in the sky, she will go out to the clothesline and neatly fold the sheets and the shirts. She will instinctively bury her face within the folds of each item and breath deeply — taking it all in — understanding simple pleasures and being happy to provide them for others.

My mom's instinct is to nurture.
Even with her bald head and her broken heart she wants to help.
Wishes she could help.
But she is too far gone.
When you can't help yourself, you can't hope to help others.

My mom does not bring iced tea in the late afternoons to the quonset anymore, but she still knows what my dad does there when he isn't in the city. She knows how he stands at his workbench, opening each drawer, but never knowing what he is looking for. The farmer has lost his function.

My mom stands at the double sink in their bathroom. When she peers into the looking glass, she sees the quonset reflected back to her from below, and in the foreground she sees her ghastly reflection and the mirror image of all that will soon be lost. The farmer's wife will lose the farmer soon.

A BREAK IN BOSTON

Sandy feels guilty for the reprieve she gets from the farm.

She moves through airports anonymously — she sits in the window seat slicing eastward through the sky, chatting to strangers about a brother in university — me. Sandy constructs her life as she needs it to be with the unknowing. It is hard for me to watch her build on a life that ended. At her hairdresser in Boston, she talks on as if nothing has happened — she can actually make herself believe what her mind tells her to be true. She likes the games that she plays.

Tricia doesn't get a break.
Everywhere she goes, people know that I am dead.
She can't play some twisted game of pretend like Sandy can.
She moves around my ghost every day.
She weaves through the gates on her slalom course of life.
Each of them knocking into her at every turn.
Crumpled red car.
Her momentum carries her forward.
Dead body.
She digs in to stay the course.
A mom with cancer.
Runaway life.
Despondent dad.
Crevices open up in her path.
Attempting to swallow her whole.
She dodges them temporarily.

BONNY

Bonny sits at the oak table in her kitchen with the matching oak chairs and the plaid cushions that are tied to the outer rungs. There is an apple crumble in the oven and the smell that wafts about her speaks loudly of my mom — she smiles at the thought. There is a roast in the crockpot, homemade coleslaw in the fridge, and vegetables roasting on the barbecue outside. At the centre of the table sits a lazy susan — sitting on top are ceramic salt and pepper shakers, a sugar bowl, some toothpicks, and some napkins, held in place by the side rails that keep them from spinning off. There is a blank card in front of her — a bouquet of lavender, tied with an apple green ribbon decorating the front.

She begins.

Dear Sandy,

She chooses her words carefully.

I wanted to tell you that the way you have been handling things is an inspiration.

She wants to impart an expression of gratitude.

You have taken care of all the details, stayed strong for Mom and Dad and kept Tricia on track with school.

She understands that Sandy has put her own life on hold to take care of others.

You have great determination.

She needs to say thank you.

I appreciate all you have done.

When Sandy receives the note, she reads it, sits down beside her mailbox on the road and sobs. Sandy knows of the deceit that she

190

hides — she knows how untrue it all is — the coping and the perceived strength. She takes the card and places it in one of her diaries. Throughout her life, she will be reminded of her sister's kind words. Unfortunately, her memory does not offer her the same rosy picture — there are all the things she didn't do and the fighting and the angry words.

Bonny feels guilt for not being able to be on the farm with our mom as much as her younger sisters. I wish I could tell her to be patient, that in time, she will give more than most people to her parents. And life will spin like one of those merry-go-rounds at the park where the kids run as fast as they can and then jump on, sending others flying — the ones that don't have a good grip.

CANCER SKIN

The effects of chemotherapy build over time. Those effects have robbed my mom's skin of all its color — she reminds me of E.T. now. Her skin has a translucent quality that makes her appear see-through. Her bones protrude in ways that make them look too big for the casing that covers them, like E.T's bony extended finger.

My mom wears clothing now that she would never have worn before — sweatpants and long sleeved shirts to cover the skin with the wavy grey veins. Everything is too big for her since the cancer extracted what it wanted.

The skin around my mom's eyes pulls away from the sockets, receding like the tide, leaving bulging islands of suffering.

The skin around her mouth blends into her lips in a puckered manner. There is no longer a line delineating her lips from her face — the color is faded — leaving her lipless.

THE FARM NOW

There are weeds in the garden that are three feet tall.
The weeping willows extend their branches like tentacles.
Draping themselves across the lane.
No one lives here, they say.
They are whimpering and wailing and everyone in the house can hear them.
We are losing the farm.
The chokecherries are asphyxiating the beds behind the house. The grass is so long that when my family walks in it, their legs are held back, like walking through water. The people who live here don't notice. The general upkeep of painting here and there, patching and hiding, improving, maintaining, left when I did.
The winter months are most forgiving.
The snow hiding the forsaken beneath.
The summer brings a growth that can't be harnessed. The neglect metastasizing across the land like cancer.

Time is not healing all wounds on the farm.
Gaping gashes expose raw flesh.
Stitches pull apart.
Scabs are picked off.

My mom does not bring the horses apple peels and bran mash in her buckets and bags anymore. She did not order seeds from the TNT seed catalogue this year, and she did not plant those seeds beneath the soil. She stands at the kitchen sink and stares through the pane in a way that makes you think she sees nothing.

The color has been switched off.
The sounds muted.

My dad moves about, but gets nothing done. He travels to the city daily now and escapes all that is missing on the farm. He used to be very politically minded, a history buff and interested in word origins and definitions. Whenever one of us kids would ask him what the meaning of something was, he would always tell us to go and get the two massive dictionaries — one labeled A through J and the other K through Z. We always groaned at the thought of discussing word definitions at the dinner table, but you didn't say no to my dad. I wish he could find his way back to some of the things that interested him in the past. In the near future, my sisters will use my dad's encyclopedic dictionaries to search for unfamiliar medical terms.

Tricia continues on with her classes at the university. Like my dad, she too feels the pull of the city and all it has to offer.

When Sandy comes to the farm, she tries to fix everything. She prunes trees and pulls weeds and cuts grass, but she can't make a dent in all that has already fallen into ruin.

When Bonny comes to the farm, she is a model of positivity and can see beyond the damage.

I am coming to terms with the fact that the farm has changed for all of us. Farms have an obvious purpose — they produce. The people who reside on the land have a purpose as well — they manage. My absence impairs them. I see the heart of our land slowing — the beat less strong — denying oxygen and nutrients — the muscles weakening.

I will never go home again.
I get that.
And home is no longer sweet.
The bitterness has won.
The farm has always been the place where I can lose myself.
The wide-open spaces pulling me in.
Embracing me.

The horses greeting me.
Pawing the earth.
Snorting free the dust that sits in their large nostrils.
The sound of their hooves carrying me across the prairies.
The wind in my hair.
Clip, clop.

The farm is dying.
And I get to witness that too.

As time goes on, I feel my anger boring deeper and deeper into the core of who I was. Tightening like a screw.
I hate myself for what I have done.

TEENAGE MORTALITY

I never thought about dying until I actually did. I had seen the commercials with the crumpled cars and the white sheets covering bodies on the ground, but I never imagined myself under one of those sheets. I think many male teenagers see themselves as invincible — it's a time to push limits, experiment, and take chances — I experimented with speed, but I never thought about the physics behind it.

Speed kills.

There are these programs that travel around to high schools near graduation and they try to teach kids about drinking and driving and speeding. They bring in a car from the junkyard that has been in a bad accident and then they have volunteers pretend to be injured and dead — they use fake blood and everything to get the attention of the driving youth. One volunteer is always dead and they cover them with a sheet. If you look at the percentage of teenagers that die in car accidents, the program isn't doing enough. I think they should make every kid lie under that sheet for five minutes, and I think before that they should have actual paramedics pretend to work on their dying bodies. Ideally, if their parents were screaming in the background that would add a nice effect.

Possible broken neck. Give me a C collar.
*Large bore I.V.'s. **NOW!***
Open femur fracture — right leg.
We need a traction splint on the left.
We need to decompress.
Possible pelvic instability.

A trip to the morgue might do the trick too. We have a place on our driver's license where we say whether or not we will donate our organs, so why not add a check box for showing our mangled bodies to teenagers? I would have volunteered.

The hardest thing about dying for me is watching my family. I force myself to be present. I force myself to experience their pain with them. Grieving for the young is not something that you "get through." It is something that you "live in." Every day my family struggles through the slime that surrounds them. The darkness is so thick that it impedes their movements.

I understand now that there are consequences to every choice made. I learned a huge lesson while speeding down a dirt road without my seatbelt on, and I will never get to make good use of the lesson learned.

CHRIS AND
MY MOM'S CANCER

When Chris comes to visit my mom, he brings his smile, a genuine love for his dead friend, and endless stories about her son. She laughs in his presence — so indebted to the young man who will venture into the past with her. He is happy to be able to take her there.

Chris and I went to a tiny little school in the town of Kronau from kindergarten to grade six. Less than one hundred and twenty people lived in Kronau at the time, and the majority of the kids who attended school there travelled on buses from surrounding farms. Our school was a bigger version of the one room schoolhouse that was used before they built the new building. There were eight kids in our graduating sixth grade class. Chris and I did every school project together that we were allowed to do. I remember one was an adaptation to the story of "The Three Little Pigs." The assignment asked that you work in pairs and change a nursery rhyme to make it politically correct. We kind of made up our own rules and instead of the wolf blowing down the houses, we had the wolf fart them down. When we read our story for the class, we could barely keep it together. I remember the teacher smiling at the back of the class. We didn't get an A, but we got a lot of laughs. My mom saved that story along with my clay handprint, every Mother's Day card I ever made, my best test results, and my most impressive artwork. She keeps them all in a box marked *Jarett* and looks at the items hiding inside more often than she should. Each of my sisters has a box too, but theirs do not hold the power over her that mine does. A part of Chris is in that box with me, and each time my mom opens it, she thinks, *Chris is still making memories for his mom to place in a box and look at whenever she wants. All of the memories in her box are happy and mine are so sad that I want to die. When I hold one of the clay sculptures Jarett made in elementary school, I cry. Chris' mom smiles when she looks at the funny things her son made.*

As time passes, Chris and my mom's relationship evolves. Initially, Chris was the calm in the storm, but as he grows and accomplishes and builds a life, he becomes all that I am not. My mom struggles to not hate him for that. The boy who grew up with me is growing away from me, and every day he is something I will never be. It becomes harder and harder for my mom to not think of that every time she sees him. Chris can feel the change coming. He knows that our lives were parallel and now they are not.

Cancer makes it harder for Chris to keep coming to the farm. My mom is needier now — she is not the mom who yelled at him and me for walking on her clean floors with muddy boots. Chris sees a sadness in my mom that haunts him — a hollowness. He stops coming around as much.

I don't blame him.

MY FAMILY

My parents and my sisters move like silent ghosts in the dance around death and cancer. They pirouette by the empty chairs, the bald head, my John Deere hat hanging on the coat rack, the barf bags, and the memories. There are pictures of me ad nauseam, but no one looks at the face that doesn't age.

No one likes to look at the face without hair framing it either.

I know their thoughts.

I hope she wears a wig or a scarf today.

You can see the pleading in their faces.

Please say you will wear it for me.

I don't care that it is itchy or hot.

No one wants to see my mom's bald head.

A well-meaning relative recently tried to take a family photo of the five I left behind, and each of my family members shouted "No" simultaneously. The last of our family portraits hang on the walls — all of us frozen in time. My family is not ready to make new memories without me. My family does not want to see pictures of my mom without hair.

As time passes, my family talks less and less of me.

If you pretend he never existed, I will do the same.

Separately, they all mourn me, but when they come out into the light of day, they smile smiles that say, *I am okay — I am moving on.*

My sisters do not want to bring me up in a conversation, because they worry that the mere mention of my name will bring my parents to their knees.

My parents do not want to discuss the dead, for fear that they may appear uninterested in the living.

It is a circular game that they play.

Each reciting the same mantra:

You protect me and I will protect you.

The dead boy can only hurt us in solitude.

United we live in betrayal.

BONNY, SANDY, AND TRICIA

Bonny guides the farm household in stimulating thought and life-style from afar. She researches holistic approaches to cancer, imbues a positivity that not many can ignore, and stands courageously in the path of the disease. When Bonny is able to come to the farm, she is the visiting motivational speaker. The great thing about Bonny is that she truly believes that eating seaweed and visualizing your cancer cells dying can help you beat the big C.

Bonny comes as often as she can to the farm. She brings with her a library of magazine articles, a dictionary of holistic medicine the size of a coffee table, and a carton of roots and weeds and herbs. The medical doctors do not want my mom combining holistic medicine with their western treatments, but Bonny keeps preaching the benefits of a gentler approach.

Tricia is the head of our cancer department. She can deal with the gore of incisions and most importantly, she can make my mom laugh while tending to her wounds. Tricia does not cower in the corner or get queasy — she is take charge in all areas medical. She learns things about herself that will one day have her choose a different career path. There will be ulterior motives involved, though…

Sandy is in charge of research and becomes an expert on my mom's diagnosis and prognosis. She spends hours and hours reading about the drugs they give her. She does most of the talking with doctors and she asks the hardest questions, "Can she beat this?"
She is not afraid of stepping on anyone's toes, "We want another opinion."

There is an efficiency that my sisters bring to the situation — they each know where their strengths lie and they are pulled to their stations organically.

My sisters submit to the roles they play — my mom plays the lead as patient, while my dad exits the stage. I want him to stay by her side and hold her hand — she deserves that. I want to scream at him — ***Dad, help Mom.***

I hate what he does to her. How can he walk away from someone so frail, someone so needy?

I watch her roll over in bed.

Away from the window.

Where he sits outside in his diesel Chevy.

The glow plugs warming.

He waits to turn the key and escape.

The sound of the engine turning over and over in her mind.

Hoping the firing stops and he walks back up the stairs to her.

But he never does.

She buries her head in a pillow as the engine fades at the bend in the yard.

SANDY'S BABIES

Sandy's two babies have become one. Back in Boston, the people at the fertility clinic tell her that this happens frequently; if she wasn't doing fertility and having ultrasounds at such early points in her pregnancy, she never would have known that one was absorbed by the other.

The news comes to her alone.

As she is accustomed.

She is sad, as she liked the idea of two babies to focus on.

The diapers, the nursing, the bathing, blocking out the mess on the farm.

One will still give her what she needs, though.

Someone to love who will love her back.

She will make the child sensitive and kind and in tune with the world around them.

Sandy and her husband decide to find out the child's gender.

It is a girl.

They are both ecstatic.

Her husband focuses on being able to provide this child with everything — she will want for nothing materialistically.

Sandy will be the conduit for providing her with the rest — the meaty stuff — morals, work ethic, kindness, a strong sense of self.

Sandy and her husband are very different people — my death has inflicted their marriage with serious harm and those afflictions will showcase their differences over time.

For now, Sandy focuses on the nursery and buying the right stroller and filling a closet with tiny clothes.

She is so excited to have someone who will depend on her for everything. She thinks only of the child that is hers.

As Sandy's belly fills with the being of Michaela, she thinks of new life and lives moving away from life. There is a new person blooming inside of her, and at the same time my mom's body is being cut and radiated and poisoned. Sandy is bothered by the conflicting realities and how one pulls her closer and the other pushes her away.

CANCER

Cancer takes orders from no one. If I had to describe cancer as a personality, I would liken it to a corrupt warden. If anyone in the cancer circle gets out of line, cancer whips out one of its many appendages and beats them into submission. Cancer is in cahoots with the nausea, the hair loss, the missing body parts, the scars, and the fear of dying. Cancer says, *We can bring her down together,* and quite often, cancer and its allies do.

Cancer is the extrovert in the room — cancer is the aggressive *I know everything* personality that demands people listen to it. Cancer takes pride in knowing it can band together with the side effects of the drugs and control them like a mob boss. Cancer likes it when a patient looks in the mirror and they aren't acquainted with the face staring back at them. Cancer gets all giddy when people who come to visit can't hide their startled reactions. Cancer wins then.

Cancer controls the people it attacks, as well as the people who care for the afflicted. There is an obedience that reigns over the people — they don't want to piss off the cancer or the doctors or the nurses. There is an unspoken belief that if they all do what they are told, then the cancer will like them and the medical staff will think, *What a great patient she is — so deserving of a miracle.* But, cancer doesn't work that way. It shows up in a body, a life, a family, and then it controls everything.

Cancer runs Tricia's life.
It lives down the hall from her.

Cancer calls to her in the middle of the night.
Tricia. Tricia. Can you help me?
Death calls to her from my room too.
She is twenty-one — a time to be carefree and have fun.
Her friends are present, but can't relate.
She turns her attention to another friend.

NO MORE CHEMO PARTY

My mom has completed her chemotherapy — for now.

Sandy is at the farm. She and Tricia plan a surprise "No More Chemo Party" for Mom. They are overjoyed that her personal poisoning is complete. They make her favorite foods and are so pleased when she actually eats more than a bite or two. They create a rhyming treasure hunt where they ask her questions and when she answers them correctly, she is rewarded with a gift. There are fits of giggles when one of my two sisters reads the verses — they describe things that only others who have cared for someone with cancer could understand.

They give her a beautiful antique hairbrush for the new hair that sprouts on top of her head. They buy her a colorful neck scarf, and tell her to **never** wear it on her head. They find a new birdhouse to hang in the tree that shades her garden, hoping to lure her outside in the sunshine. There is a basket with new gardening gloves, some fancy hand cream, and a new wide brim hat.

I feel so proud of my mom.
But.
Her smile feels mischievous.
Like a Cheshire cat.
Tricking the people around her to believe in something she does not.

My dad is awkwardly absent.
Sitting alone in a dimly lit bar.
The three who gather to laugh and smile are not letting on that they even notice.

RADIATION

My mom is tattooed with little dots.
They are permanent.
Connect the dots and her tumor emerges as a separate entity.
Another living thing.
Radiate the dots from the outside in.
The skin burns — 1st degree, 2nd degree.

Radiation is not as hard on my mom as the chemo was. She trudges
on. Acquiescent as always.
She moves through it like a wind up toy.
Her daughters turning the clockwork key at the back.
Her movements quick and robotic at first.
Then slowing and stopping mid-stride.
The doctors in Saskatoon advise my sisters to transfer the radiation
treatments to General Hospital in the capital city — twenty minutes
from the farm. The distance has been an added burden on my mom. My
sisters see the frail woman contracting in the passenger seat and agree.

My mom's eyebrows reappear — defining the face we knew before.
Her hair sprouts like new grass in the yard.
Equal in length.
Filling the baldness on her head.
She feels a sense of pride for the fight she is fighting.
A grieving mom.
Handicapped already.
She takes up arms for the others.
But her battle cry is temporary.

THURSDAY NIGHTS

I died on a Thursday. Thursday nights have become mandatory *think of your dead son/brother* rituals. My sisters and mom light candles, no matter where they are. These four sad women sit around coffee tables, sipping on sorrow, staring at the flame before them. They shop for the same brand of candles and pay the over inflated prices — someone really cashing in on memorializing those who have travelled to the other side. As the candle burns down to a stub, my mom and sisters feel accomplished in grief, at the shrinking form before them. Within each candle is a tiny metal token — a teddy bear, a butterfly, a heart — hokey, I know. In a few years from now, they will each have a pile of candle stumps with the wicks burned out the bottom and a pile of useless shapes that someone decided are meaningful when someone dies. They put in their time mourning me and create unique ways to keep me in their lives.

Thursday 7 pm: Appointment with Jarett.

Once a year there is a worldwide event where people burn candles for the deceased. Around the globe the flames flicker — moving like a wave from time zone to time zone — one big dead head concert. My sisters and my mom participate, deciding to light their candles at the same time, even though they live in different parts of North America.

On holidays, large grief groups gather in church basements and tell their sad stories to others who will listen — my mom and my sisters attend — needing to keep the vision of me alive.

I find it strange the efforts people will go to in order to try and please the dead. My sisters discuss how weird I would find their candle burning crusade, but yet they continue on with it for years.

CHRIS' LIFE

Chris has a girlfriend — something I never had. When Tricia and Sandy meet her for the first time, instantly liking her, the sting of losing Chris to the living, leaving them with the stories of the dead, moves through their minds — getting stuck on the bitterness placed there.

Chris holds a key to my past. He is the keeper of so many stories that only he or I can tell. My sisters are afraid of losing all of that. They don't want Chris to forget about me or about them for that matter. It is hard to be left behind when others find the strength to move forward.

Chris thinks about me often, but he learns not to dwell on my accident. He is one of those teenagers whose best friend died — he will never forget me — but he will move on.

It is tough for me to watch Chris move toward the future without me, especially when our lives would have probably been close to mirror images. Chris and I both hate the city, and I can picture us living on farms beside each other as adults — our kids growing up in the country like we did. I know that we would have always been friends. I am the dead friend now that everyone is sick of hearing about. Other people have filled the friend shoes I walked in. I know that the living need to get on with living, and that the dead don't make good friends.

Chris will inherit his dad's land one day and I guess I am envious of all that lays before him. I want the chance to make my parents proud like he has. I want the chance to make mistakes and not have

212

to die for them. Every teenage boy I know has driven too fast on a dirt road. Why did my car line up exactly with a mammoth vehicle in that one split second?

I have questions that will never be answered.

My parents and sisters have the same.

I know that life chose Chris and he deserves that.

I know that death chose me.

STUCK IN BOSTON

Sandy is in her eighth month of pregnancy, and her doctor will not let her fly back and forth to Canada any more. It has been over a year since I died. Sandy will stay in Boston until the baby is born and then my mom will go and stay with her for six weeks.

Sandy swims daily.
She loves the weightlessness.
On the surface she is just a thirty-something woman.
Slicing through the water as a submarine.
Beneath the surface she moves the hidden weight.
The nine-pound child keeping her afloat.
The toxic parts of her being sending out indecipherable code, pinging off the people around her.

On Sandy's return to Boston, people do not flock in her direction to hold her steady. Perhaps it is her silence that makes people walk the other way.
She checked out of life and life moved on without her.
She is so alone.
I wonder why her friends can't see that.

Sandy sleeps more than anyone I have ever seen. Slumber has replaced the alcohol that she used before her pregnancy to numb her mind. She is able to summon a quiet mind more easily now. She read somewhere that sleeping is great for the baby, so shutting down the world benefits them both.

She spends inordinate amounts of time alone.

Moving as only Sandy can move — hushed.

Sometimes she just lies on the couch and cries — clutching at the child within.

Sandy sees her best friend for the first time since I died. They both had been trying to get pregnant for years before my accident, and now in an Italian restaurant in the corner booth, they both have trouble fitting between the bench and the table. The conversation is awkward — Sandy feels foreign, disconnected, and foggy with all that she carries in her heart, but they will reconnect in time — their children growing up together.

Sandy's husband works hard as usual — a numbers guy innately — unable to fit his wife and her emotions into a cell or a row or a column or a chart on a spreadsheet. He is thrilled to become a dad and he knows that Sandy will make a great mom.

He will be the breadwinner.

Sandy will raise their child.

He will move numbers around in Excel.

Sandy will move an infant into adulthood.

Affecting a toddler, a teenager, a woman, a grandma.

The arrangement suits them both.

The hustle and bustle for one.

The tranquility of home for the other.

One of the two will change their minds about this arrangement, when the bulk of the work is done.

MICHAELA

Baby Michaela is born to Sandy and her husband November 3rd, 1999. After twenty-seven hours in labor at the hospital, Sandy holds their child in her arms.

Her focus shifts.

The lens of her life brings her child to the nucleus.

Sandy had called my parents to tell them that she was going to the hospital, but hasn't checked in since, and now my parents and Tricia are worried at home on the farm.

Her husband has not called to update them.

Sandy is not aware of the lacking communication.

When the drugs and the emotions wane, she is angry that her family has been left to wait and worry.

She makes the call herself.

My mom answers, her voice small, "Sandy, we haven't heard anything in a day and a half. We were so worried."

The family so far away on the farm.

The empty room down the hall and the cancer telling them that dying in childbirth is possible.

Sandy understands the worry, "I am so sorry mom. I should have known that he wouldn't think to call."

Michaela started life at a whopping ten pounds four ounces, so she will never wear the newborn clothes that hang in her closet. She is strong from the start. She actually looks like a three month old — chubby and pink and very aware.

Michaela is checked for diabetes because of her size — a routine procedure — she is not diabetic. An on-call doctor notices a looseness in her hips though, the hip sockets being too shallow to hold her leg bones in place. The doctor with the poor bedside manner tells the new parents about the issue with Michaela's hips. Sandy is emotional already and the news of a potential problem sends her over the edge. After further consultation, Michaela is required to wear three diapers to keep her hips from popping out of the too shallow hip sockets. This will solve the problem in about six months, but Sandy will have Michaela's hips checked every couple of years until she stops growing — consulting the best orthopedic surgeon in Boston.

Fourteen long months have passed since my accident. Michaela is my namesake — not for my first name, but for my middle name, Michael. Sandy is pleased that a part of my name is the name she will focus on for the rest of her life.

Michaela as an infant, a toddler, a tween, a teen, and an adult.

My parents are touched by the gesture.

I am honored.

Sandy is all consumed by motherhood. She loves every task, every moment, every responsibility. She will excel in her new role. She has a new identity. She is a mom, and she gladly accepts all that motherhood offers. She sheds a layer of herself — moving away from the dead nineteen-year-old.

Sandy is possessive of Michaela. She really doesn't want to share her with anyone. She is not the typical new mom who needs time for herself. She is in fact the opposite — being away from Michaela is torture and so she never leaves her. Sandy never tires of the diaper changes, the baths, or the feedings in the middle of the night. Michaela sleeps directly beside her in a bassinet. Her dad never wakes when she cries — he will be up early to get to the gym and then to work. Sandy wakes often to check that the child is still breathing, certain that crib death is imminent.

Mother and child hunker down in the house — Sandy preferring to avoid the germs of supermarkets and restaurants until Michaela has strengthened her immune system. Sandy eats only the healthiest food. She reads to her newborn from the start, having filled a bookshelf with endless books prior to her due date. Our mom read endlessly to all four of her kids every night growing up — a ritual that Sandy replicates. There are books about the moon and bunnies that run away, books about teddy bears and endless motherly love. Sandy's favorite is *The Big Red Barn* by Margaret Wise Brown.

By the big red barn in the great green field.

There was a pink pig who was learning to squeal…

MY MOM IN BOSTON

My mom travels to Boston by herself.

Sandy stands in the Air Canada terminal while the lines of travelers pass her by.

Baby Michaela snuggles closely.

Sandy searches the crowds for our mom's face.

Unrecognizable.

When the people stop, she panics.

She finds her in the baggage claim.

The tiny woman with her luggage still circling on the belt.

Too weak to pull it free.

The look of a child on her face.

My mom steadies Sandy in motherhood and Sandy steadies my mom in recovery. They sit for hours in the two rocking chairs in the nursery — the back and forth soothing them both. They go for walks in the neighborhood and out for lunch a couple of times, but mostly they just sit and talk and be. My mom makes Raggedy Ann and Andy dolls for Michaela like her mom did for her kids. She embroiders hearts on their chest and writes *Love Grandma* in cursive. Michaela will cherish those rag dolls from her toddler years and beyond. There will be a time when her mom will convince her to stop playing with the dolls and place them on the wooden shelf in her room — the wear and tear pulling at their seams — the same wear and tear showing on the woman who made them.

Tricia embraces her freedom in my mom's absence, and while my dad is looking the other way, toward the past, she continues to experiment with the mind clearing power of alcohol. There is always a group of acquaintances that Tricia can find in the city that like to push the boundaries of alcohol consumption as she does. The rendezvous' with her sauced self being easier to fit in when Sandy and my mom are away. Tricia bats away at the things that life hands her.

No more.

Please make it stop.

But her life is like a giant punching bag — hit it and kick it and smash it with all of her might and that damn thing comes back at her every time — faster and harder, faster and harder, faster and harder.

Tricia and my dad travel to Boston to see the new baby too. They only stay for five days.

Sandy keeps asking, "What would you like to do today, Dad?"

His stock response, "Tricia and I should be getting back."

Sandy keeps trying, "Would you like to go to a museum in Boston?"

My dad won't engage, "There is so much to do at home."

I wish he could act happier for Sandy's sake. She is trying so hard.

But, he just can't show it. He is withdrawn and he can barely look at his wife with the brush-cut. Sandy prepares a huge Christmas dinner, attempting to duplicate the holidays she grew up with. She begins to build on the traditions she knows, establishing memories for Michaela. The conversation around the table is strained — my mom attempts to speak for two. My dad will not step out from the shadow of me — he stands in the darkness I cast.

LIFE ON THE FARM

Everyone is trying to merge into the lane of the living — my mom looks at the TNT Seed Catalogue but doesn't order anything. My dad brings my tractor into the warmth of the quonset, but doesn't change the spark plugs like he had planned. Tricia moves between the city and the farm but doesn't move out of my room.

All things Jarett are exactly how I left them that September morning I died. Nothing has been moved in my bedroom, and my toothbrush is still in the toothbrush holder in the bathroom. They find such comfort in seeing my things — like I might come back and use them. They feel that if everything I owned gets packed up in boxes, it will erase my existence further than they can bear. My things are there, but they don't look at them — kind of like choosing not to look at an accident when you drive by.

When baby Michaela is three months old, Sandy brings her to the farm for the first time. Bonny, her husband, and their kids are there, and having everyone present makes my absence more obvious. There is intense awkwardness in my home — such avoidance — such fear of remembering. My sisters all think the same. *Should I mention his name? Would a funny anecdote help us to discuss him? What if I sat in his chair? Would that help or hurt?* My name, my face, and my memory are all tied to their most hideous experiences. It's no wonder they don't want to discuss me. A sinister quiet still creeps through the house day and night. The rituals of bravery begin, each attempting to hide what my absence has done to them.

Michaela bounces in the jolly jumper that hangs from the door jam in the entrance to the family room — pulling in my family with her squeals of delight — her chubby arms and legs springing up and down unabashedly — the bubbles that form in her spit reminding them of the joy in the world.

Bonny is resolute with death. She stands in defiance to it, while Sandy and Tricia succumb to its forces. The people left in death's wake that can find truth in the phrase, *My brother would want me to go on, to be happy and live life,* are much better equipped to deal with death's powers than the ones who can't believe in the words. Bonny knows the words to be true. Dead people want you to believe in the words. Dead people want you to let them go, but some just can't, and so we stay near.

SOCIAL BEINGS

Sandy can't relate to anyone anymore — her friends in Canada or Boston. She passes on most invitations to gather with friends. Tricia is the opposite. She needs her friends and she is able to discuss me with them — we goofed off on the bus together — we grew up at the same time.

Sandy just wants to be with Michaela.
The light in her darkness.
The calm in her storm.
The toddling toddler charges her being.
The child consumes her and snuffs out some of the anger lurking about. It is hard to harbor rage when a chubby face plays peek-a-boo with you or when a stiff legged toddler runs from you, collapsing in a fit of giggles.

Michaela can literally recite her favorite books from cover to cover and one of those is *The Big Red Barn*. When Michaela is at the farm, she likes to sit on my mom's or dad's knees and turn the pages and say the words as if she were actually reading. My parents love hearing her little voice copying the animation her mom reads with — accentuating some words, slowing others, and ending high when needed. Sandy reads a staggering amount of books to Michaela on a daily basis. At the farm, Grandma takes over the task and Sandy lies silently beside the two.

When Michaela sleeps in the afternoons, Sandy sits and stares at her. Following stories at bedtime, Sandy returns to me.

Sandy is a loner. She gets more from the words she writes than from the words that spew out of people's mouths. She spends more and more time writing, and when I read the words, I feel the weight of the loneliness she bears.

When you speak to me I do not hear anything audible. I see your mouth form the shapes of words in spoken form, but I only see your words mired in the fog of self-aggrandizement, not in the interest of me. You scream at me with your actions and words that you are okay and I am not. I know this already. I drift in and out of consciousness, although, seemingly I am awake. I feel like I am in a bubble that distorts my vision of all people and places around me. Always returning to haunt my thoughts are the words my brother is dead, my brother is dead. The deafening sounds of these words stun me over and over. I am unwilling to hear or listen to your trivial comments about weddings, birthdays, Merry Christmas, Happy New Year, and good will to all men.

You
Sitting there looking back at me
Glad to be you
I
Staring blindly
Longing
Not to be me

SECOND SPRING

My dad returns to the fields. I long to see a tall standing crop on the farm again. The beauty of a wheat field on the prairie comes from the movement of the wheat in the wind. Billions of separate pieces moving as one creates a wave that can lull you to sleep. There is an elegance in the way that it shifts. It dances with sinewy tendrils spreading east and west, north and south. It sways in the light of day and the darkness of night. Only the farmer can understand and feel indebted to it. But, not my dad anymore.

My mom digs furrows in her garden — straight lines for the peas and the beans and the carrots. She is trying, but the weeds will devour her efforts by mid-summer.

Tricia sows her sorrows in the city after class — feeling more at home in a bar than on the farm.

Sandy's love for Michaela grows endlessly, her paranoia swelling at the same rapid rate. She worries about car accidents, terrorism, child molesters, cancer, plane crashes, boating accidents, ski accidents, birth defects, snipers, kidnappers, stalkers, fires, earthquakes, and on and on. She worries about how much she worries. It's like climbing a never-ending mountain day after day. She never reaches the top. Her husband doesn't see or understand her growing concerns and this disconnects them further. The weight of the worry she carries alone is intent on crushing her. Sandy lives moment to moment and she lives in fear — not for herself, but for Michaela. The devil has rewired Sandy's brain.

Bonny is logical enough to know that time spent worrying is a waste of time.

Tricia worries less when she is drunk, so she drinks more.

Bonny germinates new ideas about business — her personal growth burgeoning.

Chris' girlfriend is pregnant. He is starting his family without me. Chris is growing up, getting married, having kids. He feels guilty about showing his new life to my parents. He pulls back more and more from my family and our farm. He doesn't do so with any kind of intent to harm — we are all still on his mind. He has noble reasons for hiding his happiness from my sisters and parents.
His life speaks loudly to them.
Look at me — look at all that I am doing — look at all that I have. You have nothing but a dead son in an urn.

Chris is a man's man — the kind of guy who thinks that a male showing emotion is a sign of weakness. We were both raised that way. I never saw my dad show any emotion until I was dead. Chris sees his duty to my family as a storyteller — infused with humor — a distractor — like trying to get a baby to smile for a photo — waving his hands — remember this — remember this? Chris feels guilty because he has new stories to tell and I am not in any of them.

GRIEVING ON

Everyone wants to see grieving as an evolution — a progression towards something endurable. I see it as a life long handicap when the young beat their parents to the grave. Theirs is not a wound that will heal and leave only a scar. It is a vacuity. It is not conspicuous on the surface, but it is cavernous in depth. I wish there was some identifier that could define my parents to others — like the *Baby On Board* signs that tells other drivers of the precious life within — perhaps a button to wear on their lapel — *Son Died At Nineteen.* Then maybe the hairdresser at the salon will understand my mom's reaction when she asks her how many kids she has and the teller at the bank will make sense of my dad's inability to speak when he inquires about closing my account.

The advice proffered by many is that time heals all wounds. The theory may work when your ninety-year old grandmother dies, but it doesn't seem to apply here. I watch as my family learns how to get through their days without writhing in pain, awash with tears. There is a learning curve whereby they have become adept at managing grief at the grocery store or while meeting a friend for coffee. It is a thin skin that they wear now, though. Do not ask them how long it has been since my accident. Know only that they don't talk about it, because they can't. Time has done them no favors.

My family only speaks of me in terms of a memory, a personality trait, a dimpled smile, or a reference to the past. They are not a family in therapy seeking solace in shared feelings. Together or on their own they find no solace in viewing my accident from different angles, advancing years, or shared perspectives. They do not speak openly of my accident and what it has done to them individually. They do not divide and distribute their feelings amongst themselves. They have each internalized all that my absence means to them. They see the same six-foot six-inch teenager at the mall, they note the car, its color and make, they hear of ski trips to the mountains and voyages to the lake to water ski while their minds replay fragmented frames of life from our past. They look down at their plates, their hands, their shoes when they hear of graduations, birthdays, marriages, life in general. They see through the same soot-covered glasses and they feel with the same broken hearts.

The pain encases each of my family members within their own tombs of sorrow. They walk through the graveyard of life not as a family, but as broken pieces of a once monumental family. And I get all of the credit for this.

HARVEST

Tricia is studying for finals, so Sandy and Michaela return to the farm to help with harvest. Sandy will work with my dad, and Michaela will lift up my mom with her chubby cheeks, her giggles, her experimentation with solid foods smeared across her face. As they fly in from the east, Sandy watches the land billow below, the wheat swelling and dipping in the wind, waving at her, welcoming her home.

My mom is fueled by all things baby: toes and spit bubbles, arms and legs flapping simultaneously, peek-a-boo and cuddling a sleeping child in her arms. Michaela is such a happy baby that it is hard to be sad when she smiles at you. She is a chubby little thing, and the rolls on her arms and legs make you want to chuckle as she turns over and over on the floor. There is nothing dainty about Michaela at this age and most strangers think she is a boy. Sandy dresses her with pink frills and matching ribbons and bows, but people still refer to her as "he."

My dad loathes the land and all that it demands of him. There is bad blood between the two. He is not the farmer with the capable hands that I knew. The land betrayed him in ways he can't forgive. He raised a boy in the country and that boy died just up the road past the "S" curve. In the yard the trees hide the view from him, but out in the fields he can see the road from every angle.

Michaela and my mom spend time together in the house, while my dad informs Sandy in so many ways that she can't fill my shoes. It is difficult to watch them do the tasks that I should be doing, my dad swearing his head off, Sandy showing her waning farm skills, my dad reacting to the city girl before him. Things are progressing, but slowly. Sandy doesn't understand the hand signals that my dad motions to her from the combine. The oppressive air moves about her in waves — distorting the landscape and the man who flaps his arms repeatedly. I wish I could tell her that the looping hand motion means one more round and then bring the truck to unload. Harvest is about timing, about knowing what the other person is thinking before they think it; it's about working together. My dad and I have always understood each other. We think the same way and we see the same things. Right now all he sees is me and he feels intense anger because I left.

Sandy sits in the grain truck with both doors open to let the heat pass through. The Labrador sits on the bench seat beside her and the Rottweiler rests in the shade of the truck bed. The pasture fence runs to the right of her and reaches into the field where they harvest the grain. All of the horses stand clustered at the corner, leaning into the barbed wire, longing for the attention that left when I did. They call to Sandy with their whinnies, their heads rising up and down, their hooves pawing the earth. They long for the weight of the saddles across their backs, our feet in the stirrups, pushing them faster and faster across the land. Sandy walks to them when she can and strokes their muzzles, whispering her apologies, offering carrots she carries in her pockets, hoping that is enough.

My dad is flashing the lights off and on and Sandy knows that this means a breakdown. She fires up the engine and the Rottweiler jumps in for the ride. With the doors closed and the windows open, the dogs hang their heads and their tongues out the passenger side. I capture everything before me and I revel in the beauty of it all. The sound of the motor revving, the gears shifting from first to second, my city girl sister still adept at maneuvering this giant vehicle, grease smeared on her face, wearing her old coveralls cut into shorts and the engineer hat she wore as a teenager. The excitement of the dogs, the love they have for a truck ride across the field, the role they play as companion to the farmer, jumping out when the truck stops and running to the man who is everything to them, as if seeing him for the first time in days, a pat on the head ample payment for their loyalty.

The drive belt on the combine snapped. My dad gets to work pulling out the parts that hide the belt. He instructs Sandy to go to the yard and have my mom phone around and see who has the part in the city. Both dogs lie in the stubble where my dad works, opting out of a ride to rest by his side. My mom and Michaela drive to the city to get the part, and Sandy returns to the field to play assistant mechanic. She watches the dust trail behind the car as they leave, hanging heavy in the heat of the August sun; she can taste it and the grit gets in her eyes, blurring her vision. She feels the first inkling of uneasiness. My mom's blue vehicle crests the hill at the end of our property and Sandy wonders about the choice she just made.

Sandy's thoughts are unclear. They are not logical and not many will understand the leaps and turns they make in her head — catching like barbed wire — gouging at the mixed up matter in her mind — always arriving at the worst conclusion.

Sandy keeps looking at her watch. She calculates the drive to the city in her mind, allowing for traffic and a line of people getting parts during harvest.
She can't focus.
"Sandy — **Sandy** — I need the crescent wrench and the hammer," yells my dad.
Her breathing quickens and she feels a tightness in her chest.
They should have been back by now.
She keeps looking to the crest where they disappeared.
She imagines a police car with sirens.
Where are they?
She loses her grip on reality.
Crying out.
Knowing they died in a crash like me.
My dad tries to calm her as she sits in the dirt and sobs.
He knows that I did this to her.
The cage comes down around her — trapping her in her fatalist thoughts.
Anxiety owns her now.

Finally they return.
"I see them Sandy. Here they come. Michaela is okay," says my

dad in the gentlest voice he can muster.
   Sandy is distraught.
   She runs through the ditch toward my mom.
   She sees her daughter sound asleep in her car seat.
   My mom is confused — apologetic.
   Sandy's tears mixed with dirt paint the fear on her face.
   The only color in her pallet: black.

A HOUSE IN THE CITY

Sandy's husband is allergic to animals and grass and hay and anything to do with the farm. He becomes so allergic that his eyes swell shut and he has trouble breathing. When he can make the long trip to Saskatchewan, there are nights that he leaves the country in the dark to go to his parents' house in the city. Sandy spends so much time in Canada with Michaela and her family that her husband decides to buy a house in the city — a mere twenty minute drive from the farm.

Sandy looks for a house with our dad. It is a good project for the two of them, and Sandy's husband trusts them to find a house with good bones. This house will be in the family for a very long time. They find one in the east part of the city that they both favor — my dad because of the size of the lot and the perfect foundation — Sandy because the location connects her easily to the farm.

Family suppers are shared often at Sandy's city house — abandoning the memories of me in the weed-filled garden, the neglected house, the horses with their heads drooping, fat from the lack of exercise. It is easier to smile and laugh in a house free of me. I don't have a chair at the table or a room down the hall. They won't trip on my shoes at the front door.

Sandy braces herself every time she leaves the city to go to the farm. She steadies herself against the memories that stampede her. She pushes them away when she leaves and on her return they rush at her and say, *We still live here. You can't escape us.* She likes how it feels in the city — the buildings hiding the farm in the distance — the dysfunction and disorder camouflaged.

Michaela loves the animals at the farm. She especially loves feeding them. She squats in the dirt right beside their bent heads and talks to them as they chew — the horses' heads bigger than her. In her little girl voice, Michaela asks, "Do you wike it? Is it nummy?" My mom is so concerned by the fact that Michaela does not have any pets in Boston, she buys her two special kittens of her own, the farm pulling her in like it did to her mom. Michaela was four at the time and over the moon at having her own pets. She names them Olivia and Jesse — Olivia after a friend and Jesse after the cowgirl in *Toy Story*.

Michaela is the distraction that everyone loves on the farm. My dad will open the big white door on the chain pulley in the quonset to adjust training wheels and to fix broken toys. My mom will go to the garden and plant sunflowers so Michaela can marvel at the stalks that reach six feet tall and the yellow faces larger than hers. My entire family stands around the trampoline and laughs when Michaela chases the cats in circles — bouncing and falling — the cats narrowly escaping each time.

Michaela grows up knowing about me — the photos, the stories, and the regular visits to my crash site. My mom gives Michaela tiny golden angels smaller than the size of a dime to sprinkle on the memorial my two sisters made for me. Michaela loves the sprinkling — in her young mind, it's like decorating a cake. Years from now, when Michaela turns eight, her parents will buy her a platinum heart locket that she wears around her neck and never takes off.
There are not any photos in the heart shaped opening.
Michaela will put one of the golden angels in that locket.
I am the only one who knows it is there.
She understands early on what I meant to the family into which she was born.

TRICIA AND SCHOOL

Tricia is very book smart. Of my parents' four children, school comes to her the easiest. I give her so much credit for trying to keep her studies going through my death and my mom's cancer. She wavers, but then she takes up the fight again. More determined than I can describe and owing of such admiration from others that it pisses me off when people ask my family, "Oh, she still hasn't completed that degree yet?"

I want to yell at them — defend her — *You have no fucking idea what this young woman has endured before the age of twenty-two. SHUT UP.*

If they could only understand what her days are filled with and the added burdens that swamp her mind.

She makes me very proud, knowing she tries to finish it for me.

One of us needs to.

RUNNING THE HORSES

My dad used to love to ride. He especially loved to ride fast. Tricia and Sandy love to do the same. And so did I. My dad taught us four things about running the horses hard. I remember him saying, *Always cool the horses down after a hard ride. Walk them out to the evergreens and back and don't forget to loosen the saddle and take the bit out of their mouth. Lastly, don't ever let them drink water until long after their breathing has slowed and the sweat has dried on their backs.* Simple offerings for the hard work and the joy of riding an 1,100-pound animal across the prairie. My dad's rules were simple and logical and they gave back to the beasts that gave so much.

I wish I could tell you that there is some rhyme or reason to the trials and tribulations that some face on earth. I haven't found those answers yet and maybe I never will. I can tell you though that common sense exists for me here, the same as it did when I was alive.

Don't let the horses drink after a long run.

Don't give cancer to a woman who just lost her son.

Don't give the same family another horror that will swallow them whole in a short time from now.

FINDING THINGS

My mom has bouts of strength. Her garden will never look like it did in years past and her house will never be as spit-shined, but she still has surges of productivity. One day she tackles the bathroom that Tricia and I shared. She does her regular deep clean, but that clean will not involve packing up my things. She starts with the window and removes the valance first, vacuuming the dust that settles in its folds. Next she removes the screen from the window and washes it in the bathtub. I quiver in quietus as she pulls the six drawers from the cabinet — knowing what I hid there almost two years ago — hoping it stays attached to the bottom of the drawer. I see the parchment float and land at her feet. I was a decent artist, and I enjoyed sketching in pencil. The sketch lands face side-down. She stands and stares at it for almost a minute, knowing it is mine. She sits on the floor beside it and places her fingers to rest at the corner. Playing with the edge, up and down, creating a creased triangle, should I or shouldn't I. Turning it, she sees the sketch I copied from a girly magazine. I hurl tidbits of me from my deathbed, always pushing her back to the pill-popping woman beneath the sheets.

Life for my mom is a series of mazes that she works through. She looks forward to the end of the day. Calculating the hours of silence in slumber — six, sometimes seven. Letting them lay before her with the promise of anonymity, her mind devoid of thought, the pills blocking out her thoughts and the visions that fill her head.

THE WORLD

Sandy and Michaela are at the grocery store in Boston when 9/11 happens.
Oblivious.

When they arrive home, the answering machine is blinking.

My dad's voice says, "Sandy, call home."

The tone familiar.

I see her thoughts fly about her like bats in the belfry.

She lunges for the phone — her two-year-old playing at her feet in the Tupperware cupboard.

She dials the number on the farm.

A recording tells her that there aren't any lines available — the havoc released on the east coast jamming the phone lines, but she doesn't know the news, she doesn't understand.

She keeps trying.

Still nothing.

Her mind races to places all too familiar.

She tries her husband at work.

No line.

Again and again.

Nothing.

She finally gets through to her husband.

She explains the voice message from my dad — certain someone has died again.

Hysterical.

Impatiently, he says, "Turn on the TV Sandy. I am sure your dad was calling about what has happened in New York."

He can't calm her.

She needs to keep trying to reach the farm.

Time tightens about her like a zip-tie.

Each attempt advances the tie one more notch.

Unable to reverse directions.

The negative thoughts stifling the positive.

Finally, the phone rings the double ring on the Saskatchewan prairies.

My mom answers.

Sandy asks, "Is everyone okay? Dad called and left a message. I couldn't get through."

Mom assures her, "We are all fine."

My parents were concerned that Sandy's husband might have been on one of the flights from Boston to New York or that he might have been in one of the towers.

Sandy will learn that two young women she worked with before I died were on one of the flights out of Boston. The world is closing in on her and the possibilities are endless in her mind.

Sandy sits beside Michaela in the mountain of Tupperware — square and round containers, lids to match and some that don't, sippy cups and juice jugs — and cries. Michaela crawls and sits on her lap, as she is accustomed to doing.

Michaela will be in high school before she rides with the other kids on the school bus. There are no seat belts on school buses.

Michaela will never complain about the rules her mom has regarding vehicles.

Sandy openly discusses the reasons why, and Michaela has an understanding that not many could replicate.

Sandy does not venture to raise her child in a bubble — they travel, they zip-line, they hike over glaciers, they live — but cars hold a power over Sandy that she cannot combat.

MY DAD

It is March 2003.

Something is wrong with my dad. He is unsteady on his feet. He uses walls and furniture and railings to keep him on his course — bouncing from one to the other like he lives in a pinball machine. He informs my mom of his balance issues, and she conspires with him to keep it from my sisters, which is simple; two daughters live far away and Tricia lives in Sandy's house in the city now.

A sixty-year-old couple alone on the farm.
My mom a weaker version of her old self.
My dad in complete denial about the seriousness of what he is facing.
Both still crippled by the empty bedroom at the end of the hall.
It will pass.
It is nothing.
He consults again and again with his doctor, and the cause is always undefined.

Things change quickly.
Three weeks pass.
My mom helps him more and more each day.
He is losing control of his hands.
When he looks at them and tells them to open and close, they won't.
The hands my mom and sisters look to — *Fix it. Hold it. Help me.*
My mom takes him to the emergency room.
Farming will be a thing of his past.
He will never return to our land as the man we know.

Life isn't fair.

I've heard that one too.

But I look around and all this shit doesn't seem to be distributed very evenly.

Why so much on one family?

My mom calls her daughters again.

The phone lines reaching across the miles.

Strangling their lives in new ways.

My dad lies on a gurney in a hall at General Hospital.

Weak and unmoving.

Grey.

Tricia arrives first — cutting class and slicing into her future.

My dad talks to Bonny and Sandy — urging them to give it some time before travelling long distances.

"It's probably just some weird virus," he states with conviction..

"It simply needs to work through my body."

Bonny is there second.

Sandy and Michaela arrive the next day.

My dad is still in the hall.

Three daughters and my mom circle him.

Things are moving fast.

He cannot stand up.

The doctors keep testing, but find nothing definitive.

They ask about travel and immunizations and obscure things.

The doctors hate Sandy immediately — the one with all of the questions.

The devil whispers sweet nothings to my sisters in the emergency waiting room. Hiding their thoughts from the ears of our mom, sitting stoically by our dad.

The daily shifts start then.

Hospitals will own my family again.

Three and a half years will pass in a blur.

My dad's legs are the first to go.

They make him stand in a tiny box — the four walls helping to hold him up.

Like a calf in a cattle chute before it gets branded — he can't move backward or forward or side-to-side.

His legs act like a newborn colt's — buckling — shaking.

He leaves the box exhausted.

Defeated.

The doctors talk about trying to keep his legs strong, but they abandon the box torture quickly.

My dad moves from his hospital bed to the bathroom on a sling contraption that hangs from a pole on wheels.

When the nurse moves it forward, his body swings like a kid on a ride at the fair.

Nothing fun here — humiliation hangs in the air beside him.

Tricia writes her final exams.

Doing poorly.

Unable to focus.

My dad expects so much of my mom, but was so quick to leave when she was the one in the bed with the side rails.

"Where is your mother?" I watch him ask repeatedly.

She brings him home-cooked meals for lunch and dinner.

My sisters come in shifts — only leaving him at night.

They urge my mom to rest and stay healthy.

They don't want to overburden her because the cancer might come back.

But everyone is doing overtime.

Weeks pass and still no answers.

Sandy pisses off the neurologists by inquiring about second opinions.

She likes it when the doctors hate her.

My dad refuses to consider going anywhere else.

Sandy and her husband send my dad's medical records to the Mayo Clinic in Minnesota and the Neurological Institute in Montreal.

Both respond with, "We need to see the patient."

Montreal is free if my dad's current neurologist admits defeat.

Mayo wants a credit card, the first charge $30,000.00.

Sandy's husband offers to pay — he is good that way.

My dad loses control of his arms next.

He has lain in a bed for weeks now.

He has endured spinal taps, prodding, needle pricks, and endless imaging.

He is depressed, but refuses to alter his mind.

It is the one thing he still controls.

Nine weeks from the day he walked into the hospital, my dad gives in to the idea of another opinion.

Sandy arrives for her shift.

He breaks down and spits out the words, "I should have gone sooner. I should have listened to you."

So Sandy calls in the doctor that hates her and she watches as our dad begs him to go to Montreal.

His arms and legs lying immobile beneath the sheets.

The tears falling heavy, like solder in the quonset.

The Neurological Institute in Montreal is amassing a team to prepare for my dad's arrival. My family floats on the optimism of new minds trying to solve the puzzle. My mom flies with my dad and a nurse on a private plane to Montreal. Sandy and Michaela fly home to Boston the day before, and then Sandy's husband drives them the five short hours to help my mom. My parents want Tricia to stay home and try to keep on with her studies. Bonny needs to get back to work, as she and her husband have looming financial responsibilities back in Lethbridge.

One hour from Montreal, Sandy's cell phone rings in the car unexpectedly.

It is my mom.

They have arrived at the Neurology Institute.

My mom is sobbing.

My dad is struggling to breathe.

Fighting for air.

Whatever lives within him has made it to his lungs.

The doctors want to put him on a ventilator, but have cautioned him that he may never get off it.

When my dad agrees to the procedure, he speaks his last words.

"I need to do this, Joan. I don't have a choice."

And chews his last food.

Sandy finds my mom in the ICU waiting room.
She looks small and out of place.
The country mouse that came to the big city.
Forever spinning on the wheel of death.
Clawing her way.
The rungs turning faster and faster in front of her.
If you look closely, you can see the cancer cells multiplying.

My mom and Sandy call Tricia and Bonny together.
They need to tell them what is happening.
Tricia won't stay away.
She leaves her studies for the third time.
Bonny can't come.
No one judges but her.

Tricia withdraws from school.

A nurse approaches and tells my mom and Sandy that my dad is back.
He can rest now, as the machine does his breathing for him.
His eyes are closed when they enter.
Exhausted from the fight he just lost, but doesn't yet know.
It's a mechanical sound that fills the room.
Darth Vader like.
A click and a rush of air pulled in.
Two pumps.
And again.
The machine speaks to Sandy.
I am not your father…

My dad breathes through a hole in his neck now.
He underwent an emergency tracheotomy.
Clear tubing connects to the hole, and arches over the bed rail to the breathing box.
I think of the tubing behind my mom's dryer.
It stopped drying the clothes one day, so my dad and I pulled it out from the wall.
We disconnected the hose from the vent and found a bird's nest sitting inside.

The sticks and fluff and mud and horsehair were impeding the flow of air.
I wish my dad simply had something stuck in his throat.
But this is more serious than that.
His heart will be next.
And then his brain.
A click and a rush of air pulled in.
Two pumps.
And again.

Sandy's husband finds accommodations within walking distance of the hospital.
At the end of six weeks, he will pay the bill.
He is good like that.

My dad does not wake until morning.
My mom and Sandy are on either side of his bed.
Both of his hands held.
Tightly.
He squeezes gently in response.
The calluses of the hard working farmer we once knew softened.
The strength in his hands gone.
There is recognition in his eyes and thankfulness.
There is fear too.
They instruct him to answer *no* with one blink and *yes* with two.
He clearly understands.
They can see it and I can too.

Tricia boards the plane alone.
Sandy's husband makes the arrangements and pays the airfare as well.
He is good like that.
Tricia worries that she might not make it in time.
She is mad at herself for not going earlier.
She talks to me in the skies.
She begs me to help him, but I have no power where I am.
None of us do.
Tricia takes advantage of the free booze and primes herself like we do to the pump at the creek when it won't start.
She functions on the fumes.

Tricia arrives before noon.
My mom and Sandy warn her of the dramatic changes.
It has been three days.
She is not prepared for what she sees.
The man with the blinking eyes.
The man with the hands that barely squeeze back.
A click and a rush of air pulled in.
Two pumps.
And again.
I am not your father…

Tricia, Sandy, and my mom establish a routine.
One or two of them stays with my dad, while the third takes care
of Michaela.
They work in shifts.
My sisters try to lighten the load for my mom.
But she will have none of it.
She walks those hills with the determination of a girl who grew
up on a farm.
Her *I've had cancer* body taking her farther than her daughters
thought possible.
Bonny checks in at the end of her days.
"Should I come?" asks the woman who wants someone to tell her
what to do.
"It has to be your choice, Bonny."
At night, Michaela's joy refuels the three that spend their days
watching a brain fry.

The fourth night in Montreal, whatever it is that lives in my dad
attacks his heart.
The phone rings at the hotel — my mom answers.
My dad's heart is racing too fast and then dropping too low.
They use electrically charged paddles to shock his heart back
into rhythm.
The same way we jump a dead battery on the farm with jumper cables.
Charge to 100.
Clear.
Charge to 200.

Clear.

I am there to see his body jump like the grasshoppers Chris and I burned with the torch in the quonset.

My dad is losing his lucidity.
Blinking eyes don't always line up with questions anymore.
Hand squeezes are weak and random.
It has come for his mind.
No tests are definitive.
They have spent five weeks in Montreal.
My sisters are coming unglued.
My mom is losing too much weight.
They spend the light of day in ICU.
They burrow like moles in the garden at night.

My family exists in another new world.
They have entered a realm that not many can comprehend.
They walk the halls talking with other neuro afflicted families.
Parts of them dying.
Leaving their bodies.
Staring down at themselves.
That can't be us.

Tricia and Sandy do most of their shifts together now.
Urging my mom to play and color with Michaela.
The two of them walk to the toy store with the teddy bear, blowing bubbles above the sign outdoors, Michaela entranced by the vision each time. They buy trains and new books and clothes for Michaela's stuffed animals.

The team of doctors knocks and enters my dad's room.
They state matter-of-factly, "We are making the arrangements to send your dad home. There is nothing more we can do for him here."
My sisters nod and say the appropriate things and thank them for all they have done.
Across the hall there is a young girl with a brain tumor. A brain dead boy from a skateboard accident is in the room next door. A drowning victim breathes through a hole in his neck in the room to the left. My

dad is closer to a mummy than a person.

They are surrounded by insurmountable pain.

When the door closes and the footsteps move away, my sisters stare at each other.

Tricia nonchalantly says, "Time to hit the road."

Which isn't even funny.

But the two of them erupt in uproarious laughter.

They both slide down the wall and writhe on the floor in convulsive fits of emotion.

We came here with a dad who spoke and he knew us and he breathed on his own and there were still glimpses of the man we know and now five weeks later you want us to leave with this? This isn't a man and he is not our dad.

Every time they look at each other, they laugh harder.

My dad spasmodically scans the room with his eyes — not even able to move his head.

Looking for the two he knows to be present.

A click and a rush of air pulled in.

Two pumps.

And again.

My mom boards the private plane with a nurse and a very different man than she arrived with.

He lies immobile.

He no longer speaks.

He doesn't breathe on his own.

He doesn't squeeze her hand.

Tricia boards the commercial flight for home.

She sits silently in the window seat with drink and head in hand.

Time stops for her as the metal cylinder with wings bullets her westward for home.

Sandy and Michaela drive back to Boston and head for Saskatchewan the next day — sawing away at their Boston ties again.

My dad returns to the neuro ward at General Hospital.

Everyone is shocked by the ragdoll man he is now.

No one more so than his eldest, who has travelled six hours to greet him.

Bonny is unprepared for all that the sheets try to hide.

But her ability to find promise in what all others see as hopeless will propel the others forward.

They live in Fantasyland now.

All unicorns and smiley faces.

LIFE

My dad would tell you that you have lived a charmed life if …

You can spend the better part of the day outside in the sun, working the land.

You can instruct your dog to round up the cattle with a whistle and a command.

You can look to the north, the east and the south, and the land that you see is yours.

You have raised four healthy, hard working kids.

My dad is a simple man.

He is not arrogant or a spendthrift.

He believes in hard work and reward.

He does not think that everyone is worthy of a trophy.

He believes in losers as much as winners.

He never complains and will chastise you if you do.

He loves animals and thinks that children can learn about life through them.

His world is spinning too fast now.

It nibbles at his brain.

He is losing his grip.

It spins faster and faster.

He can't hold on.

His capable hands let go.

BONNY'S FINANCES

Bonny and her husband are struggling financially. They have had great success with one business and now a second will pull them under. The mortgage on their house is due and there is no money to pay it. The money that gets them through will come from an unexpected place.

Bonny takes off even more time from work to be with my dad. The bills keep coming, but she feels guilty for not having gone to Montreal.

Through it all, Bonny will maintain her positive, upbeat attitude.
The eldest daughter in our family has a fortitude that not many can match.
She keeps moving forward, never doubting that she can't.

BREATHING

The beast inside of my dad has travelled through his body.
The doctors tell us that the damage is done.
It has left huge ruts like the dualie tractor I got stuck in the slew the spring of '98.
My dad told me it was still too wet, but I drove in anyways.
I remember spinning and spinning the tires — the mud flying up all around me — revving the powerful motor — but nothing moved.

They think my dad can breathe without the ventilator.
This optimism fuels Bonny's crusade for complete recovery.
If he can breathe on his own, the potential is there for so much more.
But if your brain is mush, there isn't much you can aspire to be.
His brain is able to tell his lungs to breathe.
That is about it.
If only his brain could tell his body to die.

The respirologists wean him quite quickly from the ventilator.
They leave the tube in his neck.
The trach bobs up and down when he coughs and sometimes mucus spews out of it.
It's like sneezing through a hole in your neck.
Bonny can see talking and walking in his near future.
No one else can.

People who don't move get infections easily.
Especially when there is a gaping hole in their neck.
Physiotherapists come to treat my dad every second day.

They move his limbs and flop him around like a dead fish.
It must feel like falling backwards all of the time.
Trusting that someone will catch him.
I hope for him that they will not.
They pound on his back to loosen up the shit that pools in his lungs.
His neck cannot hold up his head.
Back and forth it falls.
Left and right it slumps.
Like a bobble head on the dashboard.

LONG TERM CARE

My dad is sent to live at a long-term care facility.

He is assessed as a level four patient.

Level four means you can't do anything for yourself.

The great minds at the hospital hope to dissect his brain one day, but for now they just want the bed he lies in.

My dad requires twenty-four-hour care.

A newborn infant is able to do more than him.

They can coo, lift their head, and move their hands and feet.

My dad spends most of his days lying in bed.

The staff moves him from his left side, to his right side, and then onto his back.

Over and over they turn him, like a rotisserie chicken.

The nurses try fruitlessly to relieve his bedsores.

Getting my dad out of bed and dressed requires two strong staff members.

Imagine dressing a six-foot beanbag.

Imagine dealing with the wires and the tubes with pant legs and armholes and sleeves.

It's one big string and ring puzzle.

Hide the piss hose in his pants.

The bag of urine is a little more challenging.

My sisters drape afghans over the edge of the bed to conceal it from their view.

Put the feeding tube in his sleeve.

But let's be real, nobody is that fucking surprised by any of this shit when they see my dad, so why do they go to such pains to camouflage it all?

The hole in his neck is impossible to disguise.

My sisters wait outside the closed door while the nurses prepare my dad for the day.

They can hear the oximeter beeping, which tells them that his oxygen has been disconnected.

They count out the time.

Knocking loudly when they get nervous.

As if his brain dead brain will miss the oxygen.

My dad can only sit in his wheelchair for minimal amounts of time.

Unable to adjust his position.

The pressure on his hips and tailbone wreak havoc on his skin.

His elbows and wrists sit on the baby highchair table attached to his chair.

They have sores too.

Imagine sitting for hours and only having minimal areas of skin bear all of your weight.

There is a tilt mechanism on his chair and my sisters and mom spend the days adjusting it to different angles.

They try so hard to do something to help him.

I wish I could tell them that he feels and knows nothing.

Their efforts are futile.

There is a head extension on my dad's wheelchair to hold up his head.

Like the u-shaped cushions that newborn babies have in their car seats to keep their heads from flopping over.

This is an adult quadriplegic version.

My sisters and I had a watercolor painting of the farm done for my parents on their anniversary a few years back.

They bring the painting and hang it on the wall directly across from where he lays.

Hoping it speaks to him.

As time passes and my family acknowledges inwardly that my dad will not be walking out of his new home any time soon, there are more and more pieces of the farm brought to him.

He has no idea what a farm even is.

His memory of me is erased as well, and for that I am grateful.

I wish I could obliterate this vision of him for myself.

My dad's food comes in a can and enters his body through a tube in his stomach.

He never smells my mom's roast cooking or tastes the tender morsels of beef, potatoes, and carrots moving around his mouth. If he had any sensory awareness, all he would hear is two cans cracking open, the glug, glug of liquid pouring into the feedbag and then the sound of the motor moving the liquid toward his belly. That is his gastronomic experience.

The staff performs chewing tests on my dad and he performs poorly.

His brain will not tell his mouth to chew or to swallow.

Tricia is so bothered by the fact that he literally has no kind of pleasure.

She becomes obsessed with getting him to respond that she creates her own experiment behind the closed door of his room.

No one is aware of what she is doing but me.

She brings ice cream to him and places it on his tongue.

She talks and she coaches, "You can do this dad. You love ice cream."

It is hard to watch her try to teach my dad to close his mouth and simply let the ice-cream melt.

The man with the capable hands who taught her everything can't even suck like a baby.

Frustratingly, she tells him, "Just close your mouth and press your tongue up."

Tricia flirts dangerously with doing something she has been told not to do.

Hoping the man with the capable hands can prove them all wrong.

He is not brain dead.

He will listen to me.

I can teach him.

My dad rides a swing on a motorized lift to be placed in the bathtub.

He has no cerebral or visceral reactions when placed in the warm water.

He does not know that if the sling he lies in lets go, he will drown.

I secretly wish the person in charge would look away and that he would slip beneath the water, bubbles reaching the surface, as he leaves the body that chains him here.

My dad will never be in another photograph.

He looks nothing like the husband and the father he was.

No one wants to capture a visual of this and keep it in a box marked *Memories*.

My dad was always the one telling Sandy to go back to Boston and re-engage in her life there. Without his voice reminding her, Sandy stays longer and longer on the prairies — giving Michaela a view of the life she led and the people she loved.

A view that is fleeting and flawed.

MY DAD'S TRUCK

Every four years, my dad buys a new four-wheel drive, extend-a-cab, long box, three-quarter ton truck. My mom gets a new car about every ten years. The truck is a working vehicle — it has farm plates — so he can justify the expense. He jumps between Chevys and Fords, depending on the changing body and the front grill. His current truck is a bronzed brown with dark leather interior. It has every bell and whistle.

I can't imagine my dad driving any other vehicle. He has a ruggedness about him that says, *I drive a truck.* My dad has always taken great pride in his trucks. He keeps the interior as clean as a farmer can keep it and he has always passed off the exterior cleanliness to his kids. There was a lesson about a job well done in that task, and I never realized it until now. My dad would always inspect the truck after you said you were done, and almost every time there was something missed. Once, I washed his truck after a day of hauling bales in the mud, and the tailgate was down when I started. He walked around the truck two times looking for shoddy work and stopped at the back to close the tailgate. As he lifted and *Slam,* I saw the mud dripping down the outside. He had a way of making you feel ashamed that pushed you to try harder the next time.

Three of his kids have only ever wanted his praise. Bonny came back for it when she hit thirty, and now the ones left behind are all seeking it from a lifeless man.

My dad never let anyone drive his truck, and he only ever listened to country music or talk radio. If you didn't like either, you were out of luck. He wouldn't ask you for your music preferences. My sisters and mom have his favorite country songs looping in the background all day for him now — hoping some memory will bring him back to them. It's funny what people think might help, when all of the other options are gone.

My dad will never drive a truck again.
He will never even imagine himself behind the wheel.
The rumble of the diesel engine.
The bounce over the dips in the road and the ruts.
The heaviness, the sitting high up.
His favorite song on the radio, Tom T Hall's, *I Love.*
I love little baby ducks, old pickup trucks, slow moving trains and rain.
I love little country streams, sleep without dreams, Sunday school in May and hay.

My mom instructs Sandy to sell my dad's barely driven truck.
It just sits out in the yard collecting dust and bird shit.
A cruel reminder that he will never drive again.
Never do anything again.
Ever.

PEOPLE TO RELATE TO

My mom and my sisters find people in long-term care that they can relate to.

They too have family members that no one understands.

Who people are afraid to visit.

Who people stare at.

There are some of the saddest stories you could ever hear locked away behind the walls of Main 5.

I would never share the details.

The family members, like mine, are in different stages of denial.

They pin their hopes on unlikely recoveries, miraculous occurrences, and advances in medical technology.

My family has entered another new world and the veteran families of Main 5 discuss them sometimes — not in a gossipy way — but completely concerned by their naiveté.

I wish they could see what we all see.

That poor man is gone and he isn't coming back.

My sisters and my mom are delusional. They think that my dad's green eyes, never blinking, staring forward, understand what they say.

They do not.

They think that my dad's lifeless body will move again.

It will not.

Just like teenage death, there are others in the netherworld of neuro.

Friendships develop when people from the outside cannot find their way in.

My mom accepts the truth before my sisters do.

She talks to my dad when she visits alone.

Holding his motionless hand in hers.

"I know you aren't in there anymore, Dennis. I envy you in some ways. Your mind is free of all that we lost."

MICHAELA

Michaela is almost four when her grandpa becomes a rag doll. For the next three and a half years, she will spend endless hours with him. She does not judge him and neither does she judge the people she meets in the halls — the people who move their wheelchairs by blowing into a straw — the people who shake uncontrollably — the people who can't talk. She sees my dad with the eyes of a child. She sees him in the moment and she loves him all the same.

"Can I push grandpa now, Mom?" asks Michaela.

A hand on his shoulder, she places her pink bunny — Pink Bee — on my dad's tray.

He coughs.

"Let me help you Grandpa" — gently patting him on the back like Sandy and her aunts do.

There is a tiny gift store at the long-term care facility where my dad lives and Michaela and Sandy take my dad there every day. They make a ritual out of inspecting and naming all of the stuffed animals that sit slumped on the shelves like Michaela's grandpa. Michaela is obsessed with stuffies and Sandy buys her a new one every couple of weeks. The child never complains when she visits my dad, so Sandy creates a game with the plush animals that Michaela adores — *Who will come home with us next?* Each visit they discuss the eyes, the texture of the fur, the color, and the volume of fluff inside.

Sandy always feels guilty about taking Michaela to see my dad so much. There aren't any other options though. When Michaela is older, Sandy will understand that the people her child grew up

262

around will have molded her into something special. Sandy will be very proud.

MY DAD'S FRIENDS

Two of my dad's best friends come twice to see him.
My sisters prep him for the grand reveal.

My dad has always been concerned about how he presents himself.
His 'go to' look is jeans and a plaid shirt, with some type of loafer or
cowboy boots. In the fall and winter, his look would be paired with
a western inspired suede jacket. His wardrobe has been altered since
coming to live in a level 4 facility. No more jeans, as the stiffness of
the fabric makes it difficult for the people who dress him. He wears
sweatpants or pajamas every day, and instead of shoes, he wears slip-
pers. My dad has never been the sporty type or the man who lounges
about in sleeping attire. His plaid shirts still hang in the closet, but each
and every one is cut straight up the back, like doll clothes. I remember
the look on my mom's face when the staff explained that they would
be cutting all my dad's button down, collared shirts into giant bibs.
     Calmly, they told her, "No one will ever know that his shirts are
open in the back. All of our immobile residents have the same."

And don't forget the nametags.
My mom has to pay to have labels sewn into every piece of clothing.
D.E.SPEERS
Like we had in kindergarten.
My dad has about as much mental acuity as an amoeba.
The losses keep coming.

From my vantage point, it's as though my sisters are playing some
sick version of house with a doll figure the size of my dad — position

the articulated arms and legs just so, cover the gaping hole in his neck with a cravat perhaps, comb back his greasy hair (he only gets a bath once a week), hope to hell he doesn't drool too much and presto, the makings of a fucking tea party. There is nothing left of my dad that could be described as anything more than carbon, hydrogen, nitrogen, and calcium. My sisters dance around the facts and the gruesome science experiment before them.

Bonny leads the crusade of positivity.

But there are no more visitors.

My sisters are alone with our parents.

One as incorporeal as a ghost.

The other already living on a shelf in a closet, in an urn, with me.

T.J.

T.J. stands for Tricia and Jarett. This is the name of our black Lab, the son of Tess. Tess gave birth to T.J. in the winter, and my dad always said that the dog had brain damage. Tess died years ago and is buried with all of Tricia's cats. T.J. is one of two family dogs left on the farm and he is getting up there in age.

My mom notices changes in T.J.'s behavior that she keeps to herself. He is withdrawing from life on the farm and spends less time up on the porch. My mom knows that he spends his days lying in the trees behind the house, alone and accepting of his imminent death. He isn't really interested in food anymore and his body wiggle and his wag do not greet you every time you open the front door. My mom respects his process and lets him go about leaving her as my dad and I have already done. She checks on him throughout the day and goes to sit by his side, stroking his belly and accepting a feeble lick or two on her hand. At night, T.J. returns to the front door and my mom lets him in the house to lie on the front mat — he has concern for her, as she does for him — both of them acknowledging the death that lurks in their shadows.

My mom finds T.J. one day, cold and unmoving, hidden from view in the trees. Like so many animals, he chose a place of solitude as his final resting place. My mom sits in the trees and cries for the dog who shares my name.

Tricia and Sandy don't understand why my mom didn't tell them what was happening to T.J.

How could they know that she saw herself in the pet we all loved.

MY MOM AND THE FARM

My mom needs help on the farm.
Her husband lies like a vegetable in her garden.
A zucchini, a squash, a cucumber...
Bonny will make the move back home.
A business folds and Bonny quits her job.
She arrives with her two children and her husband.
They will try to keep the farm afloat.
They are struggling to find their way financially and so the move makes sense.
The hardest part for some is that my bedroom will become someone else's and that my dad's office will convert to another bedroom.

My mom has a friend help her pack up my room.
Tricia is aware of the packing, so she stays away.
She is filled with rage at the thought of anyone packing up my things.
My mom pleads with her to understand.
Tricia's roots in the city send out new shoots.
They extend to the pub at the U of R and numerous other bars.
She does not have much free time with two sick parents, but she always finds time for self-mutilation.

I have two large closets in my bedroom. In one, my clothes hang limp like forgotten items on a line in the rain. Tricia and Sandy want them to hang there. They need them to hang there. When they pack them up, they are burying me in another way into boxes that will sit in a musty basement. Those boxes will not be forgotten, but they will be the source of pain each and every time my sisters descend to the cellar for strawberry preserves or pickles. The silent boxes that speak so loudly with their dust and their must and their misery.

My second closet is as big as the first and it is a shrine of sorts to my hobbies, and my passions growing up. To the right are my water skis and to the left are my golf clubs. At the centre, filling the shelves, are the Lego creations, the dinosaurs, the cap guns. My guitars: the electric, the acoustic, the twelve string. Watching this, I am dying in another way. Locking my memories in boxes — so different from packing up a teenager's room for college. No promise, no future, no hope.

My mom wants to welcome Bonny and her family into her home, so she wears a brave face. She relives every moment of my short life while sitting on the floor with my things about her. The process is long and arduous. She holds every article for a time and re-acquaints herself with me at every age: the suede vest Sandy bought me when I was four that I wore every day for a year; the really old penny that I found in San Antonio on the River Walk; the cap gun my dad bought me when I was eight; the scorecard from the best round of golf I ever played, two weeks before I died. Every single item holds a memory and my dimpled smile. She packs up the remnants of me that are physical and holds tight to the ones in her mind.

My mom takes everything from my bedside table and places them in hers: my old license, a wad of Canadian Tire money, my copy of *To Kill a Mockingbird*, the leftover wallet sized school photos. She uses these as her own personal torture devices. At night they whisper grisly nightmares in her ear.

The next time Sandy is home, she freaks out at not being able to touch all of my things. She rants and she raves, and Bonny and her family feel less welcome on the farm. Sandy takes the issue to my mom and I wish she hadn't.

Sandy says angrily, "How could you pack up his clothes, Mom? How could you let them move into his room?"

Standing her ground, my mom replies, "Sandy, there are only three bedrooms in this house and your sister, her husband, and kids, need to have their own space. You keep forgetting that they are here to help me."

TEETH

My dad is a proud man, a man who likes to look his best. I never knew it until I was older, but he actually had some of his teeth pulled at a young age and a plate with fake teeth hid the fact that his mouth had holes in it. I never saw my dad without his teeth. He was very private about keeping that part of himself hidden from his kids. I remember once, when he was brushing his teeth, I saw the plate with the fake teeth in his hand, and as he spoke to me, I saw his reflection in the mirror. I was startled to see how much his face changed around his mouth and I remember not liking the way he looked. I remember the slurring and the way his voice sounded different.

My dad has not spoken for months.
And today they come for his teeth.
They are worried about him choking.
He has lost so much weight and the plate no longer fits in his mouth correctly.
They take another piece of him today.
I watch as my sisters and mom plead with the nurses.
The staff places the plate with the teeth in a bag and mark it with his name.
His face hangs from the skeletal structure beneath.
His mouth puckers and pulls inward.
His brain as dead as some think.

BATTLE SCARS

My mom has been complaining of pain in her limbs. She is scheduled for a bone scan after her routine cancer checkup. The scan lights up like the Christmas tree we no longer put up.

Further imaging shows cancer in my mom's lungs.
Chemotherapy will start again.
As the cancer comes back for my mom, each crack in my sisters grows to a crevasse.

My sisters drive here and there frantically — poisoning one parent and torturing the other with the most humiliating existence.
They are agitated and delirious as they travel between two hospitals and the farm.

My mom's brother enters the scene. The two of them share an odd relationship, close at times and distant at others. My mom wants to spend time with her brother and so she asks Sandy to host Thanksgiving at her house in the city. Sandy obliges even though she feels the same way about him as I do. Bonny and her family are not present. choosing to spend the day with her husband's relatives.

There is a huge production to get my dad to Sandy's house — the wheelchair van, the oxygen tanks, the medications, the feeding tubes, and the suction machine. The drama continues when the wheelchair won't fit through the door and so Tricia and Sandy pull off the door jam and the trim — all the while cooking a turkey and setting a table so they can sit around it and make memories that they would rather forget. My sisters finally get my dad into the family room — he can't travel beyond this point, as there are stairs to the kitchen and the dining room. Everyone takes turns sitting with my dad and treating him like a human being, except for my mom's brother and his wife.

The man they don't visit.

They think they can catch what he has.

Such a fine display of human kindness.

Jackasses.

The fighting ensues beyond holidays, mashed potatoes, and gravy.

Sandy and Bonny reach a pinnacle of loathing.

Hard times fueling hatred.

Things become territorial with Tricia and Sandy in the city and Bonny and her family at the farm. Bonny and her husband do not have the same standard of care and Sandy is critical of that. She arrives one day and finds blue paint on the cement at the entrance to the quonset. Neither Bonny nor her husband are there, but their kids are.

Sandy rages at the lack of respect for our dad's property.

She is so protective of what he built.

So intent on maintaining it for him.

She yells and screams in front of Bonny's kids — casting blame shamelessly to their mother.

She loves those kids.

She does.

She would never intentionally hurt them.

The eldest at twelve, the boy, calls his mom at the hospital.

He says, "Auntie Sandy is going crazy. She is scaring me."

Bonny screams out as if she is being murdered.

The wife of my mom's brother and Bonny drive to the farm.

My mom sits in her hospital bed amped up on meds.

No one is reacting appropriately.

There is a huge fight.

Sandy leads the crusade.

She doesn't know what she is doing.

She has lost her mind.

"This is none of your business — Get the hell out of my parent's house," she says to the meddling relative.

"How dare you deface what our dad built," she says to the eldest sister.

Bonny does not respond.

The trenches are deepening.

The casualties are growing in number.

The emotions of impending death have erased the sisters I know.

Bonny finds an ally in my mom's brother.

Someone to stand with on her side of my mom's hospital bed.

Sandy is angry for so many reasons, and she can't keep it all straight in her mind as to why, but she knows it has something to do with people living where they shouldn't be and other people not living where they should be and of course there are the dead people and the near dead people and the people who want to be dead and don't forget the people with the opinions and the words of advice and she looks at them and in her head she says *Fuck You* and at the same time her life is slipping away from her and she knows it and she can't stop it because people here need her and she needs them.

Bonny is the person she lashes out at most because she is the least like her.

Sandy and Tricia are closer than ever.

The Hatfields and the McCoys.

Placing blame.

Pointing fingers.

My sisters take the stairs to delay entry into the worlds in which their parents live.

They spend their days walking bleached halls, Purelling their hands incessantly.

They look forward to the times when they are asked to leave, so the staff can tend to our parents: change a diaper, wash a body with a bowl and a washcloth, clean a trach, tend to bedsores, and on and on. My sisters breathe momentarily when the door closes behind them and they get a break from our disfigured parents in the beds with the side rails. They find such immense pleasure in the simplest things: extra large diet cokes, hospital food from the cafeteria, five minutes on a bench alone, a vending machine that works, free burnt coffee.

Such meager rewards, but coveted all the same.

Please make it all stop.
I can't watch this much longer.

Tricia and Sandy listen to angry music as they drive back and forth between our parents.
They search for lyrics about death and dying.
The music so loud that it blocks out the truth.
Their thoughts dark, their minds necrotic.

Death is circling the wagons.
They take their last stand against the world intent on destroying this family.
Teenage death led the crusade — it drew quick and had good aim.
My sisters fight for the man who can no longer fight for himself and for the woman who refuses to fight anymore.

I don't know who will fight for my sisters.

SUCTION

My dad still has that hole in his neck.

The medical staff keeps the opening because they don't have any faith that he will ever be a functioning person again.

The hole has multiple purposes.

They use it when he needs the ventilator to breathe, but also as an entry point for a daily torture technique.

My dad gets pneumonia easily because he doesn't move.

He can't cough out all of the secretions that his body produces.

He doesn't have the strength.

And so the gunk builds up and breeds more gunk.

My dad is hooked up to an oximeter twenty-four hours a day.

It has an alarm that tells you when his oxygen level is too low.

Sandy's husband bought the medical device to bring comfort to my mom at night.

The alarm assured her that one of the night staff would come to help my dad.

In retrospect, it may have been better if he had lain gasping for breath.

Then it would have all been over.

He isn't living.

He exists.

My sisters and mom can't see that right now, but death is what he would want.

The staff trains my sisters — not my mom — to suction my dad when his numbers go too low. They sit in a chair beside him and watch the numbers on the oximeter.

If they dip below ninety-three, my sisters put on rubber gloves, un-wrap an eighteen inch sterilized tube, attach it to the suction machine, uncap his neck, and plunge deep.

My dad's entire body contorts, suffering an involuntary contraction of muscles and limbs.

They pull the tube up and out — it's called deep suctioning — the mucus stressing the suctioning motor.

My dad's shoulders curl in, his knees pull up, and his arms fold over in front of him.

He coughs violently.

My sisters hate it, but they do it because they think they are help-ing him.

Imagine torturing someone like that over and over each day.

Such are the travails of the brain dead quadriplegic and his family.

I am not sure where all of the promise has gone.

The promise we all could see in his eyes.

The eyes that used to move — one blink for *no* and two for *yes*.

The promise so fucking promising.

The promise palpable.

Now his eyes stare straight ahead.

Unblinking — but speaking volumes.

I will not let you look into the windows of my soul.

There is nothing there and I want to save you from that.

TRICIA'S FIRST HORSE

Tricia's first horse came as a surprise to the then eight-year-old girl. We had other horses, but Tricia did not raise any of them from a colt. This horse was delivered on her actual birthday, and when she exited the house to find a horse trailer, she was a little taken aback. My dad nonchalantly told her to open the back gate and see what was inside. She approached it suspiciously, because my dad was fond of practical jokes. She could well imagine that the trailer was filled with hay bales and that she would be hauling them on her birthday. When she lifted the latch and pulled, bringing lightness to what was inside, a smile stretched across her face, pushing her cheeks beyond their normal boundaries. There at the center of the trailer, lead ropes fastened to the left and the right, was a little red pony, prancing up and down, seeing its new owner for the first time.

The horses have all left the farm now. Some died, some were sold, and some went to live at the neighbors where they could get the attention they need. The barn door doesn't latch anymore and it bangs loudly when the wind instructs it to do so. One of the feed pails rolls about in the pasture and a nest of baby mice lives in the warmth of the uneaten hay bales. The water trough is filled with mud and weeds. The grass grows tall within the pasture fence line now — no animals grazing, no riders following the cow paths over hill and dale. The landscape loses another vista — the bays, the sorrels, and the palominos galloping along the crest of the hill across the creek — only the tall grass moves in the wind now.

MY MOM MOVES
TO THE CITY

Tricia finds a job to replace the education she walked away from.
A shitty dead-end kind of job.
She lives for free at Sandy's.
She left a biology degree with only two classes remaining.
She needs money for her habit.
Alcohol offers her more than education can.

Bonny is working full-time in the city teaching.
Sandy and four year old Michaela take care of my mom when the others are at work. She has chemo treatments and doctor visits and is back and forth to the hospital, so having her live in the city with Sandy makes the most sense.
With the people and the animals missing, the farm is folding in on itself.

My mom spends most of her days on Sandy's green sectional in the room attached to the kitchen. She is never alone. There are often at least forty stuffed animals, each with an intricate name, sitting with her. They are tucked all around her, on the back of the couch; some share her pillow, others cuddle with her beneath the blankets. My mom laughs with the little blond girl, Michaela, who places them there. She occupies the little girl's imagination, imprinting on her as much love as a grandma can impart. They play games — one immobile due to the fluid pooling around her organs — drowning her from the inside out — the other bouncing here and there. They play Eye Spy With My Little Eye when Michaela slows enough to sit on the couch with my mom. They play doctor, Michaela putting on her little green lab coat with the plastic name tag *Doctor Michaela*. My mom becomes the patient again, the tiny blood pressure cuff only fitting on her fingers, Michaela squeezing the small red ball that makes the dial spin round and round — "Vewy good Grwanny" — Michaela never knowing how wrong her prognosis is. Next is vet clinic. Michaela arrives at the imaginary pet hospital carrying an animal in her pet carrier. The ailments are varied and now my mom plays the medical expert.

"What brings this purple spotted monkey in today?" asks my mom. Very concerned, Michaela responds, "He wost his dots."

"Okay, let's see what we can do for him…" says the grandma.

The problems are easily solved — missing whiskers, broken tails, a thorn in a paw, a dog that won't bark.

Each of Michaela's stuffed animals takes turns speaking to my mom in the same little girl voice. They bring life to the immobile woman who lays on the couch — the cancer disguised in the giggles and the smiles. Playtime is stationary, but the memories are lasting just the same.

Walking and climbing stairs are difficult for my mom, so she sleeps in the bedroom on the main floor. Sandy encourages her to rest in the afternoons, but my mom will not let her close the door to the noises of the house and Michaela playing. "Leave the door open Sandy. I want to hear the noises of an innocent child playing."

My mom hears pieces of the farm come to life in Michaela's tiny voice. She smiles. She knows the role that the farm has played in the life of Sandy's little girl, having spent most of her first years there. Michaela sets up the corral and the large wooden barn beside the fireplace in the family room. There are three horses that are real to her. Their names are Pal and Chief and Raider — her mom's horse, her aunt's horse, and her dead uncle's. They gallop towards the couch, past the TV, and back to the corral. The grandma in Michaela's imaginative play brings the horses bags of carrot peelings and sugar cubes in her pockets.

SANDY'S HUSBAND

Sandy calls her husband often — reaching out for something.
Knowing she needs someone.
Hi — You've reached... Sorry, but I am not available to take your call...

She can't seem to reach him — literally or figuratively.
She is like an addict in need of an intervention.
Like a puppy in need of rescue.

Over time, she calls less and less.
Knowing her emotions are simply weakness in his eyes.
She reins her feelings in.
Always making others her project.
Never working through her own shit.

CHRIS

Chris is a salt of the earth kind of guy.
He is a hard worker, a man of his word and not one to complain.
He is cut from similar cloth as my dad and me.

Chris and his buddies have a weekly ritual on Fridays.
They take turns buying a case of beer.
Sitting around joking about the events of the week.
Chris has two kids now, his wife is in school, the mortgage is due, and he is down to his last twenty dollars.
Some financial setbacks involving an old pickup and a washing machine have put him behind a bit.
It is Chris' turn to buy this week.
He buys the beer because he is too proud to say he can't.
He believes in comradeship.
He would never be the one to break the chain.

Our friendship was founded on the same principles.
The friendship between Chris and my family is different, though.
It is rooted in death and it comes in waves — the current pulling him away from the ugliness, while simultaneously slamming his life and all its glory at the feet of my family over and over again — like a tide that always comes in and never goes out.

Chris doesn't come around anymore at all.
He can't see my dad the way he is.
He can't see the hands lying motionless or the likeness of me in his eyes.

He doesn't come to Sandy's to see my mom, either.
He avoids Tricia — the closest link to our friendship.
He is embarrassed by all that my sisters are enduring.
He doesn't know what to say to the family that shrinks before him.
It's easiest to just stay away.
The longer he stays away, the harder it is to return.
But Chris does not forget about them.
They are in his thoughts.
He turns left on the road that leads to our farm every day.
If he went right, he would not recognize the people or the place that exist beyond the trees.
Nobody would ever choose to be around so much sadness.
I don't blame him for turning the other way.

KINDERGARTEN

Sandy enrolls Michaela in kindergarten in Canada. She is only four, but she qualifies to go and this will be a good decision. My mom is in and out of the hospital, and Sandy longs to give her child an escape from all that is unfolding around her. Sandy takes Michaela in the mornings, walks her to class, cries in the car, and then makes her way to my mom at the hospital. She buys two double-double coffees in the lobby and a muffin for my mom — it is a ritual that offers hope for Sandy — but my mom never drinks the coffee or eats the muffin.

The doctors have stopped the chemotherapy. My mom was not able to recover after the last dose, which makes it unsafe to give her any more. The good news is that the tumors in her lungs have shrunk a bit, so the poisoning is working. My mom's hair is falling out in clumps again. She does not ask one of her daughters to cut it off, and she refuses to wear a scarf or a wig. She is a sad sight. She knows that she is in the home stretch on the road to me.

The shifts continue for my sisters with my mom at General Hospital and my dad at Wascana Rehabilitation Centre. The days are trying and they go on and on. Bonny and her family are still at the farm. Tricia, Sandy, and Michaela live together in the city in Sandy's house.

I barely recognize the people I left behind.
I should have been there to play my part.
My sisters have carried too much for too long.

Fourteen miles from the city, between Kronau and Balgonie, on a grid road before the "S" curve from Richardson, is a farm where we all lived. The land contracts in response to the dying pieces of a whole — attempting to compensate — putting strain on those that are left — *We need to save the farm.*

DYING PARENTS

My mom's head looks like a turnip from her garden — a few wiry hairs standing up on top.

She is beyond caring about what she looks like.

My dad's hair isn't much better.

He has bald spots like a newborn baby that lies around too much.

He would care if he could.

My mom is Thing One and my dad is Thing Two.

They lie two miles away from each other.

In motorized beds with side rails, their heads resting on plastic pillowcase covers.

They are both dying, but one much quicker than the other.

Their three remaining children plead with them to resist the peaceful liberation of death.

Please don't leave us.

Please don't make us pack up your lives in boxes and move them to the basement with Jarett's.

One understands, but can't oblige.

The other is already gone.

My sisters are so alone with everything that is happening to them, and they can't help but cannibalize little pieces of each other — the accusers and the foes alternating — they are the vultures flying over-head looking for an error by another. They dive bomb the aggressor and they say, *You are not doing your share, you are not sacrificing all that I am, you do not spend as much time here as I do, you don't take care of them like I do, you need to do more.* And so it goes. The destruction of a family while three die and three live. The living are left with all the bullshit, while the others just sit back and die. And let's not kid ourselves, no one wants to visit the man doll with the silly putty arms and legs, who never gets out of his pajamas and makes inappropriate noises and can't control any bodily functions, nor do they want to visit his wife who won't cover her bald head, who is gaunt and grayish and whacked out on pain meds, who is paranoid and so wanting of death, so close to death. Anyone who knows my family and dares to reach out to them wonders why my sisters are so fucked up, and I hate them for not seeing it as the bigger picture — One fucked up family portrait.

CANCER BODY

My mom has a fever.
Pneumonia has settled in her lungs.
She is back in the hospital.
The nurses drape a sheet over her thinning cancer body.
Her protruding bones hold the fabric up like tent poles.
Her skin sags like wet laundry in the rain.

Thing One and Thing Two both have pneumonia.
Thing One will let it kill her even though it doesn't have to.
Thing Two would wish that it would if he could.

My mom loses every last bit of her dignity in that bed with the side rails.
Careful now, you are about as trustworthy as an infant, so this is just like a big crib to keep you safe.
Hopped up on morphine, she says and does things that my mom wouldn't do or say.
"Bonny, hide my credit cards. The nurses and doctors are trying to steal my money."
She won't cut her tufts of hair or cover her head and she talks about dying like she is meeting death for coffee and she forgets she is leaving three women who are so afraid of being left alone with their father, her husband, and she acts like she has a get out of jail free card and they don't.
She accuses my sisters of having spent more time in the hospital with my dad than with her. "You won't miss me when I am gone. You will have more time to spend with your dad."

My mom wears one of those gowns that looks like the dark angel designed it.

She snuggles up to death like a warm bed.

The tumors are shrinking, but my mom won't go on the ventilator to help her get over the pneumonia. She only sees herself turning into my dad. I watch my sisters lie with her in her hospital bed, curled like cats about her frail body. They beg for her to go on the respirator and give the chemo a chance to work. She adamantly says no, choosing the path of least resistance — for her, anyways.

RELATIVES

My mom's brother and my dad were never really close. He doesn't go to visit my dad or try to lighten the load of my sisters or my mom. Instead, he sticks his nose where it shouldn't be. He and his wife dislike Sandy greatly — she has many traits similar to my dad's. With my dad out of the way and my mom faltering, the two see an opportunity to use Bonny as a pawn to get what my mom's brother wants in my parent's house — anything from their shared childhoods. This slithering, slimy man goes to my mom in her morphine state of mind and has her sign away the trinkets he wants from her younger years. He does not inform my sisters of the letter he has my mom write. Bonny and her family are the only ones living full time at the farm right now and so my mom's brother makes a move. Bonny, so wanting of someone to stand on her side of my mom's deathbed, can't see the treachery they are capable of. In time, Bonny will feel naïve and foolish for having trusted them. In the name of *Let us save you from your evil sister Sandy,* Bonny invites my mom's brother and his wife into my parent's home and then when she isn't looking, they transport items out to their car.

My mom's late 19th century piano bench that had been their dad's is filled with the music she played as a teenager. Sandy and my mom played the music together when Sandy was growing up — songs like "Teenage Queen," "How Much Is That Doggy In The Window," "Spinning Wheel." My mom's brother takes all of the music when no one is looking — even Sandy's beginner *Piano One* books, the pop sheet music she loved to play and the notebooks from her teachers. He takes my granddad's old readers — dated 1910 — he takes the wooden Radio Flyer wagon that was my mom's when she was a child and he takes the baby doll that cries *mama* when you tilt her body back in your arms. These are the only items my mom possessed from her childhood. He took everything else. Why does he think that my mom's things automatically become his if she dies? And let's not forget that she isn't dead yet. But he calls himself a Christian, so that makes it all okay.

Sandy tries to remind Bonny of all that they witnessed when my mom's parents died.

"Bonny, don't you remember how he taped his name on every piece of furniture? Don't you remember how Mom got nothing?"

Twenty minutes away in the city, two people that built everything on the farm stand at death's door.

Knock knock knock.

Meanwhile, two relatives are rummaging through their basement, looking for the things they want.

This entire scene baffles me.

I couldn't make it up if I tried.

Team Sandy and Tricia fight with Team Bonny about visiting hours, about the farm, about who will control the finances, my mom's brother and his wife always adding fuel to the fire.

I remember how my dad poured gasoline on the carcasses of the dead horses before he buried them.

I remember the boom when they ignited.

The burst of flame.

A cremation of sorts.

My mom is ready to pass on all of her responsibilities. Her brother jockeys for the position. Now tell me, how the fuck could he think that he would **EVER** control my dad's life and all he owns with three grown daughters? When my mom chooses Sandy, he complains to the nurses and says that she is committing some type of foul play against her own parents — the parents she gave up her own life for.

I want to yell and scream.

Mind your fucking business.
None of this concerns you.

My mom's brother and his wife keep telling my sisters that they need to accept that my mom is dying. They spread rumors to my mom's friends about her daughters' uncontrolled emotions that sometimes result in bad behavior. They should be spreading love and respect for my sisters, not hate and judgement! They just keep pecking and pecking at them like the chickens out in the yard.

I despise them.

On one occasion, my mom's brother physically pushes Tricia.

Our mom lying on her deathbed — tripping on pain meds.

Tricia stumbles backwards.

Stunned.

Bonny does nothing.

I am vapors, but I wish my anger could fuel a reincarnation.

How dare he intrude on my sister's process of watching her mom die.

Tricia runs crying to a pay phone and calls Sandy who is with Michaela at their house in the city.

Sobbing uncontrollably, Tricia says, "I can't even be with my mom as she dies. Why does he need to be there when I am? They aren't even close."

Sandy doesn't piss around.

That fucking asshole.

She is an adult — a mom — she calls the hospital and dictates that he can't be there when Tricia or she is.

My sisters are each like that 1940's baby doll — alone, crying *mama, mama.*

Two years will pass before Sandy gets the piano music back. She calls my mom's brother one day and threatens him with a lawsuit — she will drain the money from the miserly man's bank account with a long legal battle. He gives her back the music she played with our mom. The music sits in an armoire in Sandy's bedroom. She doesn't play the piano anymore, but the music speaks to her just the same.

MAIN 5

When you enter Main 5 where my dad lives, the first thing that hits you is the smell. There are glass double doors that open automatically, the second door placed six feet from the first. When the motion detector informs the second door to open, you wait for it. On some days it smells like a giant toddler room filled with kids wearing saggy diapers. Other days it smells like greasy dirty hair mixed with body odors that belong in the barn. Most people that live on this ward are 100% dependant on others. There are some incredible nurses and aids who care for the people like my dad. I give them mountains and mountains of praise. I just wish there was more they could do to maintain the dignity of the unknowing and their families.

Unit 2E is like a big X, and at the centre of the X is the nurse's station. My dad lives in one of the rooms beside the nurses station, because his oxygen dips dangerously low at times and they need to hear the alarm that screams, *I live in a lifeless body, I know nothing and I can't breathe.* Across from my dad's room is the TV room, which is completely open to the nurse's station. It is decorated with upholstered chairs, not quite pretty, but attempting to offer beauty in a place so ruled by ugliness. There's a coffee table, two side tables, a TV, and some dusty silk flowers to bring cheer to the perished people whose bodies live on. This room is used a great deal, but no one actually sits in the deep burgundy and rose floral chairs, because everyone here is in a wheelchair. No one kicks back, their feet on the coffee table, a beer on the side table, because most people's arms and legs are drooping appendages. These are the people that the nurses line up like bowling pins, sometimes facing the TV and sometimes facing the nurse's station, a change of scenery for the unaware — how nice — each of them waiting for the proverbial strike to take him or her out. *Please end this humiliation. I can't even sit where I want to. They move me about like a pawn in a sick board game.*

These are the un-talking, the visitor-less. My sisters get mad at the staff when they place my dad with this group — *He is not like them.* But he is. I have seen my sisters walk by my dad and not recognize him when he sits in his wheelchair with his peers — head slanted, mouth gaping, unresponsive, seeing and hearing nothing. My sisters keep my dad in his room as much as they can. They hide him from others — they are embarrassed for him. If he sits with the others he will be guilty by association for all that he is not. My sisters cannot live with that. They need to control something.

MY DAD'S HANDS

My dad's hands begin to curl and twist like the carrots placed too close together in my mom's garden. He held the whole world in those hands — constructing and shaping everything around him as a capable mechanic, a builder, a farmer. His hands now hold nothing but the fingers that coil into them — the tendons tightening — the tasks undone.

People talk about my sisters — friends and relatives — *Those poor girls with the vegetable father, the hairless dying mother, and the dead teenage brother.* They talk about how naïve they are when it comes to my dad — *How do those girls keep going to that place and how do they pin so much hope on this man that resembles a pile of mashed potatoes?* They only come once to see the carcass of the man they knew.

The grim reaper took the parts of my dad that mattered and left the physical likeness of him to torment my mom and sisters.

He said, *Here is the man that you know and love, but understand that he is already dead. I am a heartless heathen and some of you will spend three and a half years staring at the man who is incapable of offering you anything.*

The cloaked skeleton with the scythe lit the fires of purgatory on earth, encircling the five that will soon be three.

THE FARM

The farm is for sale.

Things are moving quickly.

Neither my mom nor my dad will ever return there.

Tricia has moved back in — alone.

Bonny and her family have left the farm — they are starting new lives in a house in the city.

They proceed onward and upward — finding new jobs — new schools — new lives.

Bonny has no regrets.

She did all that she could do and she will not let the webs of doubt weave her thoughts into traps in her mind.

Tricia and Sandy have regrets — they rue the ruins that they stand in — certain there is blame lurking about.

The farm falls further and further into disarray.

Reminding my three sisters of how incapable they are of maintaining anything from the past.

My mom offers the farm to each of her daughters.

Bonny and her husband would like to return, but can't afford it.

Tricia is too young to take on such a piece of property, she doesn't have the money either, and she would die out there alone dancing through the fields, a vodka bottle in one hand and three ghosts cavorting with her in the weeds.

Sandy can afford it, but she left the farm once already and she can't go back now.

My mom signs the papers before the bumper crop of cancer in her bones and her lungs harvest another being.

Sandy is relieved not to be the one to sign it all away.

An optometrist from the city will be the new owner.

They take occupancy on March 1ˢᵗ, which gives Tricia two months to say goodbye to the house where three of the four she lived with have left her.

The demolition of the only one left on the farm begins.

THE DAMN DAM

My dad built a dam across the creek in 1987. He built it to simplify the transportation of the farm equipment to the field on the other side of the water. The farmers that live in the path of the flowing water took my dad to court, because they said he was stealing their water. The court said that was ridiculous. After that, we always referred to the dam as the damn dam.

Tricia and I spent many a hot summer's day jumping off the dam into the water. We would go into the culvert and ride the push of the water out the other end. The view of the farmyard from the dam is one vista that has never changed, the L-shaped bank of the trees hiding the wreckage beyond. Tricia spends a great deal of time out there thinking of me. She likes to sit where we sat and imagine the yard as it used to be — the people moving about as they once did.

After both of my parents left to live in hospitals, a beaver came to live on the farm. He built a dam in the culvert, blocking the flow of water and flooding the creek-bed from the yard to the dam. The power of the contained water had the potential to wash the dam away and Tricia would not let that happen. She pulled that beaver dam apart three times, standing inside the culvert, flirting with the danger of the dam letting go, her foot getting caught and then being drowned as it all rushed past her. No one knew she was out there but me — cursing and swearing — hands and arms scratched by the sticks, the rocks, and the mud that held it all together. When the beaver rebuilt the dam a fourth time, she altered her attack. She called two friends for moral support, poured herself a stiff rum — not because she drank rum, but because that is what my dad would have done — and she took the 30/30 from the gun rack. She sat on the edge of the dam and she waited. The water lay before her — unmoving — reflecting the vision of her childhood before her. Eventually, the water rippled at the centre and the beaver popped his head up out of the water. She took aim. Her hands held steady. One shot sent the overgrown rodent to his watery grave. She was protecting what my dad built and the memories we shared.

BAD BOYS

Tricia has always been attracted to bad boys who don't care about her, but her focus has shifted down a notch or two now.

Another form of torture.

She drinks heavily whenever she can.

Footing the bill for others, so she doesn't have to drink alone.

Tricia isn't looking to build a life with someone — pick a china pattern, the white picket fence — she looks for others intent on destroying themselves. She doesn't care why.

Trying to obliterate oneself is so much more fun in the company of others intent on accomplishing the same thing.

Two of her drinking buddies will end up in jail.

When I think of the people Tricia chose to spend her lowest times with, I am shocked and stunned. There is a purposeful shift away from the things that my sisters can offer her. *I hate your sad and lonely faces. You can't help me and you know it. I will find my own way to cope and you will not be a part of it. Leave me alone,* she says in her mind.

Tricia can't forget when she is with Bonny and Sandy.

They won't let her get drunk and pass out.

So she shoves them to the curb and looks for another identity in the sewers that run through the city — seeking out the lowly, like her.

ANOTHER GOODBYE

My mom is unconscious.

She will not regain her faculties.

They call it hospice, and when it introduces itself to families, it leads with such words as *terminally ill, pain management, emotional support, refrain from prolonging life*. My sisters refuse to become acquainted with hospice — to them their mom is in a different room and that is all, but the prying relatives are there with their whinny voices saying, *She is going to die and you need to accept it and it will all be easier on you when it happens*. But the relatives forget that my sisters' dad is lying in a bed that sits in a room in a long term care facility and that people do not go there to rehabilitate themselves and that he can't talk, he can't even hold their hand with the strong farmer hands he used to have, and let's not forget about me, the brother who was burned in a box at nineteen and sits as a pile of dust with my mom's shoe boxes and the dust bunnies that are hidden like me on a shelf. So no one should dare push these three young women to willingly accept the death that they know firsthand, the death that they see, taste, and feel every day. *Stop psychoanalyzing my sisters.*

My three sisters stand beside my mom — Tricia and Sandy on one side — Bonny on the other.

The tension moves through the room like electricity.

When the body of my dying mom lurches forward, the youngest leaves the room.

She will not return.

Tricia refuses to see my mom dead.

Ironically, in the near future, she will work with the dead and dying to continue the torture.

The time is near.

The brother and his wife demand to be allowed in the room with my mom for her final hour.

They stand at the foot of the bed — imposing themselves on my shrinking family.

I hate how they position themselves there so matter-of-factly — so, *We told you this would happen* — so out of place.

Sandy whispers promises to my mom — she vows to take care of Tricia and to reconcile things with Bonny. She means what she says and my mom hears her.

Sandy leaves to check on Michaela, a phone call away.

My mom takes her last breath in her absence.

Her eldest draped across her chest.

I was there when my mom died in that salmon colored room with death lingering in all the rooms around her.

The spirit of the mom that I know meets me beyond the first barrier.

The division between life and death.

She is undisturbed by her passing.

She is aware of my essence.

Tranquil and accepting, her calm carries her away from me.

My mom welcomed her death and I fought to keep mine from winning.

We are in different realms, but know of the others' whereabouts.

Bonny stays with my mom's body.

The wife of my mom's brother meets Sandy in the hall and tells her to return to the room, "Say goodbye to your mother." Sandy screams with every once of her being, **"I have been saying goodbye to her since her son died. Don't fucking tell me what to do."**

It is telling that my mom's brother will never have anything to do with Bonny and her family after my mom is dead.

I hate that my mom used her death as an escape and not as an opportunity to impart some wisdom to the three girls she was leaving behind. They were all so desperate to be told that they had done enough, that they had loved equally, and that they should go on with their lives and be happy. They needed to be guided by the only parent who could speak — they needed her counsel, her wisdom, and her motherly love. Tricia needed her the most, but the morphine pilfered the final morsels of the woman who had been all things motherly until she lost her son.

TELLING MY DAD

My sisters walk silently to the room where their only parent sits. He offers no advice, no words of comfort, just limp hands to hold — no squeeze to say I understand. Dead hands. Hands that were once strong and able.

My sisters speak the words.
"Mom has died."
Hoping for some sign of life from within.
But nothing.

His hands lie in braces — attached to the body that fails him — and wait for their turn to leave my sisters.
Unable to hang on.
Unable to help them.

DNR

DO NOT RESCUSITATE.

There is a bold sign that hangs in my dad's room now.

A parting gift from my mom.

She asked her lawyer to draw up the necessary paper work when she knew the cancer had come for her again.

She did not want my sisters to be the ones to decide about the DNR.

She had signed the same papers for herself.

MY MOM'S MEMORIAL

My mom played a part in planning her own memorial. She chose the church, the funeral home, the reverend, the speaker, and cremation. My sisters choose the songs and the photos and the urn. They also choose to sit in a separate room where the service is telecast on a TV.

They are not able to share the hideousness of my dad with others who have not seen him.

They create a barrier to match the one that already exists.

You never came to see him, and so you won't see him now.

They hide him to protect him.

They hide him to protect themselves.

They can't hear the whispers or imagine the words spoken.

Dennis is gone too.

There is nothing left.

Those girls need to let him go.

My sisters bring him to the church in a van that can transport people in their wheelchairs.

The wheels strapped down with belts and buckles.

The living body with the dead man inside bouncing along the city streets.

His head velcroed to the headrest to keep it from bobbing about.

Wearing his Sunday best with his shirt split up the back.

It takes my three sisters to deliver the dead man to his dead wife's funeral. Watching them, I think of a slaughter house — my sisters are the cattle lined up in the chute — they can smell the blood and their eyes are bulging from all they have seen — they howl inside, but they move on for my dad. They open the white double doors on the side and they place my dad's wheelchair on the motorized ramp, slowly he moves downward like a prize piece of furniture. The ceiling is high to accommodate a person sitting in a wheelchair, so the windows are bigger than usual. Tricia and Sandy long for the drapes in the hearse that hid the pine box where my body lay when they followed me to the crematorium.

They feel like deformed fish in an aquarium.

They arrive early to insure that no one sees.

They don't think that my dad would want to be on display, and they are right.

During the service, my sisters and their kids take turns sitting beside my dad, a hand on his hand, a hand on his shoulder, showing concern and comfort, but none are received.

My family watches the bad rerun on the static filled TV set.

Bonny keeps banging the top in an attempt to clear the screen.

Hoping for a new channel.

There is no reception following the service.

My three sisters simply can't endure it.

People mutter and mumble.

Where are Joan's daughters?

The poor woman.

Why aren't they here?

Where is Dennis?

People don't seem to understand that my sisters are there.

Perhaps they should have had someone say something at the beginning to inform them of their choices.

They can't do the meet and greet again.

They can't stand stoically beside my dad and smile when all they want to do is scream, ***Why didn't you ever visit? Why didn't you try to help?***

My sisters wait until everyone has left, and then they take my dad back behind the closed doors where he lives.

Sandy places my mom's urn on the shelf with mine.

At peace at last.

EMT

Tricia decides to become an EMT (Emergency Medical Technician).

It is the beginning of December and she will start her program at the end of January.

She has tired quickly of her dead-end jobs.

My dad creeps into her head.

You deserve more.

There is something appealing to her about being on the front lines with car accidents, gun shot wounds, and hangings.

The victims of her life lie about her.

Caught in the crossfire.

Our parents wove love and work ethic and determination around us as we grew.

A thread from the cocoon of our childhood hangs loose.

Tricia grabs onto it.

She has two months alone at the farm to hang herself with that thread.

I personally tied the noose.

MICHAELA AND GRANDMA

Sandy never let Michaela go to the hospital to see my mom before she died. She didn't want her to remember her grandma that way. She didn't look like a grandma anymore; she talked funny, and Sandy thought it might be damaging to her daughter. Michaela had spent the first part of her life in and out of hospitals with both of my parents. She grew up around people in wheelchairs who had holes in their necks, people who lost their hair, people who needed to lie down a lot, but this was different. This was death and Sandy did not want to introduce her five year old to something so dark.

"Can I go to see Grandma today, Mom?" the child asks daily.
"When she gets a little better, Michaela," replies the mom who stretches the truth.

Years from now Michaela will tell her mom that she wished she could have said goodbye to her grandma — that she had thought often about it and that it felt "undone" to her. Sandy will make the same mistake twice.

Perhaps Sandy was wrong.
I don't know.
I do think that when your last vision of someone you loved is a bad one, those visual images are hard to get out of your head.
Just like my family never saw me dead, I think for a child to see their graying granny lit up on drugs, uncaring about her appearance, and so focused on leaving, erases all of the good memories instantly.
A ghost is revealed, where a granny should be.

TRICIA

Tricia won't leave the farm even though Bonny and Sandy plead with her.

She lives in that big house with her cat and her dog.

Bonny is twenty minutes away in the city, but she never goes to the farm.

Sandy is back in Boston — attempting to re-enter her life there.

Tricia does not have her own family and she feels so alone.

She lurches from side to side in the cocktail that drowns her daily.

She would swim in it if she could.

Sometimes vodka, sometimes gin.

She slumps and slouches about the house.

Seeing us everywhere.

She talks to the urns in my mom's closet.

She moves us around the house with her.

On occasion she sets us on the counter with all of the booze.

We are characters in the tragic play in which she acts.

Sandy calls multiple times a day.

Knowing the danger of letting her sister live in her nightmare alone.

Knowing she cannot make her leave the farm early.

Knowing she should have stayed longer.

Tricia digs her own grave.

Lies down.

And throws dirt in on top of herself.

I am with her when she passes out and I am with her when she wakes.

She creates a blurred world to live in.

The people foggy.
The memories out of focus.

PACKING UP THE FARM

Sandy and Michaela come back to Saskatchewan to help pack up the farm.
My sisters battle to box up our parents' lives.
Splicing good memories with bad.
Jamming them in cardboard crates.
Piling the boxes higher and higher.
Aggressively taping the flaps together.
Layers and layers of heavy duty Scotch tape that bind the memories inside.
You must stay in these boxes.
I can't look at you again.

The urns are the first to go.
They are moved to Sandy's house in the city.
My mom and I sit in a different closet now.
I don't know why they didn't just leave us on the farm where we belong.
They thought about freeing us together on the land we loved, but something stopped them.
Perhaps the potential for another to join us.
How could they leave him on his own?

My sisters avoid discarding everyday items.
What do we do with their toothbrushes?

They pack up my dad's stained glass and my mom's sewing and photo-books.
Unfinished projects.
Unfinished lives.

My mom left my birthstone necklace to Sandy's daughter.
She left her piano to Bonny's.
She wanted Tricia to have her diamond ring and earrings.
She instructed Sandy to pay off Tricia's student loans and to buy her a car that would keep her safe. She told her to use the money from her teaching pension.
My mom hated how her brother hoarded their dead mother's clothes, so my sisters donate my mom's things to people who can use them. They keep a few special things for themselves — dwelling on past occasions — swelling from within.

The clothes from my dad's closet go directly into a closet in the city at Sandy's.
They hang lifeless in the gallows like him on his motorized lift.
The normal ones without the cuts up the back.

My mom wrote in a diary most of her life — my sisters take individual piles and peruse through the life of a woman who lost a son — they get tangled in the chains I bound about her — the words she wrote choking them.
My mom addressed her last diary to me.
I can't live without you, Jarett.

My mom writes about a friend — *I've questioned why we are friends several times before this — now I really wonder — she has offered me nothing.*
The guilt of a mother — *Why didn't I sense something when you died — you were only gone a few minutes from home — I should have felt something when you left us — I am your mom.*
Christmas thoughts — *I can't buy and wrap presents. I certainly can't open any. I can't decorate or hang the stockings on the fireplace. Everything seems pointless now.*
Your dad and I are not able to share our pain. We created you together, but we can only mourn you separately.
She writes about starting 1999 without me — *We all drank alcohol — some more than others, but no one toasted the New Year.*
She writes about my sisters — *Girls need me for a few years yet, but I don't know if I can stay.*
My sisters sit too long on the floor and read.

The furniture from Mexico is divided up by room. Each of my sisters wants the fourteen-foot dining room table, but there is only one house that can accommodate it. They all agree that the table will be at Sandy's and that they will share ownership equally, hoping that one day they will create new memories around it.

My parents and I would like that.

The dishes from Mexico are boxed up and no one will use them for years. Tricia will decide one day to unpack them when there are others who sit at the table in our saddle creaking chairs.

The everyday dishes, the cookbooks, and the knickknacks are daunting — each with a story all their own. A place traveled to, a meal savored, an accomplishment revered, a tradition handed down, a gift, a celebration, a milestone. Each sister can lay claim to the reminiscence — each wanting a tangible hold on the memories.

My sisters do not fight about what is left of our lives — they are respectful of the dead and dying.

Sandy and Tricia take the memorial they made from my mom's garden.
It moves with them to the house in the city.
It does not sit in a garden.
It is placed in the garage behind the old dehumidifier.
A blue tarp hides the words that were formed by the plastic letters of a child.

Bonny digs up flower bulbs and shoots throughout the yard to plant in her own garden in the city.

My sisters leave the quonset for last.
The workbench looms large within the space.
Each tool speaking to them from the handmade hooks that hang on the pegboard.
Empty hooks.
My dad is everywhere and they see me in the silhouette he projects.
They make mistakes regarding the tools and everything in the quonset.

They leave more than they should for the new owners who push and prod my three sisters to finish — showing a lack of compassion for all that they are leaving behind.

The graineries are bursting with the wheat my dad and I grew. My sisters completely overlook them — the corrupt realtor not mentioning the wheat either — a rural realtor who knows better. My sisters can't process it all, their thoughts are not logical, they leave money in those graineries that should have been theirs. Sandy will think of it years from now, obsessing about the mistakes she made as only Sandy can.

Some come like vultures to feed on my sisters' exposed flesh.
My dad was a collector of doors and staircases and windows.
Would you mind if I took that — no one will ever use it.
I would like to buy that old truck — but never paid in full.
I don't blame Sandy for letting some things go; I blame the people who asked, knowing full well that my dad would never let the items go for free.

My sisters leave the strawberry jam and the dill pickles on the shelves in the basement. The salsa I made with my mom is pushed to the back — hidden. No one can eat what my mom left behind.

The auction company comes for the farm machinery.
Sandy makes the arrangements.
She is in charge of dismantling our lives.
They come with big flat beds and chains to hold them down.
Tricia and Bonny stay in the house packing, but Sandy needs to sign their lives away.

The swather and the combine are first.
Pulled from the land where they worked.
From the capable hands of the man who fixed them.
The dead hands now.

Sandy stands to the right of the pasture gate.
My tractor is next.

The diesel engine fires up — blue exhaust crying skyward — Sandy turns away.

She walks into the pasture.

Figments of her imagination gallop toward her — greeting her from the past.

She cries tears for us all — the dead, the dying, and the left behind.

The foreman from the auction house calls to her.

"Excuse me, Sandy, I need you to sign some papers."

Sandy composes herself and returns to the bare land where our machinery once sat.

She signs her name — feeling responsible.

Her signature alone will allow the pieces of the farm to be sold off.

The foreman yells to one of the drivers, "All set Joe. Take them to the west lot by #1."

Two semi-tractor-trailers scream to life — *Soon there will be nothing left,* they say.

The dust in their wakes disguises the new landscape.

Sandy stands and sobs until they hit the quarter mile dip in our road.

She crumples then.

My tractor sits at the back on the second flat bed — *I'm sorry to leave you too.*

It represents everything to her.

Me, my mom, my dad, and the farm.

And the young girl who left the prairies.

Sandy drives by the auction house every day to check on my tractor until it is sold. She never sits in the seat where I sat again, but she watches over this part of my life for me — a surrogate of sorts for the boy who left the prairies like her.

CITY LIFE

Tobi and Jake are the only animals left on the farm. Tobi was a puppy when I died — we had only had her for a few months and she had quickly chosen me as her master. Tobi is a Rottweiler and she is one of the sweetest dogs we have ever had. I bought Jake as a kitten for Tricia's sixteenth birthday. He is a black and white, her favorite. He is the cat we hid in her room for over six months without my dad knowing. My mom was in on the deception. She transported Jake to and from Tricia's bedroom in her laundry basket, clothes hiding the tiny ball of fluff. My mom could walk right by my dad and he never suspected a thing. Jake seemed to understand that he needed to be quiet and he always was, in the basket and in Tricia's room.

Tobi and Jake will make the move to the city with Tricia. Tobi is a true farm dog and she will have many adjustments in her new life. Jake the cat will hate the city as much, if not more, than Tobi. These two furry critters are the only remaining direct ties to me. Tricia will become obsessive about keeping them safe.

The houses in the city converge in on Tricia and the critters.
Tobi detests the confines of a fenced yard.
Jake hates being locked up in the house all day.
Tricia can't stand that other people live in our home and on our land, but she likes the easy access to drinking buddies and liquor in the city.
Tricia drives away from the farm.
Never looking back.
Vowing never to return — ever.

Tricia drinks with her cat and her dog when she can't find anyone else.
I am astounded at the amount she consumes.
She eventually passes out.
The goal achieved.
Tobi the Rottweiler licks her face to rouse her from her drunken stupor.
The cat cuddles beside her.
Concerned she may be the next to leave.

Tricia will start her EMT training soon.
She won't be able to drink like she has during the day, but the weekends and nights will be a blur.

DREAMS

Dreams.
We all have them.
Multidimensional scenes that give us what we need.
I dream about the farm.

I drive an old red pickup truck.
I bank left at the end of our half mile access — the pines curving away from me — drawing my eyes to bend with their boughs.
The light source is perfect, but it seems manipulated, as though hundreds of photography reflectors and diffusers have been set up to make my vision flawless.
Something in the distance moves towards me.
I wear a suit and a tie, which does not make the scene valid in my mind.
Typically, I wear plain t-shirts smeared with grease, old Gap jeans, and work boots.
I don't know where I am coming from, but it feels like coming home.

I hear a succession of pounding — a softness — a rhythm.
I look to my right and the horses gallop along the fence line.
Leading me.
Welcoming me back.
If I listen carefully, I can hear the faint whisper of the wheat in the fields and the trickle of the creek passing by.

I feel at ease — like I need to be here — quelling a longing.
The mass that moves toward me are people — my people.

I tower over my mom, my dad, my sisters.
I command the space about me.
We rush to embrace — to reunite.
We walk for a while as I reabsorb.
There is a sense of questioning why I left this place and these people.

The horses call to me from the pasture.
I reach for the tall Sorel who is mine — she nuzzles her huge head
in my neck.

I fear that I will be leaving soon and suddenly.
I will be dead again.
But I want to stay here.
Mostly, I want my family to forgive me.

Tricia gives me a leg up and I ride bareback into the yard — the
feeling — like floating.
My family follows.
I smell sweet grass and lilacs and the air cleans out my being.
I have lost so much.
My family even more.

The time to leave is near.
I parcel up the feelings I have for this place and these people and
put them in luggage too heavy to carry.
Life has not been fair.

I hear a succession of pounding again.
Thumping hearts in chests pleading.
A family of hearts breaking.
I prepare to leave — my body tense and rigid.
But first, a proper goodbye.
My face and body intact.
A suit to show respect.
In my dreams I give them that.

TRICIA AND GORE

Tricia completes her EMT training.

Eighteen months have passed.

She moves onto the required fieldwork.

They test her knowledge and responses to blood and guts — dead bodies and distraught family members screaming in the corners.

She is calm and cool with the carnage.

Tricia's body acts independently from her mind — moving through motions in other people's lives — she feeds on the gore — like the blood suckers we got down at the creek — latching on — sipping on slaughter.

The first call that speaks to her is a gunshot to the head.

The victim is dead when they arrive on the scene.

Brain matter everywhere.

There are others.

It's not that she likes it — the suffering and the slain.

That would be sick.

But it makes her feel less lonely.

She has the impression of being a part of something larger than my mom and my dad and me.

She is a member.

She belongs.

There are others.

Tricia sees dead people all the time.

She never saw my mom or me dead — she couldn't — so she tortures herself with other people's dead loved ones.

The stiffness.
The stillness.
Seeing faces she imagines.
There are others.

The drinking continues when it can.
Shift work is convenient when you want to go on a binge.
She drinks because of what she sees and she drinks because of me.
But the gore is gaining power.
There are others.

Tricia does her job mechanically.
She is quick on her feet and never collapses under pressure.
She sees some of the ugliest shit you can ever imagine.
One day soon she will see her first car accident on a grid road in-
volving a teenager.
She waits for it.
Knowing the power it holds.
There are others.

IT'S POSSIBLE

Everything in Sandy's mind is reduced to one question — *Is it possible?*
She answers *yes* every time.
She does not worry about herself.
She worries about Michaela.

Is it possible that Michaela could be kidnapped from school?
Yes.
Is it possible that a plane could fall from the sky?
Yes.
Is it possible that a shooter could show up at the movie theatre?
Yes.
Her life is a series of worries that she works through every day.

It's all just a phone call away.

A therapist told her once that the numbers are actually in her favor
— that the odds of something tragic happening again are lower for her.

But it only takes a knock on the door and a policeman standing there.

She knows that.
She knows the possibility.
She knows that there isn't someone out there with a calculator
crunching numbers — directing tragedy away from person A because
they have already felt misfortune.

It's all just a tap on the shoulder away — *Excuse me, are you...?*

THE FARM NOW

The farm doesn't look anything like it did when we lived there as a happy family. The yard is a mess, the fields are filled with weeds, it looks like there are towels and sheets hanging in the windows, the quonset needs paint, the porch is covered with trash, and there aren't any animals. I check on the farm from time to time; Sandy does too and so does Bonny's eldest, he is sixteen now. The farm is important to him. He wouldn't admit it, but I see him there quite often. Tricia still says that she will never return. Bonny hears about the farm from her son and that is enough for her.

The people that live on the farm now are city people — you can tell. There is no garden, as they prefer to get their produce from the grocery store, there is no pride in the yard with flower pots and baskets, and no freshly tilled earth, as they rent the land to other farmers who plant alfalfa. There is no farm machinery, and no one ever works in the quonset with the big white door open and the dogs lazing in the sun by their master. The graineries are not filled with wheat and the horses do not whinny in the distance.

Chris drives by from time to time and checks on the old Speers farm. He doesn't think that anyone is living there full time. He is right.

MY SISTERS

My sisters are moving forward with their lives.

Bonny owns and runs a Montessori pre-school, her husband has a good government job, and their kids are thriving.

Sandy's world revolves on an axis called Michaela who is enrolled full-time in school in Massachusetts. She is in grade one. Sandy volunteers at her school and loves being a stay at home mom. The two travel back and forth to Canada often and spend three straight months there in the summer. Sandy's husband travels with them when he can. They have a good life, and his efforts afford Sandy the opportunity to be a stay at home mom and she is thankful for that. Tricia is a full-time EMT now, finding new ways to torture herself and new ways to witness others' pain firsthand. She parties harder than ever and tries fruitlessly to hide it from her older sisters.

Tricia has filled the gunnysack with rocks.
She sits inside.
Tying a knot in the top.
As she rolls herself towards the water's edge.

Bonny takes a sink or swim approach — *She needs to figure it out herself.*
Sandy buys the raft she floats on, blows it up for her, patches it when she punches holes in it, replaces the oars she loses at sea, paddles when Tricia can't, bales water when it pours in — *She needs my help.*

Bonny and Sandy fight about Tricia.
You are doing too much.

You aren't doing enough.

The two are wired so differently. Sandy is ruled by regret and *What if?* Bonny doesn't let anything or anyone rule her, especially a spoiled sibling who doesn't appreciate the efforts of others.

Sandy is intent on righting the wrongs in Tricia's life. She can't do tough love on someone so lost and alone. Tough love could take someone else from her and she won't risk it.

Sandy makes appointments with therapists — Tricia never shows up.

Sandy enrolls Tricia in clubs — Tricia has no interest in new hobbies.

Sandy pays Tricia's bills — Tricia spends all of her money numbing her brain.

Sandy cleans the house that Tricia lives in rent-free. Tricia knows that Sandy hates messes.

Sandy takes her little sister's mistreatment. Tricia is often too busy to hang out with Sandy and Michaela when they come to town. She returns to the house in the early morning hours and sometimes not at all. Sandy is distraught with worry. She lies awake at night knowing that Tricia would like to be me. She calls Tricia's friends at times and they quickly tire of her mothering.

Tricia doesn't appreciate having Sandy near as much as she should. She knows that she flirts dangerously with losing the sister that can't help helping.

If my dad could think or talk, he would tell Sandy that she is enabling Tricia. Sandy would fight back strongly. She would say, *I couldn't save Jarett, or Mom, or you, but I sure us hell am going to save Tricia.*

My sisters' lives no longer revolve around my dad.

Sometimes a day passes without one of them visiting.

He doesn't know the difference.

Almost three years have passed and still he just sits and stares.

Tricia lies about being there when it is her night to spend with him.

She struggles to even look at him.

She wishes she could suffocate him.

She hates him for leaving her too.

The confines of a bottle offer her more.

Bonny speaks words of encouragement every moment she spends with him.

Sandy takes over all of the shifts when she is in town.

She feels guilty about living far from the ugliness in Saskatchewan.

The real picture of my dad zooms into focus for Sandy. When you leave and come back, things become clearer.

MY DAD

My dad struggles with pneumonia over and over. It is getting harder and harder for him to fight it off. His body has worked up a resistance to the antibiotics, having depended on them numerous times to kill the bugs that breed in his lungs.

No one comes from the physical therapy department anymore to move his limbs for him — a lost cause, I guess. My sisters rotate and stretch his arms and legs, his fingers, wrists, and elbows. Their efforts are futile. His muscles have atrophied so much that his body shape is more like that of a bean than a person. A return to the fetus.

One of our cats had seizures. I remember when I was a kid, it came into the outdoor courtyard while we were having a barbecue and it just started spazzing out under the table. It was foaming at the mouth and its eyes were crazy. It kept happening to that poor cat and so my dad took it out behind the quonset one day, with the intention of shooting it and putting it out of its misery. We all waited on the front porch to hear the gunshot, but it never came. He always used to say, *If the day comes when I can't take care of myself, haul me out to the field and shoot me.* But he couldn't even shoot the damn cat. My sisters remember that cat and watching my dad walk back into the yard with the pathetic thing in his arms.

Chris feels guilty about never going to see my dad. He has heard about the ugliness from his mom, who is a nurse in the city. He feels ashamed when he thinks about all of the demons my sisters have fought.

He can't make himself go and look at the crippled man around whom they rally.

Clinging to him and to the lives lived on a farm up the road from his.

TESS

Tess was always my dad's favorite dog. She was a cross between a Rottweiler and a Sheppard. We got her from a farmer up the road. Tess was smart, incredibly loyal, and obsessively protective. When Tricia and I were little and played outside by ourselves, she followed us wherever we went. Tess had a good life, but she was a scrapper, so she made things harder on herself than they needed to be. She had her left hind leg basically torn off by a badger; she had porcupine quills in her face numerous times; she fought a wolf or two and won; and a hawk dive-bombed her in the back once, causing a huge pocket of pus to grow. As Tess aged, she moved painfully toward the end of her life. My parents talked to Tricia and me a few times about the fact that we should put her out of her misery. I reacted the same way every time. I yelled and screamed and told them to just let her be, that it wasn't her time and it wasn't for us to decide. I let myself think that one day she might just get better and we shouldn't take that chance away from her.

My sisters treat my dad like that.
They can't let him go.

I see my dad in Tess.
I should have let her go sooner.
I know that now.

EVERYDAY LIFE

Bonny's kids are teenagers now.

They are not coddled and so they display an independence that I admire.

They are awesome cousins to Michaela, an only child. When Michaela comes to Saskatchewan, they generously play games with her that are beneath their ages.

Michaela is seven.

Sandy and her husband import pieces of Saskatchewan to Michaela from time to time — Auntie Tricia sleeping in her trundle bed on a Saturday morning — Uncle Warren hiding in the back of Sandy's car at the end of a school day.

Tricia works hard, parties harder, and develops feelings for someone who has feelings for more than one. Tricia is so in need of someone in her life, that she allows this man to gain a hold on her heart, then he yanks it up and down like a piñata in a tree.

Tricia blindfolded and disoriented.

He offers her nothing, long term.

In the end, she will take what she needs from him.

My family members are finding their footings again.

My dad is the exception.

MICHAELA'S EIGHTH BIRTHDAY

Tricia is in Boston for Michaela's eighth birthday.

My sister doesn't know it, but she carries a beacon that will lead her through the storm.

The head nurse of the unit where my dad lives calls Sandy's house in the U.S.

"You need to come home. He won't last long now."

Plans change quickly.

Two sisters and Michaela fly home to Saskatchewan.

Bonny keeps vigil while the others head north and then west.

My dad takes his last breath on Sandy's shift.

Time passing slowly.

Noises hellish to hear.

The barely rising chest wearisome to watch.

The nurses come often at the sound of the alarm.

Eventually they can't clear the airway.

Three nurses rush in at the same time.

His body succumbs quickly to the intake of air.

Well primed to be silent.

Sandy panics and steps behind the curtain — not wanting to watch.

The nurse gently says, "Sandy, your dad will be gone soon. Do you want to sit with him?"

She is frightened to think that she will see my dad dead.

She is the only one there.

She sits at the end of the bed holding his feet — her head bent down beside them.

She does not look.

She will not see him dead.

My dad knows of her presence and respects her inability to watch him die.

Sandy does not understand the proclamations of peaceful passings.

Whatever it was that ambushed my dad, it held him captive for three and half years.

It silenced him.

As his heart takes its last *thump thump*, the essence of my dad is released toward me.

He is the farmer with the capable hands again.

Our happiness and our struggles pass through us in an instant — understanding — sharing — reuniting.

My dad moves past me like my mom did — their bodies chose death and mine did not.

They understand the pull that the earth barrier has on me.

They too yanked hard on teenage death, trying with all of their might to keep me there.

There is a quiet understanding of the role I play for my sisters.

Bonny and Tricia arrive within the hour. All three hide behind the curtain — unable to acknowledge death for the third time. My sisters argue about whether or not my dad should have an autopsy. Sandy is the only one who wants to know what ate him alive.

Tricia and Bonny vote against putting his body through additional torture — on the same side for the first time.

Sandy can't fight anymore, so she gives in.

Three remain.

How do you say goodbye to so much in such a short time?

As the circle gets smaller, my remaining sisters are drawn to each other in a way that I have never seen — pulled like magnets to the sorrow they share. They are orphans now — the battle lines erased.

Sandy's husband has showered her with diamonds and jewels through the years.

She picks from one of many pieces.
Removing eighteen diamonds.
Making three platinum bands with six diamonds each.
Six diamonds for a mom, a dad, a son, and three sisters.
Three rings for three sisters.

MY DAD'S MEMORIAL

There is a sense of tranquility at my dad's memorial. My sisters finally understand that asking him to stay longer was asking too much. My dad's old country music plays in the background while his friends and relatives come to pay their respects. Another urn sits at the front on a tall, white pedestal. There is a picture of my dad standing in the sun in front of the big white quonset door — taken the year before I died. My sisters stand together for the first time and people have a hard time looking them in the eyes. People talk and they reminisce, and everyone wants to remember my dad the way he was before I died.

Sandy takes the urn to her house in the city and places my dad with my mom and me.

My sisters sit down at the kitchen table and talk for a while. They talk about me and wonder how I would have handled my parents' illnesses if I had been alive. I wonder the same. Would I have been able to rally longer in the face of cancer than my dad could when my mom got sick? Or would I have expected my sisters to handle it all like my dad did? Would I have been able to dedicate so many years to a man who could offer me nothing in return, or would I have decided that there was nothing there and moved on with my life? I know for certain that I would have carried my share of the load — whatever that ended up being — I was raised to work hard and be respectful and get the job done.

I also think that if I hadn't died, things might have played out differently, at least for my mom. I think she would have fought harder to live and that she would have beaten the cancer again. I think I could have helped her with that if the words she heard me say were from her bedside and not from an urn in her closet. My sisters know and understand the unique relationship I shared with my mom. Bonny says, "If Jarett was here, Mom would have chosen to go on the ventilator and she would have acted on the cancer sooner."

Sandy and Tricia nod in agreement.

My dad is a different story. I think there is a chance that what happened to him could have destroyed me.

My sisters agree.

Tricia says, "I am glad that Jarett never saw dad the way he ended up. I don't think he could bear it."

But, I did see what he became.

My sisters just don't know it.

I idolized that man and what life threw at him after losing a nineteen year old son, really too much for anyone. Obviously, I have a different perspective now than I would have had if I had lived. And everything that I have witnessed is different because of the grief that moves like quicksand around my family.

I live outside the earthly pain that swallowed my sisters whole.

They float above the normal people in an impenetrable bubble.

They can't pop it.

They bang on it, but the sound only reverberates back to them.

There is no entrance.

It just moved over and around them — sucking them in — GULP.

I think my sisters would have ended up resenting me if I was alive to watch my dad. I don't think I could have spent three and a half years looking at him like that. I would have taken care of the farm, but I don't think I could have taken care of him.

I think the dedication of my sisters to their parents is inspiring, and I don't think many people give them enough credit for all that they took on.

TWO WEEKS LATER

Tricia is pregnant.
She stops drinking that day.
She finally has a reason to take care of herself.
Withdrawal is tough.
She has the shakes, she can't sleep, and she sweats profusely.
But she has been through worse.
She will make it through.
The father of the child bows out quickly.
Tricia is practical — *Better now than later.*
There is a part of her that wants the child all to herself.
Needs the child to be hers and hers alone.

Tricia and I still share secrets.
She stopped taking her birth control pills months ago.
Her out of control behavior was starting to scare her.
Waking up in strange places and not knowing how she got there was getting to her.
She hears my dad's voice in her head daily.
I knew he would reach her eventually.
You can't be raised by a man like my dad and not respect what he taught you.
The most important thing you will do in your life is to have a child.
Tricia finally reached out for one of the life preservers floating around her.
She isn't sinking anymore.
I don't judge her in any way.
It's called survival.

Sandy picks up death certificates and meets with lawyers and accountants and deals with the assets her parents left behind. She takes everything they had and breaks it up into three pieces.

Bonny's family searches for a farm to buy northeast of the city. They miss the life on the farm.

TOVAH

The baby that fuels Tricia from the inside is a girl.
Her first name will be Tovah.
Tricia loved the name the first time she met Sandy's neighbor
from Denmark.
Her middle name will be Hope.

My two eldest sisters and their families provide an abundance
of support to their single mom sister who is lacking a husband and
grandparents to help. Tricia and the baby will live at Sandy's house
in the city. Bonny, a mere twenty minutes away, provides an upbeat
outlook to life as a single parent: "Of course you can do this, Tricia."
Three sisters prepare to welcome a new life into the world, the excitement building; baby booties and bonnets squelching out the sounds
of crumpling cars, IV motors, and ventilators. Tricia's belly, bursting
with child, exerts a natural force on the three left behind — attracted
like a magnet — towards the magnificence of life.

Sandy plans an elaborate baby shower at The Hotel Saskatchewan.
It is a proclamation, loud and clear —
We have something to celebrate.
In a few short months Tricia will give birth to a beautiful baby girl.
She will also deliver herself into a new world.
Finding strength in her own family.

Sandy and Tricia's friend will be present for the birth.
Sandy is appalled at how the staff treats Tricia when she does not
recognize a father on any of the forms.

Sandy keeps her mouth shut for once, knowing the nurses control the medication.

Tovah Hope is placed in her mother's arms at 10:19 a.m. on July 27th, 2007.

Tricia sees nothing but the tiny child.

No visions of a dead teenager, a bald mom, or a motionless dad.

No visions of the farm and all she left there.

Tovah is the key who unlocks the chains about her.

Tovah enables Tricia to venture into the basement and pull items from the boxes marked Jarett, Mom, Dad, farm. The Christmas ornaments will hang again on a tree when Tricia replicates scenes from our childhood. As Tovah grows, my Legos will toy with her imagination, and her creations will sit on her shelves in her room like mine did. The Mexican dishes will be placed once again on the Mexican table, and there will be new people who gather about in the creaking saddle chairs — my chair no longer empty — my parent's chairs filled with the future, not the past.

LIFE NOW

Tricia goes back to school to become a paramedic. She still feels akin to the blood and the gore, but more importantly, she wants to help people.

People that look like me and my mom and my dad.

She is building a foundation, but doesn't know it yet.

She can do some crazy shit in the field and she never flinches.

She can decompress a lung with a needle the size of the inside of a pen.

She can calm a heart that races with cardio version and quicken a heart that beats too slowly with pacing, zapping them both with electricity.

She can help you breathe with a bag valve mask.

She saves lives and she gets a rush from it.

Her new high.

Bonny and her husband buy a farm twenty minutes outside of the city. It sits ten miles northwest, past White City and Pilot Butte. Bonny's farm does not have horses and they do not plant wheat in their fields. There are regrets that their farm couldn't have been our parents'. Of my three sisters, I am actually surprised that Bonny would choose a life in the country — she never seemed as tied to the farm as Tricia and Sandy.

Sandy is all things Michaela, school volunteer and happy homemaker. She makes enviable Halloween costumes; she takes up stained glass for my dad and scrapbooking for my mom.

My sisters don't like to get together at Christmas. It affords them an opportunity to pretend that the missing half of the family is with one of the other sisters.

Two years pass and our family farm is sold to a potash company. Saskatchewan land is rich in potassium carbonate and this natural resource is used in fertilizers. Potash is the widely used term to refer to the potassium salts found in the ground. Our farm will be a part of a large mine in southern Saskatchewan that will wipe away everything we built there.

CHRIS BUILDS A HOUSE

Start at my crash site.

Head straight north.

Follow the dirt road that the semi was travelling on before it hit me.

In under two miles, you will pass Chris' house on the right.

My parents' farm — which would probably be mine by now — is less than three miles away.

Chris is building a beautiful home on a piece of his dad's land.

I watch the different stages: a basement, the foundation, framing, a roof and shingles.

Setting down roots.

Building a home for a family.

Take the grid from Chris' straight east and then south and you will end up at our farm.

There are different things happening there.

Pulling up roots.

Dismantling memories.

Taking it all away.

The creek that runs through Chris' land connects with the creek that runs across our land.

Chris has three kids now and works really hard for all that he has.

He is still a no-nonsense guy, and he doesn't take kindly to bullshit from his kids or anyone else. Chris has a couple of tattoos now. One is a big Bruins' emblem on his left tri-cep and very soon there will be another tattoo on the inside of his right forearm — I will be honored in that ink.

When I look at Chris, I see parts of my own life playing out before me.

I would have lived in the country where I belong; I would have had a wife, some kids, and two dogs. I would no doubt drive a truck and I would have taught my kids to ride like my dad taught me. I would have wanted to instill the same work ethic in my kids that my dad ingrained in me. I would have taught them respect and that the word *can't* should not be part of their vocabulary.

I would have never left Saskatchewan and the farm.

GRAVESITE

My sisters know that the three urns have stayed too long. They discuss at length what they should do with the ashes three left behind. They feel strongly about keeping them together — uniting them forever — but not floating them through the air. They need to stay intact in some way so the urns can preserve their individuality.
This is Jarett.
This is Mom.
This is Dad.

My sisters need a place to sit on sad, lonely days and talk to the three of us. They need a place to bring flowers on birthdays and death days. A gravesite will give them that place.

If my sisters could ask us, my mom, my dad, and me, we would say, *Set us free on the farm.* But we don't get a vote. This is about the people we left behind.

Sandy searches for a small plot to bury us in.
We will leave the closet soon.
Like we left the farm.
And return to the land.

Two and a half feet wide by eight feet long.
A modest thirty inches by ninety-six inches.
A blanket of grass covering what lies beneath.
Dead to the world.

My sisters don't want to bury us in the city. The three of us were farm folk at heart. Sandy finds a spot on the outskirts of town — the farm in the distance to the southeast. She shows Bonny and Tricia and they agree on the location. They choose the spot with a bank of evergreens to the right to block out the city in the west. They don't know it yet, but the urban sprawl will fill in around us one day soon and the wheat fields in the east will be gone from our view.

CAR ACCIDENT
ON A GRID ROAD

Tricia is a paramedic now.

When a serious call comes in, she takes the lead and her partner drives.

The call she has been waiting for comes through on her radio.

Code 4 (sirens on).

MVC (motor vehicle collision) one mile east of Highway 6, four miles north of the city.

Teenage driver.

Sirens blazing, Tricia and her partner leave the city on North Albert.

First professionals on the scene.

Tricia rushes to the upturned vehicle that lies in the ditch.

Sliding down the embankment — through the mud and the shattered glass.

I am so proud of her.

I can feel her determination to make this outcome different.

She reaches the car, but no one is in it.

Her partner is transporting the equipment.

Tricia yells, "I can't find the driver. Where is the driver?"

She wades through the tall grass.

I can feel her urgency.

Searching ahead and to the left and right of where the car stopped.

A seventeen-year-old boy was driving himself to school.

Driving too fast on a grid road, like me.

The stones flying up in the back.

The tires unsteady.

Unable to regain control.
Sliding.
A skid became a roll.

Tricia finds the boy.
Wearing a t-shirt, jeans, and Converse runners.
He is face down, unmoving.
No pulse.
No breath.
Tricia screams, "**Fuuuck.**"
I wonder if his shoes will go back to his parents like mine did?

The parents of the boy arrive unexpectedly on the scene.
Like Tricia did.
The police officers push them back.
Like they did to her.

Tricia speaks to the parents.
Reaching out to hold the trembling hands of the sonless mother.
A mother like hers.
Tricia is kind and she is gentle and she knows what they have become.
"I am so sorry," she says.
Tricia looks directly into the eyes of the boy's parents — hoping to impart some message of knowing how they feel.
She does not look down at twisting hands or shuffling feet like the people she works with.
The parents ask, "Can we see him? We need to see him."
Tricia responds gently, "I urge you to give that some time. My partner is with him right now."
I am so proud of Tricia.
Holding it all together.

That night she drinks.
Heavily.
So drunk she can only crawl.
The earth moving too fast for just two feet.
She still makes me proud.

Tricia attends the funeral six days later.
Sitting in the back.
Sobbing for a boy she never knew.

BURYING THE DEAD

There is something about a pile of dirt at a gravesite that is so sad.
I can't explain it.
Others feel it too.
Why else would the workers cover the dirt with green turf?
Making it resemble grass.
Living.
It's like dressing up death.

When my sisters and their families arrive at the gravesite, there are three small piles of dirt placed neatly to the right of our plot. I saw how the workers used a machine similar to the fence post auger we used on the farm — the dirt spirally upward and out — the auger digging deeper still. The gravediggers are miraculously out of sight when my family arrives, because people don't typically like to see who digs the holes or who fills them in. Burial is choreographed seamlessly.

Each of my sisters carries one of us in their arms.
They walk sedately towards the open ground.
Husbands and children walk silently behind.
The youngest carry three separate bouquets of flowers.

I have been dead for ten years.
My mom for four.
My dad for two.

This is the first time my family is seeing the flat tombstone placed in the ground.

The names and the dates make it real.
A son's name between the names of his parents.
Sheaths of wheat decorating the brass.
Wheat for the farmer.
Wheat for the farmer's wife.
Wheat for the farmer's son.
There are no blank spaces where the dates are.
The *Born* and *Died* are filled in.

The rules allow three urns to be buried together in the same small plot. The holes are perfectly spaced in a line and the depth is a mere six inches deeper than the height of the tallest urn — that would be mine.

Moving the urns from closet to closet was easier for my sisters than this ceremony is. It is an onerous task to let us go. They ponder the placement of who will go where.
Should the one who died first be placed in the first hole?
Should I be placed between my parents?
They decide on the latter.
My sisters simultaneously place the urns they hold in the earth — the circular openings cut so precisely, so neatly.
They plant the remains of three in the ground.
Three sets of eyes brimming with tears.
Droplets cresting on lower eyelids and then rolling over and down.
Falling on what was left to hang onto.
Saying goodbye again — but in a different way.

JAKE THE CAT
AND TOBI THE DOG

Tricia still refers to Tobi as my dog. She has lived for five years in the city with Tricia and has hated it. The farm was all Tobi knew until it was sold — wide open spaces and no fences. It is difficult to convert a farm dog to a city dog.

It is February 2008 and Tobi will not make it to the end of the month, her hind legs so completely paralyzed that Tricia has to walk behind her, holding up her back end whenever the poor dog tries to walk. Tobi doesn't leave her bed much anymore. She is so ashamed, ears back, with cowered head, whenever she has an accident. Tricia asks the vet to make a house call when she is finally able to let my dog go. Tricia says goodbye again and then runs upstairs to Tovah's room.

Jake is old and frail now too, but Tricia can't let him go. He is the last tie to me, to the farm, to my parents and her life. The vet has already mentioned on two occasions that Tricia should be thinking seriously about putting him to sleep. Tricia will wait until the summer.

Sandy and Michaela are in town when Tricia decides she can't torture poor Jake any longer. Sandy drives her sister and her cat to the vet. Tricia carries Jake in her arms into the examination room — lethargic and thin, the pitiful cat lies lifeless. Tricia sobs as she places him on the cold of the stainless steel table, kisses him, and then flees the room. Sandy stays with Jake, as Tricia does not want him to be alone.

Tricia has an unusual relationship with death.
She can look it in the face when the face is unrecognizable to her.

351

She can fight with it and try to beat it.

She is strong against the death that comes for strangers.

But show her a dimple she knows, blue eyes that are hers, strong hands that she held, and she crumples.

SANDY AND SASKATCHEWAN

Sandy goes home to Saskatchewan often. She has some great memories that lift her like a buoy — floating on the surface — she is calm and anchored. But then there are the other memories that dismember the connection between the anchor and the calm. At the point of disconnect, the buoy pops cheerily out of the water and remains afloat on the surface, while the anchor holds her hostage where the bottom feeders are.

She flies east from Toronto with the shade down. She keeps her eyes averted from the other open shades, but above the clouds she knows what is calling to her and she will not look at it until the descent for landing. On the three hour ten minute journey, she knows roughly when the land breaks into the flat and treeless expanse she grew up on. *Ladies and gentlemen we have begun our initial descent.* Five minutes later, Sandy opens the shade and sees nothing but white billowing clouds below her. She shuts the shade and waits. The plane is moving downward through the clouds and it bounces like the flat rocks we would skip across the creek on the farm. *Mine jumped five times, Sandy! Did you see it?*

The turmoil builds for the girl who left the prairie — the turbulence setting the stage for what is to come. She opens the shade again. They are still in the clouds, but she can see pieces of it all below her. In the summer it is the shades of green arranged perfectly to form a patchwork quilt, the grid roads of the countryside that separate our farm from yours look like the stitching lines that link it all together. In the winter, snow covered or not, the quilt is still visible, the perfect rectangular sections of land are divided by the roads that cut across every square mile to the north and every two miles to the south, the roads that the farmers move their tractors and combines on to get to the next field — the dirt paths like the one I died on.

Ladies and gentlemen, we have begun our final descent. They break through the clouds and the plane calms itself on its approach. Sandy waits for it, the sound of the landing gear locking in place. She opens the shade. The pilot banks hard to the right, the left wing tips upward and the right wing tips down. She is suspended above it all — like me — she hangs in the balance. She feels outside of herself and alone. Tilted high in the sky, as the plane continues to slice itself through the blue, the tears from her left eye run straight to her mouth. I watch her taste the sadness this place conjures up in her, the tears from her right eye roll off her face at the highest point of her cheekbone, she watches them as they fall on the right forearm that grips greedily at the armrest. It happens every time like this. It doesn't feel like home.

At the age of thirty-five, Sandy bought the burial plot beside my parents and me. Not a typical purchase for someone her age, but telling of her relationship with death. She will come home to Saskatchewan when she dies.

There is a file folder that Michaela is aware of — detailing the choices that she will never have to make.

There are letters about how life is for the living and not the dead.

There are also some strong proclamations about what she is forbidden to do.

You will not accompany my body to a crematory.

You will not keep my ashes in a closet for years.

September is still Sandy's favorite month, even though it is the one when I left.

The leaves falling gently in the breeze about them.

The crisp air of the prairies pinking up their cheeks.

The crunch of the leaves underfoot.

TATTOO

Chris is getting a new tattoo.

He is being very secretive about it, but my sisters hear the buzz amongst mutual friends.

There is talk that the tattoo has something to do with me.

Chris has thought about the design for two long years.

He travels to Weyburn to an artist he respects.

The tattoo is laid out on a grid line to keep the design centered on the inside of Chris' left forearm.

It will reach from his wrist to his elbow.

The artist transfers the stencil and begins the outline.

Working in blacks and greys.

Chris thinks out loud: *I need this to be perfect.*

The needle moving up and down 50 to 3,000 times per minute.

A foot pedal controlling the vertical movement.

Faster for the outline, slower for the shading.

Depositing tiny drops of ink one millimeter deep.

Beads of blood proclaiming the commitment.

There are three people that Chris pays tribute to on the canvas of his arm.

My mom, my dad, and me.

The sound like a dentist's drill.

Puncturing the skin.

A permanent eulogy.

Is there anything more telling of the commitment to those I left behind?

Up and down and up and down the needle pierces.

The design is medieval.

Suggestive of a violent era.

Chris brands his body with three spears — Jarett Speers — Joan Speers — Dennis Speers.

I think it is genius.

I am so proud to have called him my friend.

If you ask Chris, as many people do, what the meaning of the three spears are, he will only tell you if he thinks you are deserving of its meaning. He is very protective of the story that lives within the spears.

My best friend died when he was nineteen and then...

SPANISH HOUSE

The house my dad built is going to be auctioned off.

The potash mine owns it now.

The land needs to be cleared in preparation for the mine.

If no one is interested in buying the house or the buildings, they will all be destroyed.

My sisters will not let that happen.

If need be, they will buy it and move it somewhere else.

Either way, the house my dad built will find a new home.

There are two days when the house will be open and bids will be accepted.

Many people come to meander through the rooms we lived in.

My sisters come with their husbands and children.

This is the first time in nine years that they have entered the house.

It has been vacant for over a year, and with the new threat to destroy what my dad built, each of my sisters needs to see the house one last time on the farm.

Sandy opens the front door slowly — like it weighs a ton.

I want to go in.

I don't want to go in.

They all enter the front foyer with the view of the balcony.

The good memories greet them.

The bad memories bombard and besiege.

Tricia climbs the stairs to my room and then hers.

Tears lining her face like the bars in a jail.

Bonny and Sandy branch off in different directions — moving slowly through the hallucinations — pausing when the visions become too clear.

My dad seated at the big metal desk in his office.

My mom at the kitchen sink — vegetables from her garden piled high on the counter.

Me in the front room playing my guitar — sitting high on a stool by the pool table.

A family together in the family room.

Each of my sisters constructs elaborate visions from the past.

Individual perspectives transport the apparitions to life.

Making their way through each of the rooms, their journeys are solely independent of anyone else.

They see things as they were.

Furniture and drapes, pictures and dishes, lamps and throw pillows.

Mostly they see the people — my mom, my dad, and me.

Walking through our vacant house, my sisters stride across the floor, stepping on familiar triggers. The house screams at them for leaving. It's like walking on a land mine, the memories blowing up in their faces. The visions of the people who lived there, the furniture, the bank of reverie, pulling on the ripcord in their minds that keeps the visions contained, releasing them at a velocity that pulls them light speed to the past.

Eventually my three sisters converge in the kitchen.

They are silent and lost in their own thoughts.

This visit to their previously happy home dredges up suppressed images from the plethora of unpleasantries — never forgotten — but pushed below the surface.

They open drawers and cupboards, the memories playing merciless games.

I remember when Tricia and I put a strip of fur in the corner lazy susan and when Mom went to get the sugar, she screamed and jumped because she thought it was a mouse.

My sisters each try to hold in their emotions — creating separate mausoleums for their memories.

I laugh to my dead self when I think of how Mom let us bring all the cats in the house and we suddenly heard dad's diesel truck in the yard. Mom calmly decided we should gently drop each of them out the kitchen window, but I couldn't get the screen off and so we were all lined up holding the cats in our arms, giggling, but scared just the same.

This is the house where I watched my family mourn me.
This is the house where my mom fought cancer and lost.
This is the house where my dad left as a man and never returned.
This is the house that love built and death tore down.
I don't like the way the house feels.
If it could talk, it would say, *I am haunted by all I have seen.*

Sandy needs to get outside for some air. She walks to the place in the evergreens where she would go when she wanted to be alone, the boughs hanging heavily down and the acorns and the smell and lying back and looking up, the fresh farm air and the colors transport her back in time.

Tricia goes to the horse barn and sits in the stall labeled *Chief.*

Bonny searches for flower bulbs to dig up and take to her farmyard.

Michaela and her dad search for treasures in the old playhouse. They find some curling trophies of my dad's in the remaining rubble and Michaela chooses one to take with her. That beat-up old thing will have a prominent place in Michaela's bedroom back in Boston. It will sit on a white desk looking out of place in the bedroom with a loft. She will treasure that trophy. The farm holds a power over her.

Sandy and Michaela walk out to the tire swing — the rope is worn and fraying.

My sisters roam through the quonset.
Recognizing pieces of my dad here and there.
The vice grip attached to the workbench.
The wooden drawers emptied of the nuts and bolts and washers.
The homemade hooks on the pegboard hanging empty.

My sisters and their families all walk together out to the grid road and back. They walk slowly, their feet shuffling across the land, knowing what will become of the farm they love. Another loss binding them closer together.

THREE SPEARS

Chris still has not told my sisters about his new tattoo. For whatever reason, he is worried that it won't be enough in their minds. He couldn't be farther from the truth.

Sandy plans a dinner for everyone and their families — Chris shows up in a long sleeved shirt — hiding the ink beneath.

My sisters are afraid to ask and Chris is afraid to tell.

The evening is about to end. Chris and his family standing at the door to go.

Sandy can't take it any longer. She can't let them leave without asking.

"Chris, we have heard that you have a new tattoo and that it has something to do with Jarett. Is that just a rumor?"

"It isn't a rumor," says Chris. "I have had it for a couple of months."

"Can we see it?" asks Sandy.

"Of course," says Chris.

Chris rolls up the sleeve of his shirt and turns his arm to show the inside of his forearm.

And there for my sisters to see — etched in his skin — are three spears.

Tricia is so moved by the design and the tribute and the meaning that she asks Chris if he would mind if she copied his idea.

He is touched that she likes it so much.

Tricia's is a smaller version of Chris' — about four and a half inches long — on the inside of her left wrist.

Tricia's has color.

Tricia made one other alteration and intentionally flipped the spears to point upward on her arm — directed at her heart.

THE TREES

You can tell the seriousness of a farmer by the organization and neatness of the farmyard, as well as the trees that have been planted. Trees in Saskatchewan are sold at a discount to the farmer who wants his yard and wheat fields protected from the elements.

There was a thick stand of trees before we moved to the farm, but my mom added many more to define the spaces and replace the ones that would fall down in storms or die. The shelterbelts of trees are laid out to minimize the prairie winds from all directions. It takes at least fifteen years of growth for the trees to reach a good height. In our yard, they extend due west to the gas shed and due south past the tire swing and out to the curve where the road arcs you into their sanctuary. Within the yard there is a belt of weeping willows from the old storage shed to the corner of the concrete driveway that leads to the double car garage. Banking the horse corral is a line of box elder that divides the garden and the pasture. Beyond the four graineries that create a ninety-degree angle in the southwest corner of the yard, you will find a bank of white elm that delineate the cow pasture and the chicken coops. At the centre of it all, perched at the edge of the flower garden, stands the old dutch elm. At night it basks in the radiance of the yard light that shines brightly to show the love and care that the yard receives.

One of the trees that meant the most to me is the tire swing tree.
Most of the trees have died around it now.
It stands alone like so many others who swung beneath its boughs.
It stands there as a symbol for Sandy.

It holds up the tire that she hung on that rope.

The swing that defined this farm to this girl.

It is defiant and only the bulldozers that will fell the trees in its wake can bring it down.

As it falls, no one will notice the poetry that Sandy scrawled for me. Carved chaotically with a knife and a chisel into the bark of the tree. Where I swung as a boy. On a tire that she hung.

> *Insipid is life*
> *Tasteless*
> *Death has won*
> *You*
> *We have lost*
> *Everything*

A woman from McLean buys the house my dad built.

A man from Balgonie buys the quonset a community built.

In order to get them out of the yard, most of the interior trees come down.

It is hard to watch them fell the trees that my mom worked so hard to plant.

Chopping away at the bank of visions I have of her.

When she was strong.

When she had a son.

Trees change landscapes.

Fallen trees toy with memories.

Was it here that my sister pushed me on that tire swing?

I can see the tire Sandy hung that day I followed her.

Crushed beneath a pile of tree trunks.

Still attached to the limb onto which she climbed.

MOVING THE HOUSE

The house movers arrive with jacks and steel beams and dollies.
They start by disconnecting all things plumbing and electrical.
Severing the ties.
The exterior courtyard will not be moved.
It is detached from the house and pulled away.
The sound of the saws cut into me.
The Spanish style stucco cracking and crumbling as the bucket on the bobcat pulls it free from the house.
The guts of the rebar exposed inside.

The movers clear a twelve-foot swath around the house.
My mom's lilac trees and the ferns she planted are ripped from the earth.
The dirt is dug out from around the base of the house and the movers cut openings in the foundation walls.
Piercing into the bedrock of the man who built it.
Steel beams are inserted into the openings.
Skewering the memories inside.
Interlocking wooden posts support the house inside and out.
Bracing for what is to come.
The house was born here.

Hydraulic jacks are placed under the steel beams and they lift the house from the only place it has ever sat. The unified system raises and lowers each jack simultaneously in order to keep the house level.
Ever so slowly the house my dad built is leaving the farm.

Sliding beams are placed beneath the house and ever so gently it is pulled onto special dollies with huge rubber tires.
Like slowly pulling back a band-aid to expose the wound beneath.
The basement is revealed to the sun and the sky.
An open hole with stairs and walls.
Like a dollhouse with no roof.
The child can position her dolls where she wants.
The mom sits at her desk where she sews quilts and Halloween costumes.
The dad sits behind the door and works on his stained glass projects.
The firewood is gone from where the kids piled it high.
But there on the shelves, behind the strawberry jam and the pickles, is the salsa I made with my mom.

Next, the workers attach the dollies to a very large truck.
I watch as the house moves away from the lives we lived here on this land.
Creeping away from us all.

An entourage of workers follow the house down the road.
Out to the grid and beyond.
They move signs and raise wires.
The house my dad built will travel 33.5 kilometers to a new hole in the ground.

A small crew stays back at the farm.
Working with a backhoe, they fill the basement in with dirt.
Hiding the existence of a home.
Burying a family beneath.
Another death.

Bonny's eldest is there to watch, like me.
The workmen tell him how well the house is built.
Not one wall will crack.
He is proud, but sad.
The farm is dear to him.

In less than two months, all of the buildings will be gone.
The quonset will be taken last.

It stands alone in a yard where the wind blows hard.
Patches of the protective trees lay on the ground.

THE EMPTY FARMYARD

I am surprised that Tricia would ever go to see the empty farmyard, but she does.

She goes alone.

Showing her newfound strength.

She parks her car about a quarter mile from the bend into the yard.

She walks slowly toward the curve.

The fence line to her right lying twisted in the dirt.

Tumbleweeds caught in the wires.

Visions of her and me with the horses surging in her mind.

You never raced horses with your brother here.

She scans the horizon to her right.

Searching for the woodpile and the place where I parked my tractor.

Every piece of farm machinery gone.

You never farmed this land with your family.

Tricia stops twice before advancing beyond the remaining outer trees.

The house is normally the first thing you see when you follow the gentle slope to the left.

Finally, she steps into the life she led.

Like stepping into a framed portrait.

And there where she lived and she grew, is nothing.

She runs now — searching for something that validates the lives lived here.

But there is no evidence of anything familiar.

She cries out to my parents and me — "Everything is gone" — "How can this be?"

The dead are gone, and the living have been eliminated too.

The slate wiped clean.
The characters erased.

Tricia sits in the tall grass, where the back of the house used to be.
My bedroom would have been directly above her.
She sits and she sobs.
I am present, but she doesn't know it.

She looks out to where the quonset should be.

It shouldn't have ended this way.

A DOG HOUSE

My dad and I built a doghouse together. I was about ten years old and it was one of my first lessons in construction. We built it big and we built it strong. My dad taught me to measure twice and cut once. *There is no room for error when building a home.* We insulated the walls and the roof to keep our furry friends warm in the winter. We even fashioned a flap door, split up the middle that would open and close when one of the dogs entered or exited. The exterior was clapboard and painted crème to resemble the stucco on the main house. We shingled it with clay tiles that matched the tiles on the big house and then set it beside the driveway under the trees. In the winter we added new hay to line the bottom of the floor, and then Tricia and I would arrange some old pillows and blankets in the corners and up the walls. Our dogs loved that house.

When the farm was sold, Tricia would not leave the doghouse. It wouldn't fit on the moving truck and so Tricia paid someone to go out to the farm and haul it into the city for her. Tobi had four years in that house in the city and then it sat empty for six. Tricia filled that home again with a yellow lab for Tovah, allowing pieces of her own childhood to come back to her. Two years later she added a cat. *Every kid should have a pet to love and to take care of* — the words of my dad filling her head. The memories of all the animals she cherished on the farm filling her heart.

SANDY SAYS GOODBYE TO THE FARM

Like Tricia, Sandy returns to the farm alone. She needs to walk the land on her own. She parks at the grid and walks through the fields and the horse pasture, seeing what is real to her. She moves across the earth that mutates her memories to lies, misleading her mind to see only what is left and not what was there before, falsifying. She progresses through the tales of darkness and annihilation and focuses on the characters who are as real to her as the land she walks on — *This was a great place to grow up.*

Sandy drives into the yard. It is the hardest. She has a purpose. She pulls a shovel from the back of the suburban and digs a circle of holes where the house used to be. Six holes. She heads to my mom's garden, where the weeds and the bramble have snuffed out any signs of the love that she grew on this land. She searches for any remnants of my mom's labors: the iris' she planted along the driveway, the tulip bulbs from under the tree, the daffodils by the corral, and the bleeding hearts she planted for me. She finds many defiant flower shoots and she carefully digs them from the earth and tenderly transports them to the holes she dug over the basement. One by one, she places them in the ground above the foundation, where my dad built a Spanish home for us.

It feels like another death.

Our Spanish house sits on a farm straight east on Highway 1 from the high school Tricia and I attended.

No one from my family will ever go to see it.

TOVAH AND THE FARM

Tricia brings her daughter and their dog out to the farm now and then. She never drives into the yard, though. She tries to tell the little blond girl about her grandparents and me and the life we shared on this land. She tells her about the horses and the secrets we shared, about the hard work and the good times. She talks about the people that left.

The little girl loves to throw rocks into the water where Tricia and I jumped into the rushing creek off the damn dam. Their dog loves to swim. Tricia sits on the dam and looks across the field to the exterior bank of trees where the farmyard used to be. It looks the same as it did when we grew up here. No one could tell of all that is missing from where Tricia is seated, so she likes to spend time on the dam and imagine all that should still be behind the trees.

A NEW BEAVER DAM

A new beaver comes to live on the farm. He builds a huge dam in the culvert and the water rises quickly. Sandy and Michaela happen to be in town, and they join Tricia and Tovah on a trip to the farm. Their two yellow labs come along for the ride and they rush to the water for a swim. The water is so high that it reaches the top of the dam. If the beaver dam is not released, the dam my dad built will wash away within days.

And then where will Tricia sit and admire the view?

Tricia is frantic.

She rips off her shoes, rolls up her pant legs, and enters the culvert at the end that isn't blocked.

A massive wall of water stands before her, held in place by some sticks and mud.

Placed there by a rat-like animal with big teeth and no visible ears.

Sandy is yelling at Tricia.

"Get out of there, Tricia. Are you crazy? Don't you understand the danger in what you are doing? If that dam lets go and you get your foot caught, I can't save you. Your daughter will watch you drown and this place — this place that you love — will have lost someone else."

Michaela and Tovah chase the dogs through the fields. Tovah unaware of the danger in which her mom has placed herself.

Tricia keeps tearing at the mud with her bare hands.

I want her to get the hell out of there.

Tricia just can't let it all wash away.

So much is already gone and this is all that she has left.

A view.

I try with all of my might to reach her, but I can't.

Tovah is the only one that can.

Sandy knows it, too.

Sandy keeps yelling.

"Tricia — think about what you are doing. This isn't worth it. Michaela and Tovah are on their way back. Don't let them see you acting like a crazy person. Don't make me raise Tovah for you.

"Get out of there right fucking now!"

Tricia climbs up out of the culvert.

She has scratches on her hands and face and she looks defeated.

She lies down in the mud and cries.

Sandy grabs a huge tree branch and uses it as a crowbar to dislodge pieces of the blockage on the outside. Tricia eventually joins in and they manage to lower the level of the dam — the water rushing through the culvert with tremendous force. They need to let the massive amounts of water contained on one side flow through to the other, before they can expect to remove any more of the beaver's dam. They hope that in the next day or two, the power of the water will break up the remaining dam and push it right through to the other side.

That won't happen and I will be the only one to see what does.

THE DAM BREAKS

Tricia tried, but she couldn't stop the dam from breaking.

None of us could stop any of it.

I was there when it let go and washed the last pieces of what we had away.

It felt like there should have been some dramatic music playing in the background.

Something dark and thorny with cymbals and horns and violins.

The water peaked at the top of the dam, forming a wave that reached up and over.

It charged across the dam road and down the other side.

Digging trenches in the dirt that my dad built up.

The trenches deepened and the water filled the empty spaces.

Pushing the dirt downstream.

Away from the farm.

Quickly the land corroded around the culvert.

In a crescendo of misery the culvert flipped ass over teakettle — high in the air.

The wall of water advanced and removed the remaining damn dam.

The culvert rode the wave for a while and landed high on the banks.

Where the horses used to stand.

There among the rosehips and the goldenrod.

It's all gone now.

The people.

The place.

THREE SISTERS AND
A BROTHER

Three years have passed since the dam broke.

Tricia is finally in a stable relationship.

She buys Sandy's house in the city with her partner and they construct a life for themselves.

Tovah has a dad.

Tricia returns to university to finish what she started with me.

When she graduates, she brings her diploma to the place where I died.

She peels back the blanket of grass and digs out the Tupperware container.

Letters and trinkets and cards retelling the sadness she lived through.

She places the diploma inside the rectangular box and buries it beneath the earth.

She finished it for me.

When she was able.

And I am thankful.

Bonny plants a garden to marvel my moms.

She cans and she pickles and she preserves.

She plants trees to strengthen the shelterbelt of their farmyard.

She tends to the animals that graze on their land.

For the birthdays of her two nieces, Bonny lovingly creates recipe books, pulling from my mom's favorites, even adding the notes she scrawled in the corners.

Like my mom, Bonny believes that homemade gifts mean the most — and they do.

Bonny's kids are self-sufficient young adults now.

Her youngest works and lives in the city.

Her oldest buys a parcel of land in the country and builds a house of his own — like my dad did.

Sandy has been married for thirty-three years.

Her husband points his finger at her — casting blame for everything.

He spews words that lacerate.

Doors slamming — never talking — never explaining.

No rest after the tempest.

Another loss.

Michaela is looking at colleges.

Tricia is happy and doesn't need Sandy anymore.

Sandy pulls into herself again.

Sleeping alone in the king size bed.

An indentation on her left ring finger.

Bare.

She is alone again.

She sits and she writes about me.

The catalyst for it all.

Death for the young happens in stages.

Places and people have the power to hold the youthful dead where I am — bound by invisible ties of duty, remorse and the kind of love that one can only feel when it is too late.

The farm has released me.

Bonny and Tricia have forgiven me — they are willing and able to let me go.

Sandy is not. She carries a kind of guilt, knowing subconsciously that I wouldn't leave her like this.

We are both stuck.

I know I fucked up.

I am so sorry for what I did.

My parents wait for me in the calm of the peace they both found when they were able to shed the burdensome bodies I left them in.

My death has not provided me with the same tranquility.

I choose to stay because I should and I can and I will.

I am no angel, but I will be my sisters' guardian — I am responsible for them.

I owe them that.

THE HOUSE MY DAD BUILT BURNS

The house that moved from the farm to McLean lies in ashes.
The house my dad built.
The news comes to my sisters from a rural contact.
Another young person lying in a grave — the new owner's son.
Like me.
Parents and siblings moaned and wailed inside its walls — again.
My sisters think of the family, first.
The house they would have done anything to preserve, second.
Perhaps the house endured too much pain.
Accidental or intentional.
It doesn't matter why the house burned.
My sisters wanted what my dad built to live on, but not like this.
The house is gone now too.
Maybe it's best that way.

ACKNOWLEDGEMENTS

Without Jennifer Crystal and the Grub Street community, this book would never have been rewritten in my brother's voice. I thank each and every one of you who ever read the words that I wrote. Jennifer has personally guided me on this journey to publication, with a belief in my writing that has been unwavering. I thank her for her mentorship, her commitment to the craft, as well as her friendship.

I would like to thank Jodie Toohey and Legacy Book Press LLC, for believing that Jarett's story deserved to be read by others. Her organization and commitment to detail, as well as her willingness to answer any and all questions kept me on task.

I need to thank my parents for my childhood, the farm, every single animal we ever loved, and most importantly, for Jarett — the kid who gave us so much and then took even more without ever meaning to. We forgive you, Jarett.

To Jarett, I want to thank him for being the son and the brother that he was to the Speers family of Kronau, Saskatchewan. I will forever miss his dimples, his six feet six inches, his propensity for hard work and never complaining, his candor, and his strength of character.

It's okay if you leave now, Jarett. I am sorry it took me twenty-five years to be able to say that.

My daughter Michaela was born into a family still struggling with the loss of a teenager and then along came cancer and a brain dead quadriplegic.

Thank you Michaela for always accepting and loving my dad, even in the cruel state he was in. You were never ashamed of him and you treated him like a person deserving of love and attention. I don't know where you found the strength as a child to go to a hospital or a long-term care facility (sometimes both) every day, but I thank you for it. You never once cried or complained, knowing somehow, with your burgeoning self-awareness, that your plight was not worthy of mentioning.

Thank you for making my mom's last few weeks on that green sectional couch at our house in Saskatchewan so very special. You dressed up death with your stuffies and your little lab coat, your imagination on a continuous loop describing the farm, my mom languishing in the frivolity of your little girl voice, keeping her with us, coaxing her to stay longer and hear your stories. Michaela, you let my parents give you what they could in a very short time and still to this day, you cherish the morsels they left you — the letters, the curling trophy, Raggedy Ann and Andy, the birthstone, the love.

You saw so much with your young eyes as you watched my parents leave us, and I truly believe that they gave you more in a short amount of time than some receive in a lifetime. At such an impressionable time in your life, you picked up some of the most valued personality traits I could ever hope for you to have. You are non-judgmental, giving, humble, empathetic, delicately stoic, thoughtful, ambitious, and kind. Thank you for all that you are to me, Michaela, and all that you were to my parents.

To my very strong and capable sisters, who battled in the same trenches as I did.

I thank Tricia for all that we shared in the name of grief — without her I do not think I could have resurfaced after the first wave hit us. I also thank her for having the courage to let me write about her lowest times. I did not sugar coat anything and nor did she ask me to.

I thank Bonny for her ability to always move toward the future — her hope un-tethered, always leading us onward. Bonny has never spent one second of her life feeling sorry for herself, and for that I applaud her.

I thank Tovah for saving her mom.

I thank Chris for the stories and his permanent ink eulogy to my brother and my parents.

I thank Rue, our beloved Labrador, for always being there at my feet.

ABOUT THE AUTHOR

Sandy Speers Markwart was born and raised in Saskatchewan, Canada. She would describe her childhood as idyllic. Sandy moved to Boston, Massachusetts, at the age of twenty, but the prairies have always kept a hold on her. An avid writer, *I Want You To Know* is her first novel. Sandy lives with her yellow Lab in Back Bay, Boston. She loves anything artistic and spends her spare time creating stained glass windows, glass fused art, and woodworking. Sandy loves ripping houses apart and putting them back together. She enjoys taking classes at Boston Architectural College and North Bennet Street School. Sandy loves the outdoors (all seasons) and travelling with family and friends.